BARBER/BARBOUR GENEALOGY

THOMAS BARBER, THE EMIGRANT
1614–1662

Book 2

Compiled by

Betty Jewell Durbin Carson

DAR Member #832584

HERITAGE BOOKS
2016

HERITAGE BOOKS
AN IMPRINT OF HERITAGE BOOKS, INC.

Books, CDs, and more—Worldwide

For our listing of thousands of titles see our website
at
www.HeritageBooks.com

Published 2016 by
HERITAGE BOOKS, INC.
Publishing Division
5810 Ruatan Street
Berwyn Heights, Md. 20740

International Standard Book Numbers
Paperbound: 978-0-7884-5722-7
Clothbound: 978-0-7884-6449-2

Acknowledgement

I would like to give acknowledgement to my sister, Doris May Durbin Wooley, who worked with me on this research of the Barber/Barbour and Barclay/Barkley families for over 15 years. We visited many state archives, courthouses, bought and Xeroxed many documents, searched census records, and loved doing it as a team.

Doris died February 4, 2014, but left me all of her notes and files which I combined with mine. The Barber line is closely intermarried with the Barclay/Barkley family for many years. This book is dedicated to our deceased mother, Nellie Barkley Durbin, as it is part of her ancestry.

While there has not been any definite proof that Thomas and Samuel were related, available records would indicate a close connection. Thomas had a younger brother named Samuel and this Samuel may be a grandson or nephew. Many of the names in Thomas' manuscript as well as Samuel's have names that are connected through DNA lines.

That is why there are two Barber books. Records indicate that the American progenitor was Francis Barber, 1616/17, b. England, perhaps the one who came to VA in 1635; children: Francis 165?; Samuel 1955 m. Elizabeth Heathcoate; John; Sarah; Elizabeth; Joseph; and William 166?

Nellie Barkley Durbin - 1948

Nellie Barkley as a young woman

Table of Contents

Book 2:

Thomas Barber, The Emigrant

THOMAS BARBER THE EMIGRANT

Before coming to New England Thomas was apprenticed on 12-18-1634 for a period of 9 years (until December 1643) under Francis Stiles, a master carpenter from Millbrook, Bedfordshire, England. Stiles was contracted by Sir Richard Saltonstall to bring apprentices to Windsor, and to build houses in America for Englishmen who were to follow. Thomas Barber at the age of 21 was among the twenty apprentices plus others who sailed with Stiles for New England in the ship "Christian" (John White, Master), which left London 3-16-1634 (Julian Calendar), and arrived 3 months later in Boston, June, 1635. Each of the passengers had a certificate which read in part:"with certificate from St. Mildred, Bead Street, London, and having taken the oaths, to be transported to New England from London in the "Christian". After 10 days at Boston the Christian sailed up the Connecticut River to Windsor, arriving there on 7-1-1635. That same year Thomas was granted a lot of a few acres, extending from Mill Brook near the old Warham gristmill, north along both sides of Poquonock Avenue. After 330 years of continuous Barber ownership, the land has now all been sold.

The Pequot War in 1637, which according to the settlers was precipitated by the Pequot Indians and their continual harassment of the settlers, the friendly Mohegan Indians, and sometimes the Narragansetts, found Thomas a Sargeant, one of 30 soldiers from Windsor who were enrolled under Major Stoughton for 3 weeks and 2 days. Under the leadership of Captain John Mason, the May 26, 1637 night attack on the Pequot Fort was a complete surprise to the sleeping Pequots, and a large percentage of the tribe was massacred. Thomas Barber's bravery (he was inside the Pequot Fort at Mystic during the attack, and along with Edward Pattison, "having no time to reload their muskets, slew seven fleeing Indians with axes and knives"), gained him honorable mention from Capt. Mason, and in return for this service, in 1641 he was granted 600 acres of land in Massaco, in the western part of Windsor. Massaco became Simsbury in 1669.

On March 28, 1637 Francis Stiles (master carpenter) was ordered to teach his servants, George Chapple, Thomas Cooper, and Thomas Barber in the trade of carpentry. The year 1645 found Thomas still an apprentice carpenter. Stiles apparently was slow to finish Thomas' apprenticeship, and needed a court order to force him to do so. Shortly after that Thomas was a free man. At the time of his death in 1662, Thomas may have been making preparations to move to Northampton, Mass where he was offered a home lot and 20 acres.

Life was apparently not completely peaceful for Thomas Barber. Court records in 1649 show that he was found liable for a debt to William Franklin. Thomas claimed that he had given the money to Thomas Ford to pay to Franklin. Then in 1650 Sargeant Barber was fined 5 pounds and forced to surrender his rank, for the disorderly striking of Lt. Cooke in an argument over church matters: Thomas believed that the church had no right to interfere in temporal matters. This penalty was later canceled when apparently Thomas apologized: "he is affected with his great evil and rash passionate carriage in striking the Lt."

Thomas left an estate at over 132 pounds.

A deep mystery surrounds Jane, wife of Thomas. He married her in 1640, but the written record by Matthew Grant gives only the name Jane or Joan. Two of Thomas' sons married Coggin ladies, but there is little sign that Jane was a Coggin, as some have suggested. One report (LDS record) has it that Jane Coggin, b Bedfordshire, England 1619 was daughter of John Coggin b in Bedford, Bedfordshire about 1593.

It has also been suggested that Thomas Barber married Jane Bancroft, widow of John Bancroft who died in 1637. Jane Bancroft had ties to Windsor thru her daughter Anna, b 1627, who married 1647 John Griffin of Windsor and Simsbury, and her son John, born about 1620, who married in 1640 Hannah Dupper and had a family in Windsor. But Jane Bonython who married John Bancroft was born in 1573, and would have been way too old to have borne Thomas Barber's children. This theory against the wife being Jan Bancroft was written up in The American Genealogist, Vol 37, p 164 in 1961 by George E McCracken and more or less disproved at that time. He points out that she would have had to have borne children for too long a time span - highly unlikely, and also she would have had sons named John and 2 named Thomas -also unlikely.

Another account has John Bancroft born about 1596, died 1637, married Jane about 1622. That would have meant she was born about 1606 or before, making her about 47 in 1653 when Thomas' youngest child Josiah Barber was born - not impossible, but very unlikely.

It has been said by some that Thomas may have married the daughter of one of the Dutch traders at Old Saybrook, or Hartford, and also that the one he married was 'the first white woman to land in Connecticut".

One of Francis Stiles' sisters was named Jane, born 1605. She married in England and presumably remained there. There was a Jane Morden or Worden, age 35 (in 1635) on the passenger list of the Christian; however, nothing further is know about her. It seems she was too old to have borne all of Thomas' children. There seems as yet no way of knowing who Jane was.

FIRST GENERATION.

1.   THOMAS BARBER, whose name appears in the early Colonial Records of Windsor. Conn, was born probably in the County of Bedfordshire, England, about 1614.

He came to Windsor in 1635 with the party fitted out by Sir Richard Saltonstall, under Francis Stiles, a master carpenter of London. He was then 21 years of age, and was the first of the Barber name in New England.

The following is a copy of a portion of the London Passenger Register for the ship "Christian " in which the Saltonstall party sailed for America.

"16 March 1634

"These underwritten names are to be transported to New England imbarqued in ye " Christian" de Lo ; (from London) Joh. White Mr. bound thither, the men having taken ye oath of Allegiance & Supremacie.

Names Yeres
1 ffrancis Stiles 35
2 Tho: Bassett 37
3 Tho : Stiles 20
4 Tho : Barber 21

The ancient Jewish year which opened with the 25th of March continued long to have a legal position in Christian countries. In England, it was not until 1752 that the 1st of January became the initial day of the legal year, as it had long been of the popular year.

The "Christian," therefore, sailed on the 16th of March 1635 instead of March 1634, as the London Custom House Record states.

According to the Windsor records, in 1635 Thomas Barber was granted "a lot ten rods west of Humphrey Hyde's Mill Road, 8 acres and 22 rods wide, bounded south by Mill Brook, extending as sts.ted 2 rods wide, to accommodate Barber and Alvord, and also a way for Mr. Wareham, Minister, to go to his lot north of Barber's and Alvord's and ended in the Poquonnock Road."

It is evident from the records, that Francis Stiles failed to fulfill his contract with Thomas Barber and the other young men of his party, for on Mch. 28, 1647 the following order was made by the Court of Hartford : Ord. " That Mr. Francis Stiles shall teach Geo. Chappie, Thos. Cooper and Thos. Barber, his servants (apprentices) in the trade of a carpenter, according to his promise for their services for their term, behind 4 days a week only to saw and slitt their own work that they are to frame themselves with their own hands, together with himself or some other master workman ; the time to begin for the performance of this order 14 days hence without fail."

Thomas Barber's residence, it is stated, was located "upon an ancient road which running about southwesterly from the rivulet (near where the present road from Palisade Green comes in) intersected the Poquonnock road above the old mill." On the north side of this road were the residences of Thos. Barber, Humphrey Hyde, and Alex Alvord, and on the south side that of Jonathan Gillett.

Thomas Barber was a soldier with the rank of Sergeant, in the Pequot War ; he distinguished himself by his bravery in a number of fights with the Pequots, and particularly in the taking of a fort which the Indians considered impregnable. After describing the march and the plan of the attack, Capt. Mason gives the following account of the exploit.

"We called up our forces with all expedition, gave fire thro' the Pallisade upon them; the Indians being in a dead, indeed their last sleep. Then we wheeled off and fell upon the main entrance, which was blocked up with bushes about breast high, over which the Captain passed, intending to make good the entrance, encouraging the rest to follow. Lieut. Seeley endeavored to enter, but being somewhat encumbered stepped back and pulled out the bushes, and so entered, and with him about 16 men. We had formerly concluded to destroy them by the sword and save the plunder.

Whereupon, Capt. Mason, seeing no Indians, entered a wigwam, where he was beset with many Indians waiting all opportunities to lay hands on him, but could not prevail. At length Wm. Heydon espying the breach in the wigwam, supposing some Englishman might be there, entered; but in his entrance fell over a dead Indian, but speedily recovering himself, the Indians soon fled, others crept under their beds. The Captain going out of the wigwam saw many Indians in the lane or street; he making towards them they fled, were pursued to the end of the lane, where they were met by Edward Pattison, Thomas Barber, with some others, where seven of them were slain."

This occurred probably in June 1637.

While returning from this memorable fight Thomas Barber engaged with Lieut. Cook in a discussion on religious and church matters, and becoming incensed at some remark made by the latter, struck him, for which offense the Court adjudged that he should forfeit his military rank, and pay a fine of five pounds.

In 1641 the lands in the locality called by the Indian name Massaco, were apportioned among the Colonists. Thomas Barber was granted about 600 acres of these lands.

The records of Northampton, Mass., contain the following regarding Thomas Barber:

"A Towne Meeting 24th of 4 mon. 1661.

"The day and year abovesaid it was voted and agreed Thomas Barber of Windsor may bee an inhabitant of this Towne and grant him a home lott and alsoe liberty to looke out a platt of ground to the quantity of 20 acres, and if it doe encourage him to come they grant it (to him) upon this condition ; that he come and inhabit and make improvemente of it within a yere, after the date of " This proposition from the town of Northampton, seems not to have been considered, as Thomas died the following year at his home in Windsor.

From all that can be learned of the character of Thomas Barber, it is evident that he was a man of strong convictions, but very liberal in his views, especially so for the times in which he lived. It was his contention that the Church had no right to interfere in temporal matters, which caused the trouble between him and Lieut. Cook. He was, to a marked degree, impulsive and energetic and possessed of great shrewdness in business matters, but with an uprightness of character which won for him the confidence and respect of the Colonists. Brave, fearless and resourceful in times of peril, he was a prominent figure in the defense of the colony, and an Indian fighter of whom the savages stood in awe.

The Hartford Probate Records contain the following regarding the settlement of Thomas Barber's estate.

4

Barber, Thomas, Windsor, Invt. i:i32-14-00 ; taken 20, Oct. 1662, by Benj. Newberry and John Moore.

Court Record, Page 187—4 Feb., 1662-3, Invt. approved. Samuel was placed with his brother Thomas Barber to learn a trade ; Mercy (Mary) Barber was placed with Lt. Walter Fyler and his wife until 18 years of age, unless she marries before, with her Master's and Dame's and eldest brother's approbation; Josias Barber was placed with Dea. John Moore until 21 years of age to learn a trade; Thomas Barber doth engage to take Samuel Barber's portion and after two years from the present to allow 6% simple interest per annum. John Barber took Josias' portion upon the same terms.

Page 188— 6 June 1662, Dist. to John and Sarah jointly.

House and Home lot as their Father willed — 126-13-04

To Thomas Barber by Gift & his portion 13-00-00

To Samuel, Mercy & Josias each 36-15-00

By Capt. Newberry

Deacon Moore

Sgt. Alvord.

On Oct. 7, 1640, Thomas Barber married Jane or Joan (surname not known). She is supposed by some to have been a daughter of one of the Dutch settlers, and another authority states that she was the first white woman to land in Connecticut. He died on Sept. 11th, and his wife Joan on Sept. 10th, 1662.

Children :

    I.   John, bp. July 24, 1642.

    II.   Thomas, b. July 14, 1644.

    III.   Sarah, bp. July 19, 1646.

    IV.   Samuel, bp. Oct. 1, 1648.

    V.   Mary, bp. Oct. 12, 1651.

    VI.   Josiah, b. Feb. 15, 1653.

In the Hartford Probate records it will be observed that the name of the fifth child of Thomas and Joan Barber is given as Mercy instead of Mary, as shown above. Also some records seem to indicate that she married a Hale, but the Gillett family records furnish conclusive evidence of her marriage to John Gillett.

It is possible that in the records showing the name of Hale, her marriage was confused with that of her sister Sarah's to Timothy Hall, as a confusion of the names Hale and Hall is quite common.

SECOND GENERATION.

2. John Barber[2]; (Thomas[1]) bp. July 24, 1642. He m. 1st in Springfield, Conn., Sept. 2, 1663, Bathsheba Coggin, (sometimes given Coggen or Cousens) who d. in 1688 ; he m. 2nd May 1, 1689, Hannah, widow of Thomas Brancroft, and probably dau. of Samuel Gardner, of Hadley.

The records seem to indicate that as a very young man, he spent some time in Springfield, and was married there, but settled first in Windsor. In 1664 his father's place in Windsor was made over to him, but in 1671, he transferred it to his brother Samuel, and removed to Springfield. Burt's History of Springfield states that he had two children born prior to his removal to that place. His other children were born in Springfield. The same authority states that he served for eight years as one of the selectmen of Springfield, and he is referred to, in the early records, as Deacon John Barber.

In 1684 he removed from Springfield to Suffield. Here, according to some records, he was a deacon and also a selectman. But the records, both of Springfield and Suffield, are much confused regarding this John Barber and his family.

This has presented one of the difficult problems of the present work, and after a careful consideration of all the information obtainable on the subject, the conclusion seems inevitable that among the early settlers, both of Springfield and Suffield, there were other Barber families, descended probably from one of the Massachusetts emigrants, but certainly not descended from Thomas, of Windsor.

For instance, a John Barber, Sr., and a John Barber, Jr., took the oath of allegiance in Springfield, Jan. 1, 1678. These persons could not have been John (son of Thomas, of Windsor) and his son John, as the latter would have been but nine years old on that date.

Again, the records of Springfield contain a list of claimants to lands granted to deceased soldiers of King Philip's War. In this list there appears the name of "John Barber, son of John, of Springfield." This list bears date of June 1736, and as the mortuary records seem to give positive evidence that John,[3] John,[2] Thomas[1], of Windsor/ died in 1 690, this appears to confirm the theory that there were other families in Springfield descended from one of the other Barber emigrants. The frequent occurrence of the names Thomas and John in these families renders the problem still more difficult, and the records here given of John Barber (son of Thomas, of Windsor) and of his family, are all that research to this date, has been able to establish with any degree of certainty. It is to be hoped that some future historian may be more successful.

Deacon John Barber died Jan. 17, 1712. His will was proven in February of the same year, and it is stated that the surname very soon thereafter disappears from the records of Suffield. As will be seen by the records of the sons of this family (third generation) it is not improbable that the surname became extinct in this particular line with that generation.

6

Children :
I.	Joanna, b. Apr. 8, 1667; m. Mch. 18, 1684-5, Thos. Smith, a weaver or tanner of
II.	Ipswich or Springfield ; she d. June 25, 1688.
II.	John, b. July 14, 1669.
III.	Return, b. May 29, 1672; d. Dec. 17, 1673.
IV.	Thomas, b. Feb. 4, 1674 ; m. Sarah Ball.
V.	Mary, b. Feb. 13, 1677.

3.   Thomas Barber[2], (Thomas, [1]) b. July 14, 1644 ; m. Dec. 17, 1663, Mary Phelps, who was b. Mch. 2, 1644. She was the dau. of William Phelps, Sr., known as " Ould Mr. Phelps," and his second wife, Mary (Dover) Phelps.

The old Windsor records show that in 1664, Thomas Barber bought land in Windsor "whereon he builded, the lot of Samuel Pond, except about 1 1/2 acres next to Silver Street on which Pond's house stood, and which doubtless faced the Hollow Fall Road."

Other records show that Thomas and his brothers John and Samuel were among the original grantees of Simsbury, having received a portion of the " Meadow Lands " lying along the River Massaco, under an order of the General Court, of Hartford, of December, 1666, which stipulated that "within two years the person to whom granted should improve them by plowing, mowing, building, fencing, etc."

In 1669 Massaco was set off from Windsor and made a separate township under the name of Simsbury, to which Thomas and his brother Samuel, with their families, removed in 1670 or 1671, and began improving the lands at that place which they had inherited from their father Thomas.[1]

Thomas Barber [2] was lieutenant of the first military company of Simsbury, and was known as Lieut. Thomas. He built the first saw-mill and grist-mill in Simsbury, also the first church, regarding the location of which there was some contention among the settlers, which was finally decided by lot, and the location fixed in the southern end of Terry's Plains.

Thomas Barber died in Simsbury, May 10, 1713. His estate was valued at 488 18s 3d.
Children :
I.	John, b. Nov. 1, 1664 ; m. Mary Holcomb.
II.	Mary, b. Jan. 11, 1666.
III.	Sarah, b. July 12, 1669 ; m. Andrew Robe; no issue.
IV.	Joanna, b. 1670; m. Jan. 3, 1710-11, Josiah Adkins.
V.	Anne, b. 1671 ; m. Jonathan Higley.
VI.	Thomas, b. Oct. 7, 1672 ; m. Abigail Buel.
VII.	Samuel, b. May 17, 1673 ; m. Sarah Holcomb.
VIII.	Child, b. 1677 ; d. young.

The name of the husband of Sarah Barber, third child in the above family, is given in some records as " Roe," and it has been claimed that he was an ancestor of the Rev. A. S. Roe. The name, however, is given "Robe" in the Simsbury records, and in his will Thomas Barber mentions his daughter Sarah, wife of Andrew Robe. The evidence is also fairly conclusive that there was no issue.

William Phelps, the father of Mary, wife of Thomas Barber," was born in Tewksbury, County Gloucester, England, 1599. He removed to Somerset or Dorsetshire, England. His first wife was Elizabeth (surname not known). He came to Dorchester, Mass., in 1630, and in 1636 removed to Windsor, Conn. He applied to be made freeman, Oct. 19, 1630. He was a member of the jury impaneled for the trial of Walter Palmer for the murder of Austin Brotchus, being the first trial by jury in New England. That he was a highly respected and active citizen, is evidenced by the various positions of trust which he occupied. He was member in 1636 of the first court held in Connecticut, and of the court which in 1637 declared war against the Pequots. Was magistrate from 1638 to 1642, and again in 1658; was foreman of the first Grand Jury in 1643, and deputy to the General Court from 1645 to 1649, and from 1651 to 1658 ; was magistrate again from 1658 to 1662, and in 1641 was appointed member of a committee on lying. His 2nd wife, Mary Dover, is said to have been a fellow passenger from England with him. They were married in Windsor.

His Windsor residence is about three quarters of a mile northwest of Broad Street, on the road to Poquonnock. As late as 1859 it was owned by Dea. Roger Phelps.

4.   Sarah Barber[2],- (Thomas[1]) bp. July 19, 1646; m. Nov. 26, 1663, Timothy Hall. They settled on a part of her father's land in Windsor, but afterwards (1679) removed to Suffield, where the name frequently occurs, especially in the older records as "Hale."

The old church records also show that Hannah, dau. of Timothy Haile was baptised at Windsor, Mch. 28, 1678. This may have been another daughter belonging to this family.

5.   Samuel Barber[2] (Thomas,[1]) bp. Oct. 1, 1648 ; m. 1st, Dec. 1, 1670, Mary Coggins, who. d. May 19, 1676. He m. 2nd, Jan. 25, 1677, Ruth Drake, dau. of John and Hannah (Moore) Drake, who was bp. Dec. 6, 1657.

John Drake, the father of Ruth, was descended from the illustrious English family of that name, which had its seat at Ashe. In England the name has long been borne by many distinguished as navigators, clergymen, martyrs, and authors. Among the foremost of these English families is that which has its seat at Ashe, Co. Devon and from it descended the greater portion of the Drakes of Massachusetts and Connecticut.

In Samuel Barber's will, dated Feb. 21, 1708-9, it will be observed that he makes provision for his son John when he shall come to the age of 21 years. Now, if this son John had been born in 1676, he would have been at least 11 years old at the time the father's will was written, whereas it is evident from that document that he was the youngest son. Further, John Barber, the son of Samuel, was married in 1717, at which date, had he been born in 1676 he would have been 41 years old, and his wife, Jane Alvord, born in 1698, would have been 21 years younger than he; all of which is, to be sure, a possible situation, but hardly a probable one, in those days of early marriages.

The New England Gen. & Hist. Reg., Vol. V, page 64, makes mention of John Drake Barber, son of Samuel and Ruth, b. Jan. 25, 1676. This is the only record found of John Drake Barber. From all this evidence, the conclusion seems inevitable that if there was an older son John, he must have died young; and as to the confusion regarding the date of his birth, it is not improbable that he was the son of the first wife. At all events, the son John who was living at the time of the father's death was a younger child, and in all probabilities the youngest son, born presumably about 1694.

In Samuel Barber's will he makes unconditional bequests to his son Benjamin, which would indicate that he was of age at the time the will was made, and hence must have been born prior to 1690, as given in the above record.

Will of Samuel Barber, Sr.

Barber, Samuel-Sr.— Windsor ; Inv. ;598-04-10; taken Mch. 1709, by John Moore, Sr. Job. Drake, Sr. and Thomas Marshall- Will dated 21 February 1708-09.

I, Samuel Barber, Sr. of Windsor, doe make & ordain this, my last Will & Testament. I give unto my wife Ruth 2 acres of meadow land in Great Meadow, which I had with her to be at her own dispose ; also the use and improvement of my dwelling house and barn and out houses with the lands adjoining thereunto, and with other lands adjoining which I bought of John Saxton, John Barber & Andrew Hilliyer, and 14 acres of Benj. Gardiner & John Gillett, until my son John come to the age of 21 years.

Item. I give unto my grandson William Barber, son of my son William Barber (deceased) besides what I have already made over to him, 8 acres of swamp land. (Here follows boundary of the land and conditions under which the bequest is made).

Item. I give unto my son David the land I purchased of Mr. Buckingham, at Hebron ; also 2 acres of land at Windsor, being 2 acres of the 4 I received in the legacy given to my wife.

I give to my son Joseph at Scotland, 20 rods in breadth lying on the north side of the land given to my son Samuel. (Here follows description of sundry other tracts of land bequeathed to son Joseph) "he to pay my wife 20s. yearly in current pay during her life."

Item. I give unto my son Benjamin the remainder of my lott at the field called Wheat Field, the other part being given to my son Joseph. Also I give to my son Benjamin 3 acres in Palmer's Swamp, next to Joseph's land, running the same length.

Item. I give to my son John when he shall be 21 years of age, half my housing and half the land given to my wife (except 2 1/2 acres of meadow) and the other half after my wife's decease ; also I give to my son John when he comes to be of age, about 1 acre of land, which is called Fitch Waters bottom.

Item. I declare it to be my will that my three daughters, Elizabeth, Mindwell and Sarah, shall have 25£ apiece paid to each of them when they shall be 18 years of age, to make them equal with their two sisters who are married.

And I give to my five daughters (both those that are married and those that are not) the remainder of my estate which is yet undisposed of, both personal and real, to be equally divided between my 5 daughters, Mary, Ruth, Elizabeth, Mindwell and Sarah, to them and their heirs forever. I appoint my wife Ruth, and my son-in-law William Phelps to be executors.

Will proven Apr. 4, 1709. (Hartford Probate Records.)

Will of Mindwell Barber.

Estate of Mindwell Barber: Inv. taken Feb. 1712-13. Letters of administration granted to Joseph Barber, brother of deceased.

John Moore, John Bissell and James Eno, Distributors. By terms of the will, the estate was to be divided equally between the brothers and sisters of deceased.

Dist. File of Oct. 24, 1714. To the brothers and sisters of the deceased, children of Samuel Barber; to Samuel, William, David, Joseph, Benjamin and John; to Daniel Loomis and his wife Elizabeth; to Peter Browne and his wife Mary ; to William Phelps and his wife Ruth; to Sarah Barber and to William Barber, son of William Barber, deceased. (Hartford Probate Records.)

Settlement of Estate of William Barber.

William Barber (son of Samuel) Inv. of Estate Aug. 17, 1704; Administrators, widow Esther Barber, and her father-in-law Samuel. John Bissell appointed guardian for minor son William. (Hartford Probate Records.)

Will of Ruth Barber, Widow of Samuel, Sr.

Barber, Ruth,— Windsor ; Invt. i;84-10-06. Taken Nov. 30, 1731; Will dated Nov. 13, 1716.

I, Ruth Barber, of Windsor, thought it best to make this my last Will & Testament; After my just debts and funeral expenses are paid, my will is that what is wanting of my son Benjamin and John Barber's portion, and also of Sarah Barber's portion according to their father Samuel Barber's last Will, shall be made up to each of them out of my estate.

I freely release my son Joseph Barber from the 20 shillings per annum that he was to pay unto me by his father Samuel Barber's Will. I fully discharge my son Benjamin Barber from paying for his dyet while he has been with me, providing he demand nothing from my executors for what work he has done for me, nor for the corn and meat I have had of him.

I give to my son John Barber my mare, a steer and all my right in the oxen the sd. Joseph Barber bo't of Josiah Barber, and also hay to keep them this winter.

I give to my daughter Sarah my best bed and furniture; also a pig and 4 bushels of corn and two of rye. I give to my son-in-law Samuel Barber 20 shillings in money besides what he owes me.

I give to my grandson William Barber 5 shillings in money.

Lastly my will is that the remainder of my whole estate be divided to and among my children hereafter named in equal shares, viz; Mary Brown ; Ruth Phelps ; Elizabeth Loomis and Sarah Barbour (Barber).

I make my son Joseph Barber sole executor.

Will proven Dec. 1731. (Hartford Probate Records.)

6.Mary Barber[2], (Thomas[1]) bp. Oct. 12, 1651. In the " Hartford Probate Records " the name is given Mercy. She m. July 8, 1669, John Gillett, son of Jonathan Gillett, the Emigrant. He was b. in Windsor, Oct. 5, 1644.

Children : Born in Windsor, Conn.
I   Thomas Gillett, b. Jan. 7, 1671 ; bp. "ye 14;" d. young.
II.   John Gillett, b. Aug. 6, 1673 ; d. July 4, 1699.
III.   Thomas Gillett, b. July 18, ; bp. 23, 1676.
IV.   Samuel Gillett, b. Feb. 16, 1678.
V.   Nathaniel Gillett, b. Oct. 3, 1680 ; bp. in Hartford, Oct. 30, 1681.
VI.   Mercy Gillett, b. Jan. 31, 1683; (Old Church Records state b. Oct. 30, 1682, Hartford).

John Gillett, the husband of Mary Barber, was the son of Jonathan Gillett, the Emigrant, who with his brother Nathan came to Dorchester, Mass., with the Rev. Mr. Wareham. An interesting relic in the possession of a descendant of the Gillett family is a bible brought from England by Jonathan Gillett.

This bible is of the Geneva edition of 1599, which is known as the " Breeches Bible " for the reason that the fig leaf garment worn by our first parents is translated "breeches" instead of "apron " as in the King James version.

In the Gillett family this particular copy is known as the " Bear Bible " from the fact of its once having been used to prop open a window, and a bear in trying to effect an entrance through the opening, clawed the leaves, making marks which still remain.

7. **JOSIAH BARBER**[2], (Thomas[1]) b. Feb. 15, 1653; m. 1st, Nov. 22, 1677, Abigail, dau. of Nathaniel and Elizabeth (Moore) Loomis, who was b. in Windsor, Mch. 27, ; bp. Apr. 1, 1659. She d. Feb. 19, 1700-1, and he m. 2nd, Nov. 5, 1701, Sarah, widow of Enoch Drake, and dau. of John and Mary (Stanley) Porter, who was b. Sept. 5, 1655, and d. Dec. 13, 1730. According to some authorities he d. Dec. 14 or 24, 1733, but according to the Hartford Probate Records final settlement of his estate was made Aug. 3, 1731.
Children : All by first wife (Abigail Loomis).

I.   Abigail, b. Mch. 12, 1678; m. Dea. Cornelius Brown.
II.   Josiah, b. 1685 ; ca d. in 1729; no mention in his father's will, hence must have d. first.
III. Rebecca, b. Apr. 1 1, 1687 or 1690 ; m. Nathaniel Drake.
IV.   Nathaniel, b. Apr. 6, 1691 ; m. Mary Filley.
V.   Jonathan, b. June 4, 1694; m. Rachel Gaylord.
VI.   Aaron, b. July 20, 1697 ; m. Mary Douglas.

Abigail Loomis, mother of the above family, was a sister of Mary Loomis, who m. Joseph Barber.

Will of Josiah Barber of Windsor.
Barbour, Lieut. Josiah — Windsor — Invt. 81 7-01-00 Taken January 7th-1 729-30, by Jacob Drake, Job Loomis and Timothy Loomis. Will dated Apr. 1st 1726.

I, Josiah Barbour, of Windsor, wheelwright, do make this my last Will and Testament ; I give unto Sarah my wife for her to have and enjoy 1/3 part of my lands, some portions that I purchased of Ebenezer Gilbert and Ebenezer Spencer, and also of Ebenezer Williams, land that belonged to Mark Kelsey, and 1/3 part of the land I purchased of Josiah Cooke and Joanna, his wife. I also give unto my wife for her to have and enjoy only for and during ye time she shall happen to live and remain my widow; my parlour or lower room of my dwelling house, also ½ part of the west end of my barn. Also, I give her a feather bed, a mare and a cow, to be her owne for ever, and one year's provisions. The reason I have not given unto my wife any more of my moveable estate is because that I had none of her estate left her by her former husband, for she disposed of the same unbeknown to me, and she may dispose of my estate (if given) as she did her former husband's, and so leave herself destitute.

I give to Nathaniel Barbour, my eldest son, besides what I have already given him by deed of gift, all my land in the lower field on the west side of the road to Windsor, 1/3 part of the land I purchased of Ebenezer Williams, that belonged to Mark Kelsey 1/3 part of the land I purchased of Josiah Cook, and Joanna his wife, and also 1/3 part of the land I purchased of Ebenezer Gilbert and Ebenezer Spencer; also 1/3 part of my undivided land that shall be laid out by virtue of any right belonging to me.

I also give unto my son Nathaniel Barbour £20 in money, to be paid him by his brother Aaron Barbour.

I give unto my son Jonathan Barbour, besides what I have already given him by deed of gift, 2/3 part of the land purchased of Ebenezer Williams that belonged to Mark Kelsey, 2/3 part of the land I purchased of Ebenezer Gilbert and Ebenezer Spencer, also 1/2 part of all undivided lands. I give him £20 as money to be paid him by his brother Aaron Barbour.

I give my son Aaron Barbour my home lott, dwelling house, barn and all edifices erected on same, with other lands. Also I give him my "wheelwright" Tools. I give to my two daughters, Abigail Brown and Rebecca Drake, to each of them ; £80 in current pay or 2/3 money. I give unto my daughter Abigail £S more. I give to my grandchildren, to Elizabeth Drake if she continues to live at my house till she comes of age, the sum of £20 in currency pay or 2/3 money;

and to Hannah Drake ; £15 as money. I make my sons Nathaniel Barbour, Jonathan Barbour, and Aaron Barbour Executors.

Josiah Barbour.
Witness ; —
Charles Whiting
Samuel Howard
John Dod

A codicil dated December 9-1729; I, the sd. Josiah Barbour by this present codicil, do ratify and confirm my last Will and Testament, and do give to my wife Sarah 10 bushels of Indian Corne 6 bushels of rie, and 20 pounds of flax, and a barrel of sider, and all the pork, butter and suit in the house, to be paid to her, my sd. wife Sarah, immediately after my decease And whereas I have ordered a legacy to be pd. Hannah Drake, my will is that Elizabeth Drake shall have one of the feather beds and one of the blankets my wife made since we married, and Hannah Drake the other feather bed and two blankets which she made since she came here, and the middle brass kettle, as part of their legacies, to be valued at Inventory price ; but my wife Sarah shall have the use of them during her natural life.

Josiah Barbour
Witness ;
Elisha Pratt
Sarah Pratt
Hannah Loomis
Timothy Loomis.

Court record, pg. 8, Jan. 6, 1729-30; Will proven, pg. 49, 3 August 1731. The executors exhibit the receipts under the hands of the heirs.

THIRD GENERATION.

CAPT. NATHANIEL BARBER,(Nathaniel[3], Josiah[2], Thomas[1]) b. Dec. 5, 1717; m. Sept. 13, 1739, Hepzibah, dau. of Ichabod and Hepzibah Loomis, who was b. July 5, 1722. They removed to Torrington, Conn., about 1740, where Nathaniel d. Mch. 8, 1788, and his wife, Hepzibah, Mch. 26, 1793.
Children :
    I.   Hepzibah, b. Mch. 9, bp. 16, 1739-40 at Windsor.
   II.   Nathaniel, bp. Aug. 29, 1742 ; d. Mch. 9, 1743.
  III.   Nathaniel, bp. Feb. 19, 1744.
  IV.   Elijah, bp. May 11, 1746.
   V.   Timothy, bp. Nov. 6, 1748.
  VI.   Chloe, bp. Apr. 7, 1751 ; m. Abner Loomis.
 VII.   Lois or Lucy, bp. July 8, 1753 ; m. James Homes.
VIII.   Keziah, bp. Nov. 16, 1755 ; d. May 22, 1774.

IX.   Susan, bp. Feb. 19, 1758. Not mentioned in her father's will.
X.   Eli, bp. Mch. 29, 1761.
XI.   Ziba, bp. Aug. 14, 1764. Not mentioned in her father's will.
XII.   Jemima, bp. Aug. 14, 1764; m. Benoni Loomis.

In Capt. Nathaniel Barber's will dated Mch. 17, 1786 (Exhibited Apr. 12, 1788) he makes bequests — " To eldest son Nathaniel."
—To sons Elijah, Timothy and Eli."

" To my four daughters Chloe, wife of Abner Loomis ; Lucy, wife James Homes; Hepzibah and Jemima.

The wife Hepzibah and son Elijah are made executors, and the will contains the following clause : " If my son Eli never return, who is gone from me, I give his to his brothers and sisters, except £30 to his heirs."
The will of Hepzibah Barber, exhibited Apr. 3, 1793, makes mention of her four daughters, "Chloe Loomis, Lucy Homes, Jemima Loomis and Hepzibah Barber."

Abner Loomis, husband of daughter Chloe, was named Executor.

PETER BROWNE
Mayflower Passenger

Peter Browne was probably born in January 1594 in Dorking, Surrey, England[1] to William Browne.[1][2] He was baptized in the local parish on January 26, 1594.[2] While his brothers John (who joined him in 1632 in Plymouth Colony), Samuel, and James became weavers[2], his vocation is believed to have been a carpenter, machinist, or similar.[3] In 1619 or 1620 he was likely enlisted by William Mullins, as part of the "London contingent," whose trades and skills were necessary for the voyage of the *Mayflower* and the *Speedwell* and the creation of the colony.[4]
The Mayflower and Plymouth

Bas-relief from the Pilgrim Monument depicting the signing of the Mayflower Compact.
On September 6, 1620, Peter Browne boarded the *Mayflower* at Southampton, Hampshire, England.[4][1] With 102 fellow *Mayflower* passengers and crew, he intended to travel to "the Northern parts of Virginia" and establish an English colony near the mouth of the Hudson River.[4] Due to severe weather conditions, the ship was forced to anchor off of Cape Cod, where

the first disembarkation occurred and where the Pilgrims determined to bind themselves as a democratically governed and administered colony loyal to England through the signing of the Mayflower Compact by all eligible men on behalf of themselves, their families, and their fortunes and property.[4] Peter Browne was one of the 41 men who signed it on November 11, 1620.[4]

Mayflower in Plymouth Harbor by William Halsall (1882)

A January 12, 1621 incident is recorded in *Mourt's Relation* whereby Peter Browne and John Goodman became lost in the woods after their dogs began to chase a deer. After a sleepless night, during which time both Browne and Goodman believed they heard lions (possibly mountain lions or other large mammals such as bears or coyotes), they successfully reoriented themselves and returned safely to the site of the village on the shore.[5] Being among the half of the Pilgrims who survived the first winter, Browne was present at the First Thanksgiving in the fall of 1621, the event that set the precedent for the American Thanksgiving holiday.[4][5]

By the middle of the 1620s, Browne had married Martha, the widow of ship's master Ford of the *Fortune*, who was a passenger of that second ship to arrive at Plymouth.[1] They had two daughters.[1][4] By 1630, Martha was deceased and Peter Browne remarried to a woman called Mary.[1] They also had two children together.[1][4]

End of Life

Peter Browne's home site on Leyden Street in Plymouth, Massachusetts

The administration of the estate of Peter Browne on October 10, 1633,[1] indicates that he died sometime since the last reference to his property in the records. It is widely believed that he succumbed to the same sickness that spread through Plymouth Colony in the summer of 1633.[4][1] He was survived by his second wife Mary who acted as the executrix of his estate.[1] The Plymouth General Court determined that money was to be set aside for his daughters from his first marriage, whose care was taken up by neighbor John Donne.[6]

Descendants

Peter Browne had four children, only three of whom survived to adulthood.[1] By his first marriage to Martha, widow Ford, he had daughters Mary and Priscilla.[1] By his second marriage to Mary, he had daughter Rebecca and the child who did not survive.[1] His daughters were:

Mary Browne, who married Ephraim Tinkham and later relocated to Middleboro.[1] Priscilla Browne, who married William Allen, but had no children.[1]
Rebecca Browne, who married William Snow and later relocated to Sandwich.[1]

Though often stated in biographies of John Brown, the renowned 19th century abolitionist, it has been definitively proven that the Brown family of Ancient Windsor, Connecticut are not descendants of Peter Browne the *Mayflower* Pilgrim.[1]
Many of the current descendants of Peter Browne have been located in the Tinkhamtown section of Mattapoisett, Massachusetts since the late 1700s.[1]

References
^ a b c d e f g h i j k l m n o p q r *Mayflower Families: Through Five Generations, Vol. VII, Third Ed.: Peter Brown*. Massachusetts Society of Mayflower Descendants; Boston, 2007.
^ a b c Johnson, Caleb. "The Probable English Origin of Mayflower Passenger Peter Browne, And His Association with Mayflower Passenger William Mullins," *The American Genealogist*, Vol. 79, No. 3; Demorest, Ga., 2004; pp. 161-178.
^ *Correspondence of the Pilgrim Peter Browne Society*, Vol. I, No. I; Falmouth, Mass., 2008; pp. 3-4
^ a b c d e f g h i Bradford, William. *History of Plymouth Plantation*, Charles Deane, ed.; Boston, 1856.
^ a b Winslow, Edward, et al.. *Mourt's Relation, or a Journal of the Plantation at Plymouth*, Henry Dexter, ed.; publisher J.K. Wiggin, Boston, 1865.
^ "Inventory of Peter Brown." Pilgrim Hall Museum; on-line source, accessed 18 July 2008.

Descendants of Peter Brown of Windsor, CT.

First Generation

1. Peter Brown-[161] was born in 1632 in Duxbury, Plymouth, MA and died on 9 Mar 1692 in Windsor, Hartford, CT.

Peter married Mary Gillet-[162] [MRIN:54], daughter of Jonathan Gillet-[314] and Mary Dolbere-[315], on 15 Jul 1658 in Windsor, Hartford, CT.

Children from this marriage were:
  F   i. **Mary Brown-[163]** was born on 2 May 1659 in Windsor, Hartford,
  CT. F   ii. **Hannah Brown-[164]** was born in Windsor, Hartford, CT.
Noted events in her life were:
Baptism; 30 Sep 1660; Windsor, Hartford, CT.
  F   iii. **Abigail Brown** was born on 8 Aug 1662 in Windsor, Hartford, CT.
  U   iv. Hepzibah Brown

Noted events in his/her life were:

1. Baptism; 20 Nov 1664; Windsor, Hartford, CT.

M v. **Peter Brown Jr.** was born on 8 Jan 1668 in Windsor, Hartford, CT.

vi. **John Brown** was born on 8 Jan 1668 in Windsor, Hartford, CT and died on 2 Feb 1728 in Windsor, Hartford, CT.

M vii. **Jonathan Brown** was born on 30 Mar 1670 in Windsor, Hartford, CT and died on 26 Aug 1747 in Windsor, Hartford, CT.

M viii. **Cornelius Brown** was born on 30 Jul 1672 in Windsor, Hartford, CT and died on 26 Jan 1747 in Windsor, Hartford, CT.

F ix. **Hester Brown** was born on 30 Jul 1673 in Windsor, Hartford, CT.

F x. **Isabel Brown** was born on 9 Jun 1676 in Windsor, Hartford, CT.

F xi. **Deborah Brown** was born on 12 Feb 1678 in Windsor, Hartford, CT.
Deborah married John Hosford on 9 Apr 1696.

F xii. **Sarah Brown** was born on 20 Aug 1681 in Windsor, Hartford, CT.
Sarah married Joseph Moore.

Second Generation (Children)

Abigail Brown (Peter[1]) was born on 8 Aug 1662 in Windsor, Hartford, CT.
Noted events in her life were:
1. Baptism; 10 Aug 1662; Windsor, Hartford, CT.
Abigail married Samuel Fowler, son of Ambrose Fowler and Joane Alvord, on 6 Nov 1683 Windsor, Hartford, CT.
Children from this marriage were:

M i. **Samuel Fowler** was born on 29 Jan 1684 in Windsor, Hartford, CT. M

ii. **Jonathan Fowler** was born on 19 Oct 1685 in Windsor, Hartford, CT.

F iii. **Abigail Fowler** was born on 25 Oct 1687 in Windsor, Hartford, CT and died 1733 OR 43 in Farmington, Hartford, CT.

F iv. **Mary Fowler** was born on 22 Feb 1690 in Windsor, Hartford, CT.

F v. **Hannah Fowler** was born on 3 Nov 1693 in Windsor, Hartford, CT.

F vi. **Esther Fowler** was born on 16 Jan 1695 in Windsor, Hartford, CT.

F vii. **Sarah Fowler** was born on 31 May 1698.

F viii. **Isabel Fowler** was born on 1 Feb 1701.

F ix. **Elizabeth Fowler** was born on 7 Jan 1704.

F x. **Mindwell Fowler** was born about 1706.

Peter Brown Jr. (Peter[1]) was born on 8 Jan 1668 in Windsor, Hartford, CT.
Peter married Mary Barber, daughter of Thomas Barber and Mary Phelps, on 22 Jul 1696 in Windsor, Hartford, CT.
Children from this marriage were:

M i. **Peter Brown** was born on 28 Jan 1700 in Windsor, Hartford, CT.

F ii. **Dinah Brown** was born on 4 Jan 1702.

M iii. **Samuel Brown** was born on 28 Aug 1701-1702 in Windsor, Hartford, CT and died on 18 Jun 1785 in Windsor, Hartford, CT.

F iv. **Mary Brown** was born on 28 Aug 1708 in Windsor, Hartford, CT.

M v. **Benjamin Brown** was born on 11 Aug 1711 in Windsor, Hartford, CT.

M vi. **Ebenezer Brown** was born on 27 Aug 1719 in Windsor, Hartford, CT.

17

F vii. **Mindwell Brown** was born on 27 Aug 1719 in Windsor, Hartford, CT and died on 25 Feb 1758 in Windsor, Hartford, CT. Mindwell married David Rowley on 23 Jun 1736.

John Brown (Peter[1]) was born on 8 Jan 1668 in Windsor, Hartford, CT and died on 2 Feb 1728 in Windsor, Hartford, CT. John married Elizabeth Loomis, daughter of John Loomis and Elizabeth Scott, on 4 Feb 1692 in Windsor, Hartford, CT.

Children from this marriage were:

F i. **Elizabeth Brown** was born on 11 Feb 1692 in Windsor, Hartford, CT and died on 12 Aug 1715 in Windsor, Hartford, CT.

F ii. **Mary Brown** was born on 11 Sep 1694 in Windsor, Hartford, CT.

F iii. **Ann Brown** was born on 1 Sep 1696 in Windsor, Hartford, CT and died on 22 Sep 1696 in Windsor, Hartford, CT.

F iv. **Hannah Brown** was born on 24 Aug 1697 in Windsor, Hartford, CT.

M v. **John Brown** was born on 11 Mar 1700 in Windsor, Hartford, CT.

F vi. **Ann Brown** was born on 13 Aug 1702 in Windsor, Hartford, CT. F
vii. **Sarah Brown** was born on 22 Jan 1704 in Windsor, Hartford, CT.

M viii. **Isaac Brown** was born on 17 Mar 1707 in Windsor, Hartford, CT and died on 8 Sep 1775 in Wintonbury, Windsor, Hartford, CT.

M ix. **Daniel Brown** was born on 29 Jan 1709 in Windsor, Hartford, CT.

F x. **Margaret Brown** was born on 8 Mar 1711 in Windsor, Hartford, CT.

F xi. **Esther Brown** was born on 17 Mar 1713 in Windsor, Hartford, CT.

Jonathan Brown (Peter[1]) was born on 30 Mar 1670 in Windsor, Hartford, CT and died on 26 Aug 1747 in Windsor, Hartford, CT. Jonathan married Mindwell Loomis, daughter of Nathaniel Loomis and Elizabeth Moore, on 1 Oct 1696 in Windsor, Hartford, CT.

Children from this marriage were:

F i. **Mindwell Brown** was born on 8 Jan 1699 in Windsor, Hartford, CT.

M ii. **Ephraim Brown** was born on 5 Aug 1712 in Windsor, Hartford, CT.

F iii. **Ruth Brown** was born on 11 Jan 1702 in Windsor, Hartford, CT.

F iv. **Martha Brown** was born on 7 Sep 1704 in Windsor, Hartford, CT. Martha married Isaac Brown, son of John Brown and Elizabeth Loomis, on 5 Mar 1729 in Wintonbury, Windsor, Hartford, CT.

M v. Jonathan Brown was born on 20 Jun 1707 in Windsor, Hartford, CT and died Died Young in Windsor, Hartford, CT.

M vi. David Brown was born on 8 Mar 1709 in Windsor, Hartford, CT.

F vii. Eunice Brown was born on 16 May 1715 in Windsor, Hartford, CT.

M viii. Jonathan Brown was born on 10 May 1718 in Windsor, Hartford, CT.

M ix. Benjamin Brown was born on 14 Jul 1721 in Windsor, Hartford, CT.

Cornelius Brown (Peter[1]) was born on 30 Jul 1672 in Windsor, Hartford, CT and died on 26 Jan 1747 in Windsor, Hartford, CT. Cornelius married Abigail Barber, daughter of Josiah Barber and Abigail Loomis, on 4 Dec 1701 in Windsor, Hartford, CT.

Children from this marriage were:

F i. **Abigail Brown** was born on 6 Sep 1702 in Windsor, Hartford, CT.

F ii. **Rachel Brown** was born on 21 Nov 1702 in Windsor, Hartford, CT.

F iii. **Rachel Brown** was born on 21 Nov 1704 in Windsor, Hartford, CT.

F iv. **Mabel Brown** was born on 21 Nov 1704 in Windsor, Hartford, CT and died on 8 Dec 1704 in Windsor, Hartford, CT.

M v. **Cornelius Brown** was born on 1 May 1707 in Windsor, Hartford, CT.

F vi. **Hildah Brown** was born on 17 Nov 1709 in Windsor, Hartford, CT.
U vii. **Hepzibah Brown** was born on 19 Jan 1712 in Windsor, Hartford, CT.
M viii. **Titus Brown** was born on 11 Nov 1714 in Windsor, Hartford, CT.
F ix. **Ellizabeth Brown** was born on 1 Oct 1717 in Windsor, Hartford, CT.
M x. **Aaron Brown** was born on 21 May 1725 in Windsor, Hartford, CT.

IMMIGRANT ANCESTOR

JONATHAN GILLETTE
Immigrant 1633 on the "Recovery"

Jonathan Gillette Sr., son of Rev. William Gillette, died 23 August 1677 at Windsor, Ct. His will was dated 8 August 1677, proved 6 September 1677. Inventory taken by Matthew Grant (Ancestor of Ulysses S. Grant). Married at St. Andrew's Church, Colyton, Devonshire, England 29 March 1634 to Mary Dolbere, daughter of Rawkey and Mary (Mitchell) Dolbere, born 7 June 1607 at Colyton, England, and died 5 January 1685 at Windsor, Ct., also spelled Dolbiar. Name listed on the passenger list of the "Recovery" of London, 31 March 1633 from Weymouth to New England. He later returned to England to marry, and returned to New England again in June of 1634. Freeman 1635. He settled first at Dorchester, Ma., but later removed to Windsor, Ct. He gave 4s. 6d. to the fund in aid of sufferers by the Indian war at Simsbury and Springfield, and was one of the committee of distribution. Constable 1656.

Last Will and Testament:
I Jonathan Gillett Sr., of Windsor, do make this my Last Will and Testament: Imprimis: My will is that my wife shall be my sole Executrix, and my son Josiah Gillett to take the care for ye improvement of his mother's estate for her use and benefit that I shall leave her whilst she lives, which she shall have ye use and benefit that may be made of the houseing and lands of both my house lotts, my one and that which was my brother Nathan Gillett's, which are both 9 acres, also at ye upper end of ye 1st meadow, or that which is Timothy Phelps. All that remains of yt to me, I set out 3 acres to my son John. My will is that after my decease, as I have expressed, that my son Josias shall take ye care on him, to be an help and ayde to his mother in what shee needs his labor to manage her ocasions, and after her decease he shall injoy for his owne, for himselfe and his heirs forever, my now dwelling house and all the appurtenances with it, with 5 acres of house lands and all other parcels of land, as are expressed to be his mother's for her use whilst she lives, only excepting the house and 4 acres of ye houseland to it, which my sonn Jeremy shall posses for his owne after my wifes decease; ye 6 acres in ye 2nd meadow I set out to him, he is to possess for his one at present. Thirdly, my will is that if the Lord should take me and my wife both of us away by death within this 4 years after ye date hereof, my son Josiah shall pay some legacies, as to his brother Jonathan Gillett L4 and a gunn, and to his brother Cornelius Gillett L4, and to my daughter, Peter Browne's wife, L2, and to my daughter, Samuel Fyllyes wife, L2, and to ye two children which I have taken that ware my son Joseph's, Dec'd, as ye little son Jonathan L5, and ye garle L5. My son Jonathan is to have the other 20 acres of Woodland joining to ye 20 acres expressed to my wife. He is to have his 20 acres next to Thomas Barber, 10 acres of it I give him, ye other 10 he hath bought. Also Jonathan and Cornelius my sons are to have my 11 acres without ye west bounds of Windsor, betwixt them, after my decease. And my son John Gillett to have six acres of ye other parcel without ye bounds at present, and Jeremie to have the remainder of it.
Signed: Jonathan Gillett. Witness: Nathaniel Chauncey, Matthew Grant
Court Record, p. 164, 6 September 1677: Will exhibited.

Children: Jonathan b. 1634 "about half a years after coming to land" (abt. Dec.), d. 5 Sept 1708, m. 22 Apr 1661 Mary, d. of Wm. Kelsey.
Mary d.y., Mary, Jonathan, William. He m. 2nd, 1676 Miriam Dibble. Ch: Thomas, Ebenezer d.s., Samuel, Hannah, Jonathan, Miriam.
Cornelius b. 1635, m. Priscilla Kelsey.
Ch: Priscilla d.s., Priscilla, Abigail, Cornelius, Mary, Esther, Sarah, Joanna, Daniel.
Mary, twin, b. Dorchester, m. 15 July 1658 Peter Brown.
Ch: Anna b. 29 Dec, d. 18 Nov 1711 Windsor, m. 1663 Samuel Filley
Joseph b. 25 July 1641, d. aged 34, killed at the Bloody Brook Indian massacre at Deerfield, Ma., m. 1664 Elizabeth Hawkes, d. of John Hawkes.
Ch: Joseph, Elizabeth, Mary, Jonathan, John, Nathaniel, Hannah.
Samuel b. 22 Jan 1642 Windsor, d. aged 33, killed at the Turner's Falls, Mass battle with the Indians.
John b. 4 Oct 1644, of Windsor, m. 1669 Mary Barber, d. of Thomas Barber. Ch: John, Thomas, Samuel, Nathaniel, Mary.
Abigail b. 1646, d. 1649
Jeremiah m. Deborah Bartlett
Josiah bp 15 July 1650, d. 29 Oct 1736 Colchester, Ct., m. 30 June 1676 Joanna Taintor, d. of Michael and Elizabeth (Rose) Taintor. Ch: 11

THE LOOMIS FAMILY

Comment: the original spelling of the name was probably LOOMYS, as Joseph was probably of Dutch ancestry (many skilled Dutch were brought to England to work in the textile industry).

Joseph Loomis was born in 1590 in England. He emigrated on Apr 11 1638 from London. Ship "Susan and Ellen" He immigrated on Jul 17 1638 to Boston, Massachusetts. from Descendants of Joseph Loomis by Elias Loomis, LL.D., Prof Natural Philosophy & Astronomy in Yale College... "It is mentioned in the town records of Windsor, vol.1, that on the 2nd. of Feb., 1640 he had granted him from the Plantation 21 acres adjoining Farmington river, on the east side of the Connecticut, partly from the town and partly by purchase. he therefore probably came to Windsor in the summer or autumn of 1639, and he is generally supposed to have come in company with Rev. Ephriam Huet, who arrived at Windsor Aug 16, 1639. He brought with him five sons and three daughters. His house was situated near the mouth of Farmington river on the Island, so called because at every great freshet it became temporarily an island by the overflowing of Connecticut river. ...

Joseph Loomis was a woolen draper, a merchant engaged in the purchase of cloth from the many weavers who wove on hand looms in their cottage homes. He had a store in Braintree, Essex, Eng., stocked with cloths and other goods which a draper usually dealt in. These products he sold both wholesale and retail to tailors and consumers in general. Braintree and near-by towns were centers of the cloth manufacture, as many weavers from Flanders had been induced to come to England by Edward III and they had been followed by others in the latter part of the sixteenth century, who had settled in Essex, not far from Braintree, in 1570. Joseph Loomis was in prosperous circumstances and his father-in-law, Robert White, was a man of considerable means for those times. Elder John White was a son of Robert White, and the wives of John Porter and Elder William Goodwin were also daughters of Robert White. Joseph Loomis settled at Windsor near the junction of the Farmington river with the Connecticut, on the island. The island was high land and so called because it became an island at every great freshet of the river. His house has been in the perpetual possession of the family down to the present time and is probably the oldest one now standing in Connecticut, which is still owned by the descendants of the pioneer builder. It was on this island that Capt. William Holmes and a few other men of the Plymouth colony established a trading house in 1633, which was the first permanent English settlement in Connecticut.

In 1874, James C. Loomis, Hezekiah B. Loomis, Osbert B. Loomis, H. Sidney Hayden and his wife, and John Mason Loomis were constituted a corporate body by the name of the LOOMIS INSTITUTE. This institute is designed for the gratuitous education of persons of the age of twelve years and upwards, and is to be located on the original homestead of Joseph Loomis on "The Island", in Windsor, Conn. This homestead is situated on elevated ground on the west bank of the Connecticut river, and commands an uncommonly fine view of the river and valley. Since the death of Joseph Loomis this site has always been in the possession of some one of his lineal descendants to the present time. It is the design of the corporators to do what they can to endow this Institution and in this they desire the Co-operation of all the Loomis family, that the Institution may become a lasting monument to the memory of Joseph Loomis, and a blessing to the town which he selected for his refuge from the annoyances to which Puritans were subjected in the mother country."

He moved on Aug 16 1639 to Windsor, Connecticut. He died on Nov 251658 in Windsor, Connecticut. He was a Woolen draper. Parents: John Lummys and Agnes Lyngwood.

He was married to Marie White on Jun 30 1614 in Messing, Co. Essex, England. Children were: Lt. Samuel Loomis, Joseph Loomis, Sarah Loomis, Elizabeth Loomis, Mary Loomis, John Loomis, Thomas Loomis, Nathaniel Loomis.

That pioneer Joseph Loomis was a man of "respectable pecuniary means" is also evidenced by the fact that his name appears on the tax list of Braintree, England, for building a ship of 800 tons, to be built at Portsmouth, March 1, 1636, said ship to cost ?8,000, the parish of Braintree being assessed ?951-12-4 1/2. Moreover Joseph Loomis's father-in-law, Robert White, was considered a rich man for his time, and this is fully verified by his will, which see hereinafter.

It is already known, of official evidence, that the "Joseph Lummys" ("Lommys"), who resided in the town and parish of Braintree in Essex, England, left that place in the spring of the year of 1638; also, that without any appreciable delay thereafter, he became a passenger of record in a vessel of goodly register, known as the "Susan and Ellen," and that this vessel did depart on the eleventh day in the month of April, of that year, from the port of London, bound for Boston in New England, carrying quite a number of other voyagers with their personal properties.

In this connection it is the writer's duty to deal with facts that have not been made manifest hitherto--with respect to the scenes and circumstances amid which he lived; and as well, to the elements contributing chiefly to his taking leave of England. Thereunto let attention first be directed to the ways and the means by which Joseph Lummys, with his family and worldly goods, had "come up to London" from Braintree. By the sworn deposition, or affidavit, of one Joseph Hills of Charlestown, in the Massachusetts Bay Colony (see herein page 21), made thereat on the 30th day of July, 1639, he, (Hills) being the "undertaker"--the manager or promoter of this particular vessel, voyage or emigration--it is learned that the various parcels embracing the goods of Joseph Loomis (we shall principally refer to him as Loomis hereinafter) were "transported from Malden, in the County of Essex, to London, in an Ipswich hye." This place of "Malden" being Maldon, the Essex port, and an "Ipswich hye" meaning a smart craft of small size and especially engaged, we may retrace the journey of the said Loomis, his family and friends, from London, viz: down the Thames, up the Essex coast, across the Maplin and Foulness Sands, into the wide and long reach of the mouth of the river Blackwater, and continuing thence up the river some ten miles, and so, back to Maldon. This small port was one through which there long had passed commerce and people between England and the Continent. That Joseph

Loomis and family attended personally the transportation, from Maldon in this hye, of their eleven separate and varying pieces of baggage and "divers other goods," which the above-noted deposition recounts, may well be believed.

The inland Blackwater river, though but a very small stream of only a few feet in width, reaches northwestward from Maldon, to and past "Six Bells Corner" in the end of Bocking parish, by Braintree. But by so devious a route does it flow, that Joseph Loomis, in his journey seaward, only followed it in its lower half, viz: from Witham to Maldon. The "River Brain,"--a mere brook--lightly slips down direct from the southern slope of Braintree to Witham, there uniting with the Blackwater. So it was that the emigrants came out of Braintree by the pleasant highway, paralleling the Brain. They passed through Black Notley, White Notley and Faulkbourne,-- all sparse hamlets strung along the gently undulating road, above the stream, yet each little settlement with its handy inn. Thus was reached Witham, then on the great Roman road between London and the northeast. Thence out of Witham, they followed the course of the Blackwater by Wickham Place, through.

Langford and Heybridge to Maldon. Some fifteen miles in all from Braintree it was, and over a favorite route for bicyclists nowadays. Alternating copses and fields, freshly furrowed for the seed-sowing, marked the way between the snug hamlets and the occasional houses plastered in white or yellow beneath their low-browed roofs of thatch. Some of these houses still exist along the way, and pretty much the same sort of people as of yore still abide in them.

This longest way around, of 100 miles to London, may have been both an easier and a quicker progress than by the forty miles of the shortest highway thereto, by the way of Chelmsford. It should have been less costly a journey than that which necessitated frequent stops at taverns for rest and refreshment. Very well-ordered seems to have been the Loomis's departure. Many a stop was made at gate and door, in those familiar fifteen miles, to give and receive blessings and farewells--the last of earth--repeating what had but just happened in Braintree church and market-place.

Braintree scarce could afford to lose such a citizen as Joseph Loomis; but America needed him more, and he knew it. Just that same need was exactly why he went away. Verily, it was not merely religion, not all prospect of gain, not great dissatisfaction with home,--not any one of these things that chiefly moved him to arise and go to set himself down three thousand miles from the ease of home. Broader than any of these causes was the reason. To help found a new country, with fairer laws and wider liberties, where the ordinary man might be more supreme-- that was the Great Idea that possessed him, and many others. As of the non-conformist faction out of the church of England they wanted to dominate the church at home, which power they could not quite attain to there. But deeper than that desire in the breast of Joseph Loomis was the spirit that moved him. He felt himself equal to the task that other men had set. The challenge of their example stirred him. The appeal of Opportunity decided him. It convinced his mind that he was one of "the chosen" for the Great Purpose. And the apparently unlimited possibilities, to him and his, of the natural resources of an unclaimed land, hovered in his imagination. He had all the money that he would require to pleasantly establish his family in America. Let us dismiss, as being insufficient, the idea of "a band of Christians fleeing from persecution" --save with respect to the Mayflower's Pilgrims mostly. To the so-called Puritan settlers, the comforts of religion were vastly more of a necessity and more relished in the New than they had been to them in the Old England. Daily spiritual refreshment kept them to their hard tasks, soothed the longing for a return to the beautiful land they had forsaken, and, in fact, the church was the keystone that held up the arch of the early colonization.

"John Lummys," the father, and tailor, is shown by his will, dated 1619, to have been a tradesman and real-estate holder in comfortable circumstances, and a citizen of esteem in the church and community. His son Joseph advanced the fortune of the family. Contemplating his means and position in England, and his situation in America, it seems entirely fair to say that he was a prosperous man in England, and of the better class of settlers in New England. Long it has been seen that he was independent in Windsor--and particularly so as to the location of his estate there.

Not driven out of England, not forsaking duties or obligations there, not an enthusiast or Puritanical extremist in religion was Joseph Loomis. He came to America on general principles, after long deliberation. As a practical business man of the world his decision so to do, it will be now agreed, was the apotheosis of wisdom. A study of his life in America prys up no indication that he regretted his transplantation, as did many other settlers, with cause.

St. Michael's church. Here for forty years or more Joseph Loomis passed in and out. Here he was baptized between 1585-1592--undoubtedly. Here were proclaimed the banns before his marriage-day,--the wedding having been consummated as per this entry in the parish church of Shalford:--
"Anne Dni 1614
"Joseph Loomys was married unto Marye whight the XXXth Daye of June anno pr dicte."

Inv't. ?178-10-00. Taken by Henry Clark, John Moore. Ct. Records, p. 115. 2 Dec. 1658. An agreement for a Division of the Estate by the Children of Joseph Loomis, Dec'd and approved by this Court of Magistrates to be an equal Division. To Joseph Loomis, to Nicholas Olmsted, to Josiah Hull, to John Loomis, to Thomas Loomis, to Nathaniel Loomis, to Mary Tudor, to Samuel Loomis.

This agreement of the children of Mr. Joseph Loomis respecting the division of the Estate of ye father deceased, approved by the Court 2 Dec. 1658: We whose names are hereunto subscribd doe by these presents testify that it is our mutual and joynt agreement to attend an equal division of the Estate of Mr. Joseph Loomis, Our father, lately deceased, wch said estate being distributed in the equal prption we doe by these presents engage to set down Satisfied and Contented respecting any future trouble or demands about the foresaid estate now presented by Inventory to ye Court of Magistrates.

Witness our hand, 2nd December, 1658. Joseph Loomis, Josiah Hull, Thomas Loomis, Mary Tudor, Nicholas Olmsted, John Loomis, Nathaniel Loomis, Samuel Loomis.

Abstract of the Disposition of the Estate of Joseph Loomis, Windsor, Connecticut Found in Original Records, Vol. 2, page 115-116, and in the printed Digest of Manwaring, Vol. I, page 135. He died Nov. 25, 1658.

Inv't. ?178-10-00. Taken by Henry Clark, John Moore. Ct. Records, p. 115. 2 Dec. 1658. An agreement for a Division of the Estate by the Children of Joseph Loomis, Dec'd and approved by this Court of Magistrates to be an equal Division. To Joseph Loomis, to Nicholas Olmsted, to Josiah Hull, to John Loomis, to Thomas Loomis, to Nathaniel Loomis, to Mary Tudor, to Samuel Loomis.

This agreement of the children of Mr. Joseph Loomis respecting the division of the Estate of ye father deceased, approved by the Court 2 Dec. 1658: We whose names are hereunto subscribd doe by these presents testify that it is our mutual and joynt agreement to attend an equal division of the Estate of Mr. Joseph Loomis, Our father, lately deceased, wch said estate being distributed in the equal prption we doe by these presents engage to set down Satisfied and Contented respecting any future trouble or demands about the foresaid estate now presented by Inventory to ye Court of Magistrates.

Witness our hand, 2nd December, 1658. Joseph Loomis, Josiah Hull, Thomas Loomis, Mary Tudor, Nicholas Olmsted, John Loomis, Nathaniel Loomis, Samuel Loomis.

The following is a copy of the original draft (unsigned) of the deposition of Joseph Hills of Charlestown, taken 30th July, 1639:(*)

"Joseph Hills of Charlestowne, in New England, Woollen Draper,** aged about 36 yeares, sworne, saith upon his oath that he came to New England undertaker in the ship called the Susan & Ellen of London whereof was master Mr. Edward Payne, in theyeare of our Lord one thousand six hundred thirty and eight, the 14th yeare of the raigne of our Souraigne Lord the King that now is and this dpt knowes that divers goods and chattells, victualls & commodities of Joseph Loomis late of Brayntree inthe County of Essex, Woolen-draper, wch were put in three butts, two hogsheds, one halfe hogshed, one barrel, one tubb & three firkins, transported from Malden in the County of Essex to London in an Ipswch Hye, were shipped in the said ship uponthe eleventh day of Aprill in the yeare abovesayd, and this deponent cleared the said goods wth divers other goods of the said Joseph Loomis and other mens, in the Custome-house at London, as may appeare by the Customers bookes, and this deptsaith that the said goods were transported into New England in the said ship where she arrived on the seaventeenth day of July in the yeare aforesayd."

(*)The N. E. Hst. and Gen. Reg., Vol. VIII, p. 309, contains the Will of Joseph Hills, lawyer, late of Maldon, Mass. He d. Feb. 5, 1687-8.

**So designated by Savage, Vol. II, p. 417

Children of Joseph Loomis.--Joseph Loomis had five sons and three daughters, whose marriages are recorded in the town records at Windsor, as also the births of their children, but as the date of the birth of Joseph's children is not recorded, it is difficult to determine the order of seniority.

In the Records of Particular Court for the colony of CT, vol. 2, p. 115, is recorded the agreement of the children of Mr. Joseph Loomis respecting the division of the estate of said deceased, as approved by the court Dec. 2, 1658. This agreement is signed by the children in the following order:

Joseph Loomis.
Nicholas Olmsted.
Josias Hull.
John Loomis.
Thomas Loomis.
Nathaniel Loomis.
Mary Tudor.
Samuel Loomis.

It is believed that the above order indicates the relative ages of the sons. Joseph Loomis, the younger, and John Loomis had land granted to them from the Windsor Plantation in 1643. The other sons acquired no land until several years afterwards. The names of the five sons are repeatedly mentioned on the records at Windsor and Hartford, as jurors, freemen, troopers, etc., and these dates lead to the conclusion that Joseph and John were older than the other three sons.

Sources

Ancestors of Peter Paul Dziekan, Jr., (Peter P Dziekan, 64 Wayside Inn Rd, Marlborough, MA 01752, 508-481-7421, dziekan@ultranet.com).

Charles W. Manwaring, Digest of the Early Connecticut Probate Records (Hartford District), (Hartford, 1902). Vol 1, p 136-137.

Loomis, Elias, Descendants of Joseph Loomis in America, (1909.) p 98.

Parsons, Samuel H., Record of Marriages and Births in Windsor, CT, (New England Historical & Genealogical Register, Vol 5, January 1851, p 225-230; April 1851, p 225-230).
5. Records of The Particular Court of Connecticut, 1639-1663, (Hartford, 1928). p 18-19.
6. ibid. p 108.
7. ibid. p 99.
8. ibid. p 195.
9. Ancestors of Larry William Strutz, (Larry William Strutz, 535 S. Erin St., Ridgecrest, CA 93555, 760-375-7636, strutz@ridgecrest.ca.us).

10. anonymous, The Children of Robert White of Messing, Co. Essex, England, Who Settled in Hartford & Windsor, (New England Historical & Genealogical Register, Vol 55, January 1901, p 22 & subsequent). citing Parish Records of Shalford.

WILLIAM NATHANIEL BARBER

171. CAPT. NATHANIEL BARBER,(Nathaniel[3], Josiah[2], Thomas[1]) b. Dec. 5, 1717; m. Sept. 13, 1739, Hepzibah, dau. of Ichabod and Hepzibah Loomis, who was b. July 5, 1722. They removed to Torrington, Conn., about 1740, where Nathaniel d. Mch. 8, 1788, and his wife, Hepzibah, Mch. 26, 1793.

Hepzibah, daughter of Ichabod and Hepzibah Loomis, is mentioned in her parents' wills as Hepizbah Barber (page 14). She married William Nathaniel? Barber.

WILLIAM[1] BARBER, 170?. He may be the same William who was in Anson Co NC with brother John, and had children Keziah and Cassandra. (See Family of John and William Barber of Anson Co). [Ref: Lt Dick Wilson - quotes IGI of NC; Gene Barber]

KEZIAH[2], 1750; m William Henry Cone.

Birth: 1750
                      Pee Dee (Anson County)
                      Anson County
                      North Carolina, USA
Death: 1810
                      Ivanhoe
                      Bulloch County
                      Georgia, USA

Keziah Eudel Barber Cone was born about 1750 in the Pee Dee Station area of North Carolina. She was the daughter of William Nathaniel Barber and Hepzibah Loomis Barber and sister of Cassandra Barber Carter. Some of her ancestors were said to have come to America aboard the *Mayflower*. About 1765 at the Pee Dee Station in North Carolina, Keziah married William Henry Cone, who was to become a farmer, landowner, justice of the peace, and Baptist minister (of the Little Ogeechee Baptist Church), and who became a Revolutionary War hero known as the "Fighting Parson" (while fighting with Francis Marion, the "Swamp Fox," of South Carolina). Keziah and William became residents of Cheraw County, South Carolina before migrating to Effingham County, Georgia and later to Bulloch County. They had nine children: Aaron Cone, Sr., Jane E. Cone, William Cone, Jr., Joseph Cone, Keziah Cone Dampier, Sarah Cone Knight, Nancy Ann Cone Hagin, Mary Cone Lee, and Elizabeth Cone. Keziah and William resided in the Ivanhoe Voting District (Briar Patch Census District) of Bulloch County, Georgia. Preceding her husband in death, Keziah died in 1810 in Bulloch County and *probably* was buried in a now unmarked grave in the Old William Cone-Barber Family Cemetery (Captain William Cone Cemetery) adjacent to the old Barber family homestead on the east side of the Old River Road near the Stagecoach Road on the western bank of the Ogeechee River south of Georgia Highway 119 (Guyton-Stilson Road). In 1985 a bridge across the Ogeechee River linking Bulloch and Effingham Counties was named in honor of her husband. Among her many notable descendents was a son, Aaron Cone, Sr., who was a courier during the American Revolution; a son, William Cone, Jr., who served in both the Georgia and Florida legislatures; a daughter Nancy Ann Cone Hagin, a founding member of three Baptist churches and a poet; a grandson, Aaron Cone, Jr., who assisted naturalist John Abbot in exploring Bulloch County; a grandson, William Haddock Cone, who was a Confederate veteran and a Florida state senator; a grandson Peter Cone who was a Major General in the Confederacy; a grandson Daniel Newman Cone who was a law enforcement officer killed in the line of duty; great-grandsons, Paul Robert Cone and John Slater Cone, Confederate soldiers who died from wounds received at the battle at James Island, South Carolina in June 1862; a great-grandson, Frederick Preston Cone, Governor of Florida from 1937 to 1942; a great-grandson Aaron Donaldson Cone, a Confederate veteran; a great-grandson Joseph Smith Cone, a Lt. Colonel in the Confederacy and a Georgia state senator; a great-grandson James Basil Cone, a dentist; a great-great-grandson Reamer Hamilton Cone, a teacher; a great-great-grandson Howell Cobb Cone, a founder of Georgia Southern University; a great-great-great-grandson William Henry Cone, a World War II veteran, a Lt. Commander in the Navy, and an attorney; a great-great-great-grandson Harry McClelland, a World War II veteran; a great-great-great-great-grandson Pernell McClelland, Jr., a World War II veteran; a great-great-great-great-grandson Waldo Floyd, Jr., MD, a physician; a great-great-great-great-grandson James Howell Cone, a Lutheran minister; a great-great-great-great-grandson John Cone, an accountant; and a great-great-great-great-great-granddaughter Sharlotte Neely Donnelly, PhD, a professor and author of *Snowbird Cherokees*; to name but a few of Keziah Barber Cone's descendents. Thanks so much to the dozens of Cone family genealogists for much of this information.

Burial:
Old William Cone - Barber Family Cemetery
Ivanhoe
Bulloch County
Georgia, USA

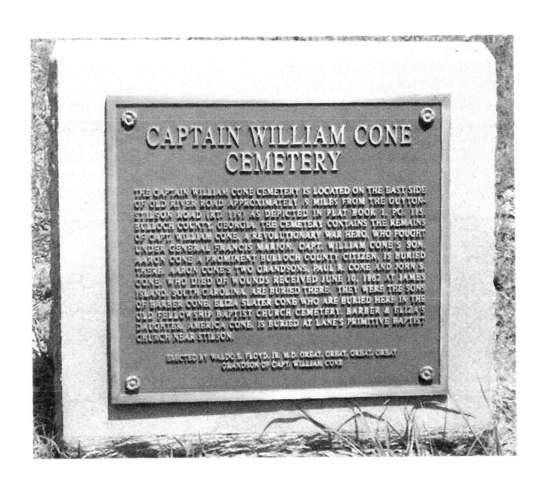

CAPTAIN WILLIAM CONE CEMETERY

THE CAPTAIN WILLIAM CONE CEMETERY IS LOCATED ON THE EAST SIDE OF OLD RIVER ROAD APPROXIMATELY .9 MILES FROM THE GUYTON-STILSON ROAD (RT. 119) AS DEPICTED IN PLAT BOOK I, PG. 115, BULLOCH COUNTY, GEORGIA. THE CEMETERY CONTAINS THE REMAINS OF CAPT. WILLIAM CONE, A REVOLUTIONARY WAR HERO, WHO FOUGHT UNDER GENERAL FRANCIS MARION. CAPT. WILLIAM CONE'S SON, AARON CONE A PROMINENT BULLOCH COUNTY CITIZEN, IS BURIED THERE. AARON CONE'S TWO GRANDSONS, PAUL R. CONE AND JOHN S. CONE, WHO DIED OF WOUNDS RECEIVED JUNE 10, 1862 AT JAMES ISLAND, SOUTH CAROLINA, ARE BURIED THERE. THEY WERE THE SONS OF BARBER CONE, ELIZA SLATER CONE WHO ARE BURIED HERE IN THE OLD FELLOWSHIP BAPTIST CHURCH CEMETERY. BARBER & ELIZA'S DAUGHTER, AMERICA CONE, IS BURIED AT LANE'S PRIMITIVE BAPTIST CHURCH NEAR STILSON.

ERECTED BY WALDO E. FLOYD, JR. M.D. GREAT, GREAT, GREAT, GREAT GRANDSON OF CAPT. WILLIAM CONE

30

Captain William Cone bridge

Little Ogeechee Baptist Church

THE CONE FAMILY

The following history of the Cone Family was taken from excerpts from *Men of Mark in Georgia* by Bernard Suttles, 1905, Contributed by Nell Campbell:

The Cone Family

For one hundred and thirty years the Cone family has been contributing in each generation splendid citizens and soldiers to the service of Georgia and Florida. Previous works of history and biography have dealt with this family in a very meager way, as will appear from the record.

William Cone, the Elder.

Daniel Cone, who settled at Haddam, Conn., in 1662, was the American progenitor. One of his descendants moved south and located on the Pee Dee River in North Carolina. Here in 1745 was born William Cone, the Revolutionary soldier, who is generally believed to have been a son of William, though this is not altogether certain, as his father's name may have been Aaron. Previous to the Revolution, William Cone married Keziah Barber, moved to Georgia, and was among the pioneer settlers of Bulloch County. He was an ardent patriot and during the Revolution saw service in McLean's regiment and under Gen. Francis Marion. This Capt.

31

William Cone was a terror to the Tories, as several incidents will show. When the notorious Tory, McGirth, and his followers were terrorizing that part of the State, it was learned that one Cargill harbored the Tories and gave them information about the Whigs. Cargill was advised that it meant death if he was again found in company with McGirth. Not long after, when William Cone was hunting deer on the Ogeechee he saw them together in the woods. He shot Cargill, but McGirth escaped, and the next day when they went to bury the dead man it was found that the wolves had almost devoured his body.

At another time the Tories fell on an unsuspecting settlement, stole the settlers' horses, and carried away everything possible. Headed by Captain Cone, the settlers pursued them down into what is now Tatnall County. Finding after a shower of rain that they were close on their heels, they sent forward one of their number to reconnoiter. The approach of this man became known to the Tories through one of the stolen horses, and one of their number, starting out to learn the cause of their confusion, was shot dead by the scout, who was concealed behind a log. This was the signal for an attack, and the patriots rushed forward, drove the Tories into the Ohoopee River and recovered their stolen goods. It is said that this raid broke the power of the Tories in that community.

At the close of the Revolution, Captain Cone returned to the pursuits of peace near Ivanhoe, and in 1796 was foreman of the first grand jury raised in Bulloch County. He died in 1815, about seventy years of age. It is a tradition in the Cone family that three brothers of Capt. William Cone fell in battle during the Revolutionary War, William being the sole survivor of the four brothers. He reared three sons and nine daughters. Of his sons, Aaron Cone was the only one who remained in Bulloch County, and he was the father of six sons and six daughters.

Peter Cone

Gen. Peter Cone was the eldest child of Aaron Cone and grandson of Capt. William Cone. His father, Aaron Cone, was born October 31, 1766, before the family left North Carolina. In 1788 he married Susan Marlow, and Peter Cone was born at Ivanhoe, Bulloch County on August 6, 1790. His father was a wealthy man, owned large landed estates with many slaves, and carried on extensive planting operations. He was much esteemed in Bulloch County, a member of the Baptist church, and died at Ivanhoe, Bulloch County on June 6, 1835, being then nearly sixty-nine years old. When the War of 1812 began, inheriting the family trait, Peter Cone enlisted, became a captain, and was stationed at Fort Sunbury. In 1818 he served under General Andrew Jackson in this Florida campaign. At the outbreak of the Civil War, Peter Cone was the senior major-general of the militia of the State of Georgia. Early in the thirties he became a member of the General Assembly and remained in that body continuously for thirty years. It is said that this is the longest continuous service by one man in the history of Georgia. he was a most influential man in his section of Georgia, and absolutely dominated Bulloch County for thirty years. A notable character in his day, he was held in much esteem by the public men of that time and lived until the year 1866. He never married.

William Cone, the Younger

When the break-up occurred in the family of Capt. William Cone, the elder, after the Revolutionary War, Aaron remained in Bulloch County. Joseph moved to Thomas County, and William, junior, moved to Camden County. William, Jr. was a very notable man. He represented Camden County for twenty three years in the Georgia legislature. He was born in 1777, and when the War of 1812 broke out was a man of thirty-five, in the prime of life. He inherited the reckless courage of the Cone family and became a captain in that war. It is related that in his infancy a body of Tories and British came to his father's house seeking the elder Cone, cut open a feather bed upon which the baby was resting, and poured baby and feathers out together, and the little fellow was nearly suffocated before he was rescued.

His military career in fighting the British, Indians and Spaniards was even more notable than that of his father. In the War of 1812 he served under General Newnan on the St. Mary's and St. John's Rivers. He was a participant in a campaign against the Alachua Indians, engaging in a hand-to-hand fight with an Indian at Alligator, killing his antagonist with clubbed musket after he had exhausted his ammunition. Returning form this expedition, they had to live on horse meat for quite a time. He took part in the defeat of the British naval expedition on St Mary's river, and in the operations against St. Augustine so incurred the hostility of the Spanish that they offered a reward of ten thousand dollars for his head. One of the brilliant exploits of that war was his defeat of the British on the St. Mary's in 1815. Twenty-three barges loaded with British soldiers ascended the river for the purpose of burning Major Clarke's mill. The enemy intended to land at a place called Camp Pinckney and march to Clarke's mill on the Spanish creek some three miles distant. Captain Cone with twenty-eight men was concealed in the palmettoes which lined the river banks, and his men being expert riflemen, opened fire on the barges. The bargers replied with cannon and small-arms fire, which was ineffective. For several miles Captain Cone's men took advantage of every turn of the river and at every shot brought down a man. Finally the British unable longer to stand the fire, retraced their course to St. Mary's. Upon their arrival at St. Mary's they reported one hundred and eighty men killed and as many wounded. Sometime after the war Captain William Cone settled in Florida and as late as 1842 represented Columbia County in the Florida State Senate. He died at Benton, Columbia County, Fla., on August 24, 1857, and was buried at Prospect church cemetery in Hamilton County. He was eighty years old at the time of his death. He had married Sarah Haddock, in Camden County, GA, about 1815.

William Burrows Cone

Judge Wm. B. Cone was a grandson of the fiery old Tory-hating captain, through the son who moved to Southwest Georgia [Joseph]. His mother was a Wadsworth. The family settled in Dooly County in 1832, and the father dying soon after, the lad became the mainstay of his mother, who had the children to rear. In 1835, then just a man, he married Elizabeth Mobley and settled down to farming. In a few years he became one of the leading men of this County, which he represented in the legislature in 1847 and 1850, and there met his kinsmen, Judge Francis Cone and General Peter Cone. Returning home from the general Assembly, he was elected Judge of the Inferior Court of Dooly County, which position he held continuously until the close of the

Civil war. After the War he lived in retirement at his handsome country home until his death in 1877, leaving the reputation of a horrible, capable man and a pure patriot.

The Later Generations

William Cone, the younger, left a family of sons who made a remarkable military record. His oldest son, B.N. Cone was captain of a company during the Indian wars in Florida, a daring and reckless officer. Another son, Capt. William H.[William Haddock] Cone, served as captain during the Seminole war in 1857 and made the most important campaign and capture of Indians during that war. later he served as captain of a cavalry company in the Confederate army. Another son, Peter Cone [Simon Peter], was lieutenant in the Indian war and served as first lieutenant in the Confederate army. The fourth son, J.B. Cone [James Barnard Cone], was considered the most powerful man physically in the State of Florida. He served in the Indian war of 1857 and was lieutenant of cavalry in the Confederate army. The fifth and youngest son, C.F. Cone [Charles F.], served as lieutenant in the Indian war of 1857 and was captain of a cavalry company in the Confederate army. D.N. Cone [Daniel Newsome], a son of Capt. B.N. Cone and a grandson of Capt. William Cone, served the entire four years as a member of the Confederate army, and his son, Hutch I. Cone, entered the United States navy and has shown such brilliant qualities that he has risen by rapid steps to be chief of the Bureau of Engineering, with the rank of rear-admiral. F. P. Cone, now a member of the Florida State senate, is another grandson of William Cone, Jr. T. J. Cone, now a prominent citizen of Florida, is a descendant of the old Revolutionary captain through the son who moved to Southwest Georgia, being grandson of Judge Wm B. Cone.

Going back to Georgia, we find that Gen. Peter Cone had a brother James. Col. J. S. Cone [Joseph Smith Cone], son of James and nephew of Peter, entered the Confederate army in 1861 as a lieutenant, later promoted to captain, and for distinguished bravery in the battle of Chickamauga was, on the recommendation of Gen. John C. Breckinridge, promoted to major. At John's Island, Colonel Cone was the leader of the assault; he commanded the fort at Secessionville in the fall of 1864, and in the battle of Honey Hill was badly wounded an promoted to lieutenant-colonel. His name appears on the Chickmauga monument, and Camp 1227, United Confederate Veterans, bears his name. from 1870 to 1875, Colonel Cone, following in the footsteps of this distinguished uncle, served his district in the State senate of Georgia. Depressed by the death of his devoted wife and business losses, he with drew from public life, and has since lived a retired life in Bulloch County. His old regiment, the Forty-seventh Georgia, bore the brunt of many a hard struggle. When sent to the relief of Vicksburg, it mustered 1,100 men. Later on, when sent to Charleston, Colonel Cone, then in command reported 150 muskets.

The record above given shows that this family has been represented numerously in all the struggles of our country from the Revolutionary War down, and that in times of peace it has had many strong members of the various legislative bodies. The family record is indeed a remarkable one and worthy of preservation in our annals for the great qualities shown--bravery, patriotism, good business capacity, sound legislative judgment, and unfailing loyalty to country. --Men of Mark in Georgia by Bernard Suttles, 1905.

William Cone came to North Carolina to South Carolina and then to Georgia. He was born about 1745 and died in 1822. The latter part of the war he fought Tories in this section of Ga. He lived in what is now Bulloch County and died in Ivanhoe. Hs grave is east of Joe Cone's field in a thickly wooded section between the Old River Road and the Ogeechee River. It is identified by a marker erected by the DAR. He was married to Kesiah Barber. *Story of Bulloch County* Pub. by Bulloch Co. Historical Society, 1973.

The Civil War in Bulloch County was generally a time of fear and hiding for civilians. Yankee soldiers coming through the area killed live stock, stole their food, and destroyed what they could not carry off. Of the 750 white men of Bulloch County at the time, 600 entered the military service of the Confederate States of America. It is doubtful that any County paid a higher price to the Confederacy. The U.S. Census of 1870, four years after the war ended, show less than 10 percent of the population of Bulloch County was made up of white men between the ages of 22 and 40. T.Y. Aiken from Bulloch County was in the 47th Regiment of the Georgia Infantry. He won the honor of being the ugliest soldier in the Confederacy from a soldier in the 60th Regiment. The commanding officer was the final judge. *Spirit of a People*.

Ivanhoe in Bulloch County, Georgia no longer exists. All that is left is an old abandoned house and some fields. It was located at 32- 17; N 81 28 39; W, Elevation 94 feet; GA-119 CONN. near GA-119, Ivanhoe, Bulloch County, Georgia. A right turn onto GA-119, a few feet ahead, will take you to the bridge that separates Bulloch and Effingham Co.

Notes for WILLIAM CONE, Revolutionary Soldier, Pioneers of Wiregrass Georgia, Volume 5, Huxford:

William Cone, R.S. married Keziah Barber who was the sister of Casandra Barber. Casandra Barber and her husband Mathew Carter moved to Mississippi. William, R.S. served in the Revolutionary War as Major, 1st. Battalion, Richmond County militia. In 1779 he moved to Cheraw District of South Carolina and later to Effingham County, Ga. On Feb. 28, 1784 he was granted 250 acres of bounty land in Washington County, Ga (see p. 48, Knight's Roster of the Revolution in Georgia). He died in 1822 and was buried in the Cone Cemetery in Bulloch County, Ga.

Corrections, Volume 5, Huxford (p. 544):

Cone, William, Sr. (pp.64-66 Volume 2)

In doing research in the Minutes of Camden Superior Court within the last three or four years, the compiler has ascertained that he married a second time - a fact never mentioned and evidently not known by any of the Cone family historians. In deed book "I", p.13 of Camden County, is the record of a separation agreement dated Jan. 8, 1812, between William Cone and his wife Martha, in which it was agreed that thereafter each should hold his and her own property free from any claim on the part of the other "as though never married". The Minutes show that the same year William Sr., filed suit for divorce against his wife, Martha Cone. The original papers in the suit having been lost, it cannot be learned when they married or what her maiden name was or where married or the grounds for divorce - matters usually set forth in divorce proceedings. The Court dockets show the case was continued from term to term from 1812 until the October 1816 term when the docket shows the case was dismissed, it being stated that "suit was abated by the death of the plaintiff."

William Cone, Sr. returned to Bulloch some time between 1812 and 1816, and it was there on June 24, 1816, he deeded all his property to his son, Aaron Cone. The deed of gift, recorded in deed book 4A, p. 311, Bulloch, conveyed 1,000 acres of land in Bulloch; one half interest in 350 acres in Glynn County granted him and John Hagin (Vol.1); seven slaves, one horse, all his household goods, crop plantation tools, rifle and all money on hand or due him. This apparently was made about the time or during the last illness of the old patriot as he was dead before the following October term of Camden Court.

William Cone, Sr. was a representative from Glynn County in 1804 and shortly thereafter moved to Camden. He was appointed Justice of Peace in the 35th district of Camden in 1806 but resigned in 1808 and was succeeded by his son, William Cone, Jr., Feb. 25, 1808.

William Cone, Sr. was drawn to serve as a grand juror at the October Term, 1809, of Camden Superior Court, but was excused from duty on account of being over 60 years of age as shown by the court minutes.

The year of his death as published in Vol. II should be changed from 1822 to 1816. The 1822 date had been arrived at from the circumstance that his son Aaron had been appointed administrator of his estate on January 6, 1823.

Article printed on Thursday, March 13, 1930 in the Savannah Morning News

D. A. R.'S UNVEIL MARKER FOR CONE

Exercises Saturday at Revolutionary Hero's Grave in Bulloch County, Ga. Captain William Cone's resting place to be marked.

Statesboro, Ga. March 12. The Briar Creek Chapter of the Daughters of the American Revolution will unveil a marker at the grave of Captain William Cone, Revolutionary Hero, in Cone Cemetery at Ivanhoe, Saturday, March 13. At this time Honorable M. E. Wilson of Savannah, will be the principal speaker.

The D.A.R. is planning to place the several markers in this section of the state to Revolutionary heroes and expect to hold their second unveiling shortly after the Cone program on Saturday. Captain William Cone, a native of North Carolina, settled in this section of Georgia before the outbreak of the Revolution and was an officer whose name is linked with many brave exploits against the Tories. The Tories used Bulloch County as a retreat, coming up from Florida through the Okefenokee Swamp. Captain Cone gathered together a party of men from this section, drove the Tories back into Florida and warned them to keep out of this community, which they did. Many people have often wondered why this section and particularly

Bulloch County was late in being settled. The settlers did not care to come to a section that was used as a hiding place for the Tories and it is due to the brave exploits of Captain Cone that Bulloch County came to be settled and afterwards densely populated.

William Cone was living in Bulloch when the county was organized. The extracts from the minutes of the first court ever held in this County read as follows: "At a Superior Court began and held at the house of Stephen Mills, in and for the County of Bulloch on Tuesday the 16th day of May, 1737, the Honorable William Stephens, Esq., one of the Judges of the Superior court of the State of Georgia, presiding. The Court opened in due form and proceeded to the organization of the same by calling the grand and petit jurors. The Grand Jury presented William Cone as their foreman. Captain Cone's grandson, General Peter Cone, served continuously in the legislature of Georgia for 30 years and was the most dominant figure in the County until the time of his death. At the outbreak of the Civil War he was a Major General in the state militia. William Cone, Jr., another grandson, became a Captain in the War of 1812 after which he settled in Florida, went to the legislature and fought against the Seminoles. Captain William Cone, grandson of the old Captain, had a large part in one of the most remarkable feats ever recorded in the War of 1812. Captain Cone commanded 20-8 men who caused 23 British barges to retreat when entering the St. Marys River in 1815. Though the ships fired large cannons, the palmetto on either side of the river served as a screen for Cone's men who in this manner harassed the British causing them to retrace their course.

William Cone's name was also a familiar one in the religious of the time. In the record of the Hephsibah Baptist Centennial from 1794 to 1834 this appears: "William Cone is first brought to our attention in 1792 as pastor of Little Ogeechee Church in Screven County and its messenger to the Georgia Association. The tradition speaks of him as the instrument in God's hands of building up the Baptist church in the above-named County, also in the counties of Bulloch and Tattnall. His name is a familiar one for many miles around Ogeechee Church."

Mrs. J. R. Roberts of the Briar Creek Chapter of D.A.R. is chairman of the committee for marking graves of Revolutionary Soldiers. Mrs. Julian C. Lane of Statesboro is chairman of the program committee and has arranged a very interesting program which will be held in the Cone Cemetery at Old Ivanhoe at 2:30 o'clock on Saturday afternoon. The program will open with taps by the Boys Scouts of Statesboro and follows.

Prayer. Rev. J. D. Peebles, Pastor of the First Baptist Church of Statesboro and ex-chaplain of the Sons of the American Revolution of Virginia.

Placing of the Wreath and the United States Flag on the Grave. Dr. R. L. Cone of Statesboro and W. C. Crumley of Brooklet.

Unveiling. Mrs. Alice Hodges, Frances Cone, and Betty Jean Cone.

Presentation of the Regent. Mrs. Julian C. Lane, Statesboro.

"Marking Historical Spots." Mrs. Charles Kopp, Regent D.A.R.

Response and Presentation of Speaker. Hon. Howell Cone, Statesboro.

Address. Hon. H. E. Wilson, Savannah.

Song. "The Star Spangled Banner."

Military Salute. State staff enlisted detachment of the Georgia National Guard.

Notes for WILLIAM CONE, Revolutionary Soldier

Pioneers of Wiregrass Georgia, Volume 5, Huxford:

William Cone, R.S. married Keziah Barber who was the sister of Cassandra Barber. Cassandra Barber and her husband Mathew Carter moved to Mississippi. William, R.S. served in the Revolutionary War as Major, 1st. Battalion, Richmond County militia. In 1779 he moved to Cheraw District of South Carolina and later to Effingham County, Ga. On Feb. 28, 1784 he was granted 250 acres of bounty land in Washington County, GA (see p. 48, Knight's Roster of the Revolution in Georgia). He died in 1822 and was buried in the Cone Cemetery in Bulloch County, Ga.

April 16, 1811, Matthew Sr., Jr., & William along with William, Edmund & James Goff, (all from Bullcock County, GA) were issued Georgia Passports to travel through Creek Indian Territory in migration to Mississippi.
In a dcoument entitled "Officials Who Were the First to Serve," there was a letter dated June 11, 1811, by Matthew Carter Sr. to his daughter, Susannah Carter Mizel & her husband, Griffin, about his move to Mississippi. It reads: "In five weeks and two days we arrived at Chickawawhay without any loss or disappointment of note. We expect in a few days to set out for Pascagoula (River) where I have choosed me a place and there expect to settle myself, my son William, and William Goff, near together. Matthew has gone on to Pearl River but expects to return at the fall unless he likes it there extraordinary well."

Corrections, Volume 5, Huxford (p. 544):

Cone, William, Sr. (pp.64-66 Volume 2)

In doing research in the Minutes of Camden Superior Court within the last three or four years, the compiler has ascertained that he married a second time - a fact never mentioned and evidently not known by any of the Cone family historians. In deed book "I", p.13 of Camden County, is the record of a separation agreement dated Jan. 8, 1812, between William Cone and his wife Martha, in which it was agreed that thereafter each should hold his and her own property free from any claim on the part of the other "as though never married". The Minutes show that the same year William Sr., filed suit for divorce against his wife, Martha Cone. The original papers in the suit having been lost, it cannot be learned when they married or what her maiden name was or where married or the grounds for divorce - matters usually set forth in divorce proceedings. The Court dockets show the case was continued from term to term

38

from 1812 until the October 1816 term when the docket shows the case was dismissed, it being stated that "suit was abated by the death of the plaintiff."

William Cone, Sr. returned to Bulloch sometime between 1812 and 1816, and it was there on June 24, 1816, he deeded all his property to his son, Aaron Cone. The deed of gift, recorded in deed book 4A, p. 311, Bulloch, conveyed 1,000 acres of land in Bulloch; one half interest in 350 acres in Glynn County granted him and John Hagin (Vol.1); seven slaves, one horse, all his household goods, crop plantation tools, rifle and all money on hand or due him. This apparently was made about the time or during the last illness of the old patriot as he was dead before the following October term of Camden Court.

William Cone, Sr. was a representative from Glynn County in 1804 and shortly thereafter moved to Camden. He was appointed Justice of Peace in the 35th district of Camden in 1806 but resigned in 1808 and was succeeded by his son, William Cone, Jr., Feb. 25, 1808.

William Cone, Sr. was drawn to serve as a grand juror at the October Term, 1809, of Camden Superior Court, but was excused from duty on account of being over 60 years of age as shown by the court minutes.

The year of his death as published in Vol. II should be changed from 1822 to 1816. The 1822 date had been arrived at from the circumstance that his son Aaron had been appointed administrator of his estate on January 6, 1823.

The following account of the mystery of the William Cones of 18th century Georgia is by a William Cone of 2002:

This account of Captain William Cone is just an example of how we all have come to see the life of William Cone, spouse of Keziah Barber and later the second wife. who was Martha Tyson, an elderly woman of property listed as such on a Camden County tax roll in 1809.

Transcribed from the text of the History of Effingham County 03/04/2002.

William Cone served as a private under General Frances Marion in the North Carolina Milita, later he served as Major in the 1st Battalion of the Richmond County Georgia Milita under McLean and even later as Captain under Colonel Sabriel in the Camden County, Georgia Milita. He is reported to have killed Cargile, a Tory spy, and led forces that drove Tories out of a region of Georgia that is today known as Bulloch County.

On February 28, 1784 he was granted 250 acres of bounty land in Washington County, Georgia on a certificate of Colonel James McNeil, On April 24, 1784 he claimed 287+ acres of bounty land in Richmond County on a certificate of Colonel James Martin. On September 18, 1784 the Governor of Georgia signed a grant of 287+ acres in Washington County Georgia. On December 16, 1784 there was a newspaper account of Captain Cone's men fighting horse thieves and retrieving the stolen livestock. The following day the minutes of the executive council recommended that Captain Cone and his men be rewarded for their several instances of suppressing robbers in the state.

From 1785 - 1787 Captain Cone served in the state legislature as a representive of Effingham County. On March 11, Captain Cone was appointed tax collector by the Superior Court of Effingham County. On May 10, 1788 the newspaper gave an account of Captain Cone's capture of the notorious Daniel McGirth. In 1791 he was appointed Justice of the Peace for Effingham County. On May 16, 1797 he served as foreman for Bulloch County's first grand jury. On August 9, 1798 he was appointed Justice of the Peace for Bulloch County and reappointed in 1799. In 1804 he was elected representative from Glynn County for the state legislature. In 1806 he was appointed Justice of the Peace in the 35th district of Camden County. In 1808 his son, William succeeded him.

In 1811 his wife Keziah died. His second wife was a woman named Martha, but a separation agreement was filed within a year. In 1816 he signed all his property over to his son, Aaron, in Bulloch County. He died the same year. He was buried at Ivanhoe in Bulloch County near the community of Hubert, on route 119.

William Cone served as a private under General Frances Marion in the North Carolina Milita, later he served as Major in the 1st Battalion of the Richmond County Georgia Milita under McLean and even later as Captain under Colonel Sabriel in the Camden County, Georgia Milita. He is reported to have killed Cargile, a Tory spy, and led forces that drove tories out of a region of Georgia that is today known as Bulloch County.

On February 28, 1784 he was granted 250 acres of bounty land in Washington County, Georgia on a certificate of Colonel James McNeil,

Note: William is 26 years old.

On April 24, 1784 he claimed 287+ acres of bounty land in Richmond County on a certificate of Colonel James Martin.

Note: William is 26 years old.

On September 18, 1784 the Governor of Georgia signed a grant of 287+ acres in Washington County Georgia.

Note: William is 26 years old.

On December 16, 1784 there was a newspaper account of Captain Cone's men fighting horse thieves and retrieving the stolen livestock. The following day the minutes of the executive council recommended that Captain Cone and his men be rewarded for their several instances of suppressing robbers in the state.

Note: William is 35 years old on this date.

From 1785 - 1787 Captain Cone served in the state legislature as a representative of Effingham County.

Note: William is 36 Years old and finishes the term at the age of 38 years old.

On March 11, 1788 Captain Cone was appointed tax collector by the Superior Court of Effingham County.

Note: William is 37 years old

On May 10, 1788 the newspaper gave an account of Captain Cone's capture of the notorious Daniel McGirt.

Note: William is 37 years old.

In 1791 he was appointed Justice of the Peace for Effingham County.

Note: William is 42 years old.

On May 16, 1797 he served as foreman for Bulloch County's first grand jury.

Note: William is 49 years old.

On August 9, 1798 he was appointed Justice of the Peace for Bulloch County and reappointed in 1799.

Note: William is 50 years old.

Note. Nancy is born in Cheraw County, SC October 16,1782. William moves to Effingham County and then Mary is born April 10, 1787 in Effingham. So within the 5 years was the year William relocated from Sc, to Ga. William is not of age to register land as was Aaron and Joesph along with William in Effingham County.

In 1804 he was elected representative from Glynn County for the state legislature.

Note: William is 27 years old and William, his father is 55 years old.

In 1806 he was appointed Justice of the Peace in the 35th district of Camden County.

Note: William is 57 years old.

In 1808 his son, William succeeded him.

In 1811 his wife Keziah died. His second wife was a woman named Martha, but a separation agreement was filed within a year. In 1816 he signed all his property over to his son, Aaron, in Bulloch County. He died the same year. He was buried at Ivanhoe in Bulloch County near the community of Hubert, on route 119.

Now with this in spread and color as noted to each William in that this information has been gathered from several sources yet it is without a doubt put together as 2 men mainly to be the dates and occurrences of one man's military service and public service during his lifetime. We have to recall that William was somewhere in the age of his late 30's when he got to GA. This is reasoned that only one child and that being Mary, his last was born in Georgia 1787. Aaron, Elizabeth and William were born in North Carolina and the remaining born in Chestefield, Cheraw County, South Carolina.

Last Will and testament of Aaron Cone January 14, 1832

In the name of God, Amen, I Aaron Cone of the State of Georgia and County of Bulloch, being infirm in body but in perfect memory, thanks be to God, calling into mind the mortality of my body and (wet stain)-wing that it was appointed for all men to die. I make and ordain this my last Will and Testament that is to say principally and first of all I give and recommend my soul into the hands of the Almighty God that give it and my body to the ground to be buried in a decent and Christian manner and from at the discretion of my friends and Executors nothing doubting but I shall at the last general resurrection receive it again by the favor of Almighty God; and as touching such worldly estate wherewith it has pleased God to bless me with in this life I do give and dispose of in the following manner. ___

Firstly, I do give and grant unto my son Peter Cone the following tracts of land, one surveyed for and granted to William Denmark, (then in Effingham County but now in Bulloch ,) on the 25th of December 1770, then so deeded from Wm. Denmark to Stephen Denmark, from Stephen Denmark to Simeon Travice, from Simeon Travice to Matthew Carter and from Matthew Carter to myself, also I give unto my son Peter Cone the three tracts of land which he deeded to me, also I give him all the debts due from him to me; likewise one negro man named Tom, also one bed and furniture._____

Secondly I do give and grant unto my son James Cone one negro man named Jack, one rifle gun and one large pot, he has had his bed and furniture.

Thirdly, I do give and grant unto my son Robert Cone, one negro boy named Dick, one large pot and one rifle gun, he has had his bed and furniture.

Fourthly, I do give and grant unto my son Barber Cone three tracts of land surveyed for myself in Bulloch County joining the Call's land and great Ogeechee, one tract of five hundred acres granted to me on the 14th of October 1813 and two other tracts of land, one contains four hundred forty four acres; the other or last tract contains six hundred acres, each one of the last mentioned tracts were surveyed and granted to me on the 16th of November 1813; likewise one negro boy named Charles and one bed and furniture, also one large pot and blacksmith tools.

Fifthly, I do give and grant unto my son Aaron Cone the following tracts and parcels of land. Viz the first tract granted originally to Rheuben Bynarm, (then Effingham County but now Bulloch for two hundred acres, the grant is dated the 31st of December 1784 and deeded by said Bynarm to Asael Farmer and his deed is last, and deeded from said Farmer to me, his deed is dated the

42

26th of April 1799; the second tract granted to Valentine Hollingsworth, (then Effingham County but now Bulloch,) for two hundred acres, the grant is the16th of November 1793, by said Hollingsworth deeded to Elizabeth Ryall; Mrs. Ryalls heirs deeded it to me; the third tract granted originally to John Goldsmith, (then Effingham County but now Bulloch) for three hundred acres, the grant is dated the 10th of November 1795; on that tract my house now stands, said Goldsmith deeded in his last will and testament, the deed is dated the 16th of march 1796; the fourth tract granted originally to John Caswell, (then Effingham County but now Bulloch) for one hundred seventy nine acres, the grant is dated the 10th of November 1795, and is deeded by said Caswell to John Goldsmith, the fifth tract granted to myself for two hundred acres of land, the grant is dated the 9th of November 1799; the sixth tract granted to myself for fifty acres of land, the grant is dated 30th of October 1801; the seventh tract granted to myself for four hundred acres of land, the grant is dated the 14th of October 1813; the eighth tract also granted to myself for fifty acres of land, the grant is dated the 16th of November 1813; likewise one negro boy named Amos, one bed and furniture, also one large pot, also one musket gun, (ineligible) I do give unto my grandson John Goodman one bed and furniture.

Seventhly I do give and grant unto my grandsons Joseph Cone and William Cone jointly the following tracts or parcels of land Viz; the first tract granted originally to Nathaniel Lundy, (then Effingham but now Bulloch County) for two hundred acres of land, the grant is dated the 22nd of February 1794, the second tract granted originally to William Pool for five hundred acres of land, being only that part of the land that lies north of Cary branch, the grant is dated the 19th of March 1795, (then Effingham County but now Bulloch); the third tract granted to Matthew Carter for one hundred fifty acres of land, the grant is dated the 19th of March 1795 (then Effingham but now Bulloch) the fourth tract of land granted to Matthew Carter for one hundred acres; the grant is dated the 10th of may 1798, (then Effingham now Bulloch County) likewise one negro boy named Ezekiel, also each one of them one bed apiece. The land and Negro boy named Ezekiel which I have given to my grandsons Joseph Cone and William Cone are to be kept for the use of my family until William Cone becomes twenty-one years of age, for I do not want to have my little grandsons to pay for their board. I wish my grandsons John Goodman, Joseph Cone and William Cone to be sent to school whence a school is within reach, from July until March in every year and their tuition paid for out of the family land as long as it does last, afterwards out of their own property.

Eighthly, I do give and grant unto my daughter Sarah Goodman one negro girl named Lindy and her Bed and furniture. _

Ninthly, I do give and grant unto my daughter Ann Jones two negro girls named Polly and Sharlet, she has had her bed and furniture.___

Tenthly, I do give and grant unto my daughter Keziah Sheffield two negro girls named Zilpha and Amy, she has had her bed and furniture.__

Eleventh, I do give and grant unto my daughter Frances Cone two negro girls named Phebe and Eliza and her bed and furniture.___

Twelfth, I do give and grant unto my daughter Susannah Cone two negro girls named Lucy and Sarah and her bed and furniture; and I charge and direct my sons James Cone and Barber Cone to act as guardians for Susannah Cone, John Goodman, Joseph Cone and William Cone until they come of age, or choose their own guardians.__

My stock of cattle are to remain on the plantation for the use of my own family, except thirteen cows and calves for Joseph Cone and William Cone jointly next spring; and to John Goodman ten cows and calves next spring, also ten cows and calves and five cows and yearlings to my beloved wife (Hannah Cone) next spring, and also to her teen steers of this description, four three year old steers and six two year old steers.__

First I want to have as many of my steers sold as will pay my debts, and the remainder of the steers from two years olds and upwards to be left for the use of my family. The balance of my stock of cattle to be divided as follows, First to Sarah Goodman, secondly to Barber Cone, Thirdly to Frances Cone, Fourthly to Aaron Cone, Fifthly to Susannah Cone, to each one of these five but last mentioned grand sons six cows and calves apiece. The remainder of my she cattle and sucklings to be equally divided between my following children Sarah Goodman, Ann Jones, Barber Cone, Keziah Sheffield, Aaron Cone, Susannah Cone.__

Robert Cone is to have a beef every year, and Barber Cone is have a beef every year after he leaves the family out of the stock left for my family.__

The balance of the steers are not to be made use of only as the necelaties of the family calls for them. I leave my stock of hogs, sheep, goats, bee hives and crop for the careful use of my family; also my horse, mule, and oxen.__

My horse fed and Sony, wife's saddle, her bed and furniture I give to my beloved wife Hannah Cone.____

Also I leave a sugar mill, two carts, hand mill, plantation tools, household and kitchen furniture, are all to be left for the use of my family,__

Also it is with my daughter Sarah Goodman to have the management and control of everything about the house, except my wife's room, she is to have the privalage of that.__

Also it is my wish for Barber Cone to have the management and control of everything on the plantation as long as he lives with the family; When Barber leaves the family, the management and control of the plantation will fall on Aaron Cone.___

I leave my negro man Dick and Mary his wife are to work for my family until my grandson William Cone arrives at the age of twenty one years. ____

After that I do intend that they (my negro man Dick and Mary his wife) shall belong to my son Aaron Cone; like wise the household and kitchen furniture to belong to my son Aaron Cone.____

44

I wish my son Barber Cone to pay to Mr. George Mitchell five dollars; I have paid him all, but the five dollars for finishing the wood work for a wagon; and when it is finished for Barber Cone to iron it off, afterwards to sell it and to take his pay for the work he does to it, out of the money which he gets for it; the surplus of the money to go for the use of my family.__

I wish my son Barber Cone to sell my mill irons and still to appropriate the money which they fetch for the use of my family.____

My daughter Sarah Goodman is to have the command of everything about the house except she gets married.

My son Aaron Cone must after Barber leaves the place try to make support for the family with the hands that are left on the plantation; unless he does marry; if he does, he is to have the privilege of the little room, and a sufficient quantity of land to tend, together with an equal part of the cow penned land; also he is to have my mark and brand,___

If my beloved wife cannot stay with the family, I want her to have the sixth part of my stock of cattle willed, for the support of my family.

I do appoint James Cone, Allen Jones, and Barber Cone my lawful Executors to have full power over my estate (ineligible) to carry my will into complete effect.

In witness herewith I have set my hand and seal In presence of us January 14, 1832

William Wright
Aaron Cone   (SEAL)
 Levi Davis   (mark of unC)
Stephen Thorne

Aaron Cone's Last Will and Testament
 Clerk office Bulloch County
Recorded in Book B.
page 404 this 13th
March 1835

CASSANDRA[2], m Matthew Carter. 1. Matthew[1] Carter was born Abt. 1725 in North Carolina. He married Patience.

Children of Matthew Carter and Patience are:

1. Matthew[2] Carter (Matthew[1]) was born 1745 in Cumberland County, North Carolina, and died April/02/1812 in Jackson County, Mississippi. He married Cassandra Barbour, sister of Keziah who married William Cone, and daughter of William Barbour. She died Aft. 1832.

Children of Matthew Carter and Cassandra Barbour are:

i.   Susannah[3] Carter, born 1778; died August/31/1848 in Bullock County, Georgia. She married Griffin Mizelle 29 May 1797.

ii.   Jane Carter, born 1779; died May/31/1856 in Jackson County, Mississippi. She married Joshua Everett October/07/1797.

iii. Matthew Carter, Jr., born January/26/1781 in North Carolina; died 15 Dec 1852 in Jackson Co., MS

iv.   William Barbour Carter the second son born to Matthew Carter and his wife **Cassandra** Barbour Carter.
He was given his mother's maiden name, Barbour. This is the spelling used in Wm Barbour Jr's family Bible. William was born 13 June, 1783 probably GA., and died 10 October, 1852 in Jackson Co. MS. He married Mary Goff, 20 November, 1810 in Bulloch Co. Georgia. Mary was born 15 February, 1788 Duplin Co. NC., and the daughter of William Goff and wife Sabra Mathis Goff. The Georgia passport list William with a wife, no children were given.

William and Mary were the parents of thirteen known children, the second and third being twins. All of William and Mary's children were born in Americus, MS.

1. Sabra Carter, born 30 October, 1811 died 1848. She married after 1837 to a Mr. McDonald, and was living in Jasper Co. MS., in 1846.
2. Ann Nancy Carter, 28 April, 1813 married William Davis
3. Cassandra V. Carter, 28 April 1813 married Reuben T. George
4. John Carter, 20 November, 1814 married his cousin, Mary Carter, daughter of Matthew Carter and wife
Ann Goff Carter. She was born 8 August, 1824 MS. and died 3 March, 1907 MS.
5. William Barbour Carter Jr. was born 17 January, 1816 Jackson Co. MS. and died 1 May, 1887 Jackson Co. He married 5 January, 1854 to Susan Davis, born 11 April, 1834 MS.
6. Susannah Carter born 17 March, 1817 MS. died 16 April, 1887 MS. married Wesley G. Evans, born 16 September, 1818.
7. Mary Ann Carter, born 27 May, 1818 MS. m. E. Fairbanks.
8. Simeon Carter, born 24 October, 1819 MS. d. 28 Oct. 1834.
9. Martha Carter, born 15 May, 1821, died 4 March, 1823.
10. Seaborn Pierson Carter, born 19 Nov. 1823, died 2 Oct.1826.

11. Elizabeth Carter, born 23 November, 1826 MS. and died 26 June 1892. She married October 1845 to Alexander Archibald McKay, born 17 September, 1821 and died 17 August, 1902.
12. James Griffin Carter, born 1 March, 1829, d. 15 Oct. 1836.
13. Jepthah Carter, born 10 February, 1834, died 24 Oct. 1834.

Many of the names and dates were taken from the William Barbour Carter Jr. family Bible. Founding Florida Pioneers & Their Descendants

v.   Naomi Carter, born Abt. 1789; died October/04/1829 in Jackson County, Mississippi.
vi.   Cassandra Carter, born 1790.

The Cone Brothers
2nd Florida Cavalry

James BARNARD Cone   WILLIAM Haddock Cone
Sgt.   3rd Seminole Indian War 1857   Captain
2nd Florida Calvary   Conferate States of America

Photograph circa 1860

Four Cone brothers fought in the Battle of Olustee:
- Captain William Haddock Cone, 2nd Florida Cavalry, Co. G - Benton, Columbia Cunty
- Lt. Simon Peter Cone, 2nd Florida Cavalry, Co. K - Simon had fought previously with CSA forces outside the state of Florida. He settled in Nassau County after the war.
- Charles Floyd Cone, 2nd Florida Cavalry, Co. G - White Springs, Hamilton County. Charles enlisted as a farrier and had fought previously with CSA forces outside the state of Florida.
- Sgt. James Barnard Cone (called Barnard), 2nd Florida Cavalry, Co. K - White Springs, Hamilton County

From the 1857 Muster Rolls of William's company of mounted volunteers (Seminole War), three of the brothers are described as:
- William Haddock - 33 years old, 5' 11", blue eyes, light hair and a farmer
- Charles Floyd - 23 years old, 6', blue eyes, dark hair and a farmer
- James Barnard - 28 years old, 6' 1", blue eyes, red hair and a farmer

Muster Roll of Capt. WILLIAM H. CONE'S Company in the 1st Regiment of Mounted Florida Volunteers commanded by Col. SAMUEL ST. GEO. ROGERS called into the service of the United States by the President under the Act of Congress approved May 13, 1846, from the 23rd day of July 1857, (date of this muster) for the term of 6 months.

Note: This muster roll has nine columns ; rank, age; when mustered, where, by whom, term, horse and horse equipment.

1. WILLIAM H. CONE, Capt., 33, 23 July 1857 at Alligator, Fla. by Capt. CONE for 6 mos; $200-$25
1. JOHN FRINK, 1st Lt., 30, 23 July 1857 at Alligator, Fla. by Capt. CONE for 6 mos., $200-$25
1. CHARLES F. CONE, 2d Lt., 23, 23 July 1857 at Alligator, Fla. by Capt. CONE for 6 mos., $175-$30
1. DAVID S. BRIAN, 1st. Sergt., 21, 23 July 1857 at Alligator, Fla. by Capt. CONE for 6 mos.; $180-$25
2. JAMES B. CONE, Sergt., 28; July 23, 1857 at Alligator, Fla. by Capt. CONE for 6 mos.; $200-$25

Page 26

Descriptive Roll of Capt. WM. H. CONE'S Company Regiment of Mounted Volunteers mustered out of service January 22, 1858.

Note: There are eight (8) columns that show Town or County, Born State or Kingdom, Height (feet and inches), complexion, eyes, hair, and occupation.

Capt.   WILLIAM H. CONE, Columbia, Fla., 5'11", light, blue, light, farmer
1st Lt. JOHN FRINK, Hamilton, Fla., 5'11", dark, blue, dark, farmer
2nd Lt. CHARLES F. CONE, Columbia, Fla., 6', light, blue, light, farmer
1st Sergt., DAVID S. BRIAN, Columbia, Fla.; 5' 11-1/2", light, blue, dark, farmer
Sergt. JAMES B. CONE, Columbia, Fla.; 6'1", light, blue, red, farmer
Sergt. WILLIAM H. LONG, Columbia, Fla.,6'1", light, blue, dark, farmer
Sergt. HENRY H. HERRING, Columbia, Fla.,6'1". light, dark, dark, farmer

name or, state, height, skin, eyes, hair, occupation

Captain William Haddock Cone was the father of Fred F. Cone who was the governor of Florida during 1937 to 1941. William Haddock Cone has been confused with his father, William Henry Cone. William Henry Cone married Sarah Haddock of Nassau County. They lived in Camden County, Georgia from 1810 to 1835 then moved to upper Columbia County, Florida near the small town of Benton. William Henry Cone, a Whig, was a Georgia state legislator in Camden County prior to 1835, a Florida Territorial legislator from Columbia County during 1841-1842, and Florida State Senator (13th District) in 1854 and 1856. William Henry fought in the 1st and 2nd Seminole Wars and taught his sons the rudiments of swamp guerilla warfare. He was a guide for Col. Newnan in a campaign (1812-1814) that included a battle southeast of Gainesville, Florida. William Henry died in 1857.

In 1857, three of his sons - William, Charles and James Barnard - participated in a raid during the 3rd Seminole War that did some damage to Seminole Chief Billy Bowlegs.

"... Captain W.H. Cone, with 115 men, surprised a party of Indians, killed one warrior, and captured eighteen women and children along with large quantities of provisions. No Americans were killed in this encounter but many of the men came out of the swamps ill and exhausted." - from <u>The Florida Wars</u>, by Virginia B. Peters, ISBN 0-20801-7194

"In November, Captain William Cone and a force of militiamen mostly from Columbia and Alachua Counties, moved into the area west of Okaloacoochee Swamp and south of Fort Doane and struck the first heavy blow felt by Billy Bowlegs and band. With experienced woodmen leading the way, the small force followed an Indian trail and discovered on November 19, 1857, a cluster of dwellings and some unforewarned Seminoles. The two guards put up a fight and were killed but the others, including the one wounded warrior, five women and thirteen children, were captured. Several nearby villages containing as many as forth dwellings and stores of corn, rice and pumpkins were destroyed. Proof that the Indians were from Bowleg's band was seen among the captured items fifty bushels of corn, one hundred bushels of rice, some oxen, and hoes and assorted items belonging to Billy Bowlegs - - a suit, an 1852 tintype showing Billy in Washington, a shotbag and a turban.

Heartened by their success, the militiamen pushed their way through the maze of cypress trees along the Okaloacoochee and were able to inflict more damage. On the day following the capture of the Seminoles, a field containing corn, pumpkins and rice was discovered and laid waste. It took much strength and endurance to wade through the waist deep water and push through the heavy growth of grass, trees and bushes. At night, the men climbed into trees and slept just a short distance above the water. The fatigue was so great that eighteen men found the struggle too much for them on the first day and on the following day, sixty-two were forced to turn back. The remained followed a trail along the river and discovered twelve sunken dugouts. Looking about they discovered a village and some unsuspecting Seminoles cooking their meal. A wild charge carried the soldiers into the cluster of homes and two Seminoles were killed in the melee. One old Seminole named Tigertail vowed that he would never leave Florida alive and although carefully watched, was able to steal, crush and devour a glass bottle at Punta Rassa. He had kept this word and died on the Florida sand.

Cone's raid was the first really effective blow struck at the well-concealed Mikasiuki band and the Seminoles vowed their revenge. They followed the militiamen along their return route to Depot Number One and attempted to ambush them, but without success. On November 26, a herd of horses grazing in Billy's garden situated about one mile's distance from Depot Number One was attacked by the Indians and thirty-six of the animals killed."

- from <u>The Billy Bowlegs War, 1856-58: The Final Stand of the Seminoles Against the Whites</u>, by James W. Covington, 1982, ISBN 091312-2068

All information and images on the Cone brothers and their family
was provided by Kenneth B. Cone, of Islamorada, Florida.
Kenneth Cone can be reached at <u>kbcone@bellsouth.net</u>.

WILLIAM[2], 174?; m Sythe ---.
According to another source, William[2] is the son of <u>MOSES</u>, b Perquiman, Co NC 1729; and
Elizabeth (**Jones**) BARBER. [Lt: Jack Thompson]

Descendant Register, Generation No. 2

4. <u>Moses Barber</u> (William Barber[1]) was born ABT 1784, and died ABT 1828 in Bryan County,
   Georgia, United States. Black Creek Cemetery, Pembroke, GA. He married <u>Mary Barber</u>. She
   was born in Montgomery County, Georgia, United States.

   BARBER, MOSES - First granted land in Montgomery County in 1817, Landowner 55th
   Mont. Co. 1811/2.
   Moses had land in Bryan County, GA on the middle prong of Bird Mill Creek. He also had
   land on Anthony Branch which was sold to his son Moses, Jr. by his siblings in 1828.
   BARBER, AARON - 1797/8 Landowner, first granted land in Montgomery County in 1812,
   may have been granted land in Burke County in 1788, 1804 Jury member 55th, Landowner
   55th Mont. Co. 1805/06/11/12, Unfortunate Drawer 1805 Land Lottery, Land Lottery Winner,
   1807. *Montgomery, pp. 44, 49, 56, 64, 74, Grants, p. 28.*

William Barber signs land over to son Moses Barber
County Chatham, North Carolina

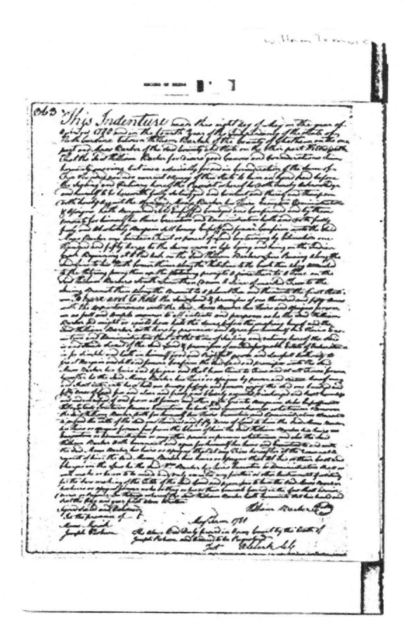

...m To Richard

RECORD OF DEEDS

This Indenture made this eighth day of May in the year of our
Lord 1780 and in the fourth year of the Independency of the State of North
Carolina between William Barber of the County of Chatham on the one part
and Richard Barber of the said County and State of the other part Witnesseth
That the said William Barber for divers good causes and considerations him hereunto moving (but more especially for and in consideration of the sum of five
hundred pounds current money of this State to him in hand paid before the
sealing and delivery hereof the Receipt whereof he doth hereby acknowledge
and himself therewith to be fully satisfied and content and thereof and therefrom
doth hereby acquit the aforesaid Richard Barber his heirs Executors Administrators and Assigns) hath bargained sold enfeoffed conveyed and confirmed and
by these presents for himself his heirs Executors and Administrators hath and do
doth fully freely and absolutely bargain sell enfeoff and forever confirm unto
the said Richard Barber one certain tract or parcell of land containing by esti-
mation one hundred acres be the same more or less lying and being on the Indian Creek Beginning on the branch at a post oak Running to the said William
Barber that his then along said line to his that corner thence down to the branch
thence up the branch to the first station. To have and to hold the said land and
premises of one hundred acres with the appurtenances unto the said Richard
Barber his heirs or assigns forever in as full and ample manner to all intents
and purposes as he the said William Barber did might or could have had the same
before the making hereof and the said William Barber doth hereby promise
and agree himself his heirs Executors and Administrators that at the sealing
and delivery hereof the said William Barber is and stands seized of an indefeasible
estate of Inheritance in fee simple and hath in himself good and rightfull power
and lawful authority to grant bargain and sell and forever confirm the said land
and premises with the appurtenances unto the said Richard Barber his heirs
and assigns and that from time to time and at all times forever hereafter he the
said Richard Barber his heirs or assigns by power and virtue hereof may and
shall enter into have hold use occupy possess and forever enjoy the said one hundred
acres free and clear and freely and clearly acquitted discharged exonerated kept harmless and
indemnified of and from all former and other gifts grants bargains sales enfeoffments
title entails jointures dowries executions extents and incumbrances whatsoever
moreover the said William Barber doth for himself his heirs Executors and
Administrators covenant to defend the title of the said one hundred acres to
him the said Richard Barber his heirs and assigns forever free from the claim of
him the said William Barber his heirs Executors and Administrators and any
other person or persons whatsoever and also the said William Barber doth covenant and agree for himself his heirs and Executors to and with the said
Richard Barber his heirs or assigns that at any time hereafter at the reason-
able request of him the said Richard Barber his heirs or assigns that at
his or their charges in the law he the said William Barber his heirs Executors

50

Map of Bryan County, Georgia

UPPER BLACK CREEK
PRIMITIVE
BAPTIST CHURCH
Constituted August 15, 1802

SUNDAY SERVICES   WEDNESDAY - 7:30 PM
BIBLE STUDY - 10:00 AM   THURSDAY BEFORE
WORSHIP - 11:00 AM & 6:00 PM   THIRD SUNDAY - 7:30 PM

PASTOR: ELDER KEITH HAMILTON

12. Isaac Barber (Moses Barber[2], William Barber[1]) was born ABT 1802 in Bryan County, Georgia, United States, and died ABT 1854 in Bryan County, Georgia, United States. He married Catherine Francis Sikes ABT 1820, daughter of Edward Sikes and Catherine McGee. She was born ABT 1803 in Bryan County, Georgia, United States, and died ABT 1864.

19. Henry Obadiah Barber (Isaac Barber[3], Moses Barber[2], William Barber[1]) was born 25 JUL 1825 in Bryan County, Georgia, United States, and died 28 DEC 1909. He married Nancy Stephens. She was born 19 FEB 1829, and died 6 NOV 1874. He married Matilda Tatum. She was born 9 SEP 1848, and died ABT 1898. He married Martha Ann Kight. She was born ABT MAY 1872.

Children of Henry Obadiah Barber and Nancy Stephens are:

+ 27 i.   James Israel Barber was born 28 MAR 1852 in Bryan, Georgia, United States, and died 22 OCT 1926 in Ware, Georgia, United States.
+ 28 ii.   Julie Ann Barber was born 12 DEC 1849 in Bryan County, Georgia, United States, and died 14 JUL 1923 in Brantley County, Georgia, United States.
+ 29 iii. Laura Emily Barber was born 20 JAN 1855, and died 15 AUG 1942.
  30 iv.   Elizabeth Isabelle Barber was born 18 MAY 1856 in Georgia, United States, and died 2 MAY 1942.
+ 31 v.   Nancy Angeline "Angie" Barber was born 25 JAN 1861, and died 27 MAR 1924.
+ 32 vi.   Edmond Obadiah Barber was born ABT 1866 in Pierce County, Georgia, United States, and died 26 DEC 1931.
+ 33 vii. William Albert Barber was born 23 NOV 1857, and died 14 JAN 1898.
  34 viii. Lydia Lavina Barber was born 31 MAR 1869, and died 12 JUN 1887.
  35 ix.   Charlotte Barber was born ABT 1868, and died ABT 1880.
  36 x.   Mary Marjory Barber.
  37 xi.   Ella Barber was born 4 MAR 1864, and died 9 MAR 1938.

Children of Henry Obadiah Barber and Matilda Tatum are:

  i.   Charles F. Barber was born 24 APR 1884, and died 26 AUG 1904. He married Rosa Howell.
  ii.   Perry Barber was born 2 MAY 1882, and died 12 AUG 1958. He married Elizabeth O'Neal.

iii. Samuel Jackson Barber was born 20 MAY 1889, and died 9 FEB 1967. He married Gertrude Robinson.

iv. Virginia Barber was born 8 JUN 1879, and died 10 NOV 1971. She married Noel Skeickland.

v. John H. Barber was born ABT JAN 1893, and died ABT 1900.

vi. Rose Verbie Barber was born 15 AUG 1877, and died 1 JUN 1900. She married Joseph Yeomans.

vii. George Cleveland Barber was born ABT NOV 1885, and died 20 DEC 1931. He married Annie Laurie Smoak.

viii. Lucinda Barber was born ABT 1875.

ix. Henry Lee Barber was born ABT SEP 1887, and died ABT 1909.

Okefenokee Folk: "A kinder, or more hospitable people do not live."
By C.T. Trowell.

Today the Okefenokee is primarily a wildlife refuge, but the great swamp has a long history of being sought out by people attempting to escape from some real or imagined threat. Isolated, over the years, the Okefenokee became a cultural sanctuary as well.

It appears that Indians occupied the Okefenokee around 4,000 years ago. The population reached a peak between around A.D. 500 and A.D. 1200. A band of Timucuans fled into the center of the Okefenokee as refugees from Spanish Florida during the 17th century. The Creeks avoided the swamp. One, Hopoithle Tustannugee Thlucco, moved with his family into the swamp as refugees during the American Revolution. Their livestock was ravaged by bears and panthers; they sought refuge elsewhere. Although many Indian families, Creeks and Seminoles, wandered through and around the swamp during the late 18th and early 19th centuries, with one exception, their names are unknown.

An old Indian named Billy, or "Indian Billy from Ware County," lived on Billys Island during the early 19th century. He was murdered around 1827. His murderers, unlike many of the unruly cattle rustlers living along the Georgia-Florida line, were arrested and jailed. They escaped, but some of them were recaptured several years later in Florida. This episode was probably the origin of the legendary Billy Bowlegs in the Okefenokee Swamp. The catchy name led to media attention which fed local stories about Indians in the swamp. Instead of calling Indians Indians, people referred to Billy Bowlegs in the swamp.

Documentary sources depict life and work on the Okefenokee frontier during the 19th and early 20th centuries. Surveyors, soldiers, journalists, scientists, and other visitors have commented on the life of the people Francis Harper, a naturalist who with his family spent many years documenting life in the swamp, called the "Okefinokee Folk."

Several sources are especially useful. The diary and reports of General Charles R. Floyd and other Army officers during the Second Seminole War provide glimpses of life around the Okefenokee during the 1830s. Reports, diaries, and articles by surveyors during the 1850s contain information on life around the swamp at this time. Two letters and maps of the Mansfield Torrance survey, when they marked the unsurveyed Ware County lots in the Okefenokee Swamp in 1850, described the swamp frontier at mid-century.

During the summer of 1854, Alexander A. Allen of Bainbridge, Georgia was commissioned to meet with Benjamin F. Whitner of Florida and determine the correct location of the Georgia-Florida boundary. Allen kept a diary of his travels and observations as he made his way through the plantation lands and culture of Southwest Georgia to the emerging tourist center and culture at the Suwannee Springs spa in North Florida. He also recorded his impressions of the Okefenokee lands and the stockminding folk of the Cracker culture that he found living on the southern fringe of the swamp.

The Georgia Legislature authorized an exploration of the Okefenokee in 1856. Richard Hunter, in charge of the survey, prepared a report in 1857. An assistant, Miller B. Grant, wrote an illustrated article on the explorers' experiences for Frank Leslie's New Family Magazine in 1858. Grant's observations of the people are especially useful.

Charles R. Pendleton's newspaper articles, reminiscing about life around the Okefenokee in 1860, and his letters written during his exploring expeditions in 1875, including the Atlanta Constitution exploring expedition, provide some of the most detailed data on landscape and culture when the area was still a frontier. These journalists explored the jungles of South Georgia while Henry M. Stanley explored the jungles of Africa.

Although change was under way by the 1880s, Howell Cobb Jackson, writing as a special correspondent for the Atlanta Journal, found much of the Cracker culture intact in 1890 as he made his way around the Okefenokee with the surveyors marking the boundaries of the lands to be purchased by the Suwanee Canal Company. His letters to the newspaper are some of the most interesting I have found. Francis Harper compiled probably the most extensive profile of the Okefenokee culture in his field notebooks and a manuscript he called "Okefinokee Folk." Harper's labor of love was edited by Delma Presley and published as a book called Okefinokee Album.

Life On The Frontier

The frontier culture of the Okefenokee was a piney woods Cracker culture. The people, men and women, possessed and fostered a self-sufficient life style, a strong sense of independence in thought and behavior, and a commitment to family relationships and traditions. Their descendants still usually ask "Are you related to ...?" instead of "What do you do...?" or "Where do you live...?" Confident in who they were and what they could do, and in the promise of the future, they produced large families.

On his map in 1769, Samuel Savery, a Royal surveyor, noted that these lands were "Low Pine Barrens and Cypress Ponds - only fit for Cattle Range." Savery's note was prophetic. The lands in and around the Okefenokee came to be perceived to be worthless bog. The surrounding piney woods were used as a vast cattle range for the following two centuries. During the late 18th and early 19th centuries, the forests east of the swamp also sheltered roving bands of renegades, rustlers, revolutionaries, and banditti, but their interest was in Spanish lands and Seminole cattle in Florida, not in the Okefenokee.

The earliest white settler documented who was associated with the Okefenokee was Israel Barber. He moved to the Georgia Bend (the tip of Georgia, created by the St. Marys River, which dips into Florida) in 1807. He was interviewed by members of the Georgia-Florida Boundary Survey in 1831. Barber said he was familiar with the recesses of the southeastern corner of the Okefenokee because of his "habit of hunting gaters and herding cattle and hogs throughout the country." He died in 1833.

The Creek Indian Lands in South Georgia were acquired by the State of Georgia in 1802 and 1818. The lands were surveyed into 490-acre rectangular lots. They were organized as Wayne County in 1805 and Appling and Irwin counties in 1820. But few families moved to the Okefenokee area. Most of the Okefenokee Swamp was not surveyed because of the impenetrable vegetation. Nothing was known about its interior.

During the 1830s the Second Seminole War in Florida spilled over into Georgia. A band of Indians sought sanctuary from army patrols in the recesses of the Okefenokee in 1838. The warriors soon turned to plunder and kill families living on Okefenokee rim. Widely scattered settlers fled in panic to Center Village and Trader's Hill (about three miles southwest of Folkston) for refuge.
A ring of forts was constructed around the swamp during the summer of 1838. In the fall of 1838, General Charles R. Floyd launched a series of search and destroy operations to kill or drive the Indians from the swamp. A lucrative military-agricultural complex developed around the Okefenokee between 1839 and 1842. Militia units were mobilized to investigate "Indian sign" time after time between 1839 and 1842, but found no Indians. The Federal government finally refused to pay

for the mobilizations. In 1842, the Georgia Legislature ended the war by refusing to pay for any more militia expenses.

The area was very sparsely settled during this period. The census taker recorded 29 families living in the Georgia Bend area in 1840. Following an Indian raid from Florida, he wrote to the Governor that most members of three families had been killed and they should be removed from the census. Life on the frontier during this time was described by John C. Murray, 82, in an interview in 1897. He moved to the Okefenokee frontier with his father in 1833. He served as a soldier in the Indian War and in the Civil War. He recalled the following about life during the early years:

Centerville [located] below Folkston [was] the trading center. Traders' Hill also was a good business town. Among the enterprising merchants at Centerville were Mr. Guckenheimer and Mr. Epstein, who, after leaving Centerville, located in Savannah...
Cattle were not so plentiful as deer, and venison and beef sold for 2 cents and 2 1/2 cents per pound. A bag of salt, a pound of powder and a few bars of lead were all the articles wanted by the settlers when they carried their dried beef and venison to the market...
There were numerous wolves and panthers. Mr. Murray said, in those days, and they killed many calves and cattle.
There were no country schools, nor doctors nor churches. All the clothes worn by the people were spun and wove at home by the wives and daughters of the farmers. All the houses were built of round sapling logs, and the flooring for the cabins was of hewn logs.

Mansfield Torrance and one of his surveyors, probably William Nichols, wrote long letters to the Columbus and Milledgevile newspapers in 1850. The writers, who wrote mainly about the plants and animals, included the following notes on life around the swamp at this time. They observed the difficulty in clearing palmetto lands, but went on to note the following:

... but little land is cultivated; the chief productive wealth of the country is beef cattle. As stock is the chief wealth, agricultural pursuits are subservient to it. Enough corn and cotton is raised for home consumption. The black seed cotton is exclusively cultivated, and is ginned with hand roller gins fixed by uprights into a common stool. It is turned with one hand and fed with the other.
Sugar grows well and is cultivated for domestic supply.
Small grain does poorly, except rice. [But] I saw but two patches of rice and both were planted in Cyprus ponds, well ditched and drained.
The gardens, like they are all over Georgia, with but few exception, are below mediocrity.

Four years later, Alexander Allen visited and took testimony from several families living along the upper St. Marys River. Allen was a University of Georgia graduate who grew up in Cotton Plantation Up-Country Georgia. He compiled the following observations and impressions of the Cracker culture in 1854:

Mr. [Tarlton] Johns kindly invited us to dine with him which of course we did. Here we met Mr. George Johns 68 years of age healthy old man. a large stock owner & gathers his own cattle. he is father to Tarlton Johns. ... The old Gentleman is loquacious & fond of rough jokes. Tarlton & family are fair specimens of pine country simplicity. goodhearted people but know very little of the world The dinner consisted of coffee without milk or shugar, corn bread venison bacon & beans. The people appear very kind. mostly hunters & stock minders & owners.

A few days later (July 6), Allen camped at the home of George Combs:

The people are perfectly destitute of any of the modesties of more refined society. We find them here as elsewhere bare-footed both men & women. Nurse their children in your presence without the least sense of impropriety. There are at this house 4 young babies & I have not seen a house not even filled with children. The population must therefore increase rapidly
The country is infested with gnats, flies, fleas & all other insects.
On July 8, at Mr. Kennedy's house, Allen wrote:
At this house as at others a gang of strapping lazy fellows are loitering with nothing to do or nothing that they would do. This whole population is lazy & indolent as far as I have seen. A crowd of lazy fellows have met at Kenedy's to shoot for beef.
On July 16, they went to the Cruise [Crews] house on the southern fringe of the Okefenokee "to get the clothes we had washed. Mrs. Cruise very much distressed. Cruise had gone to a whiskey burner & most probably drunk and he had not returned. A big strapping girl boasts of her cotton picking."

Following Richard Hunter's survey of the Okefenokee from 1856 to 1857, Miller B. Grant, his 17 year old surveyor, described a typical Okefenokee frontier homestead and its inhabitants as follows:

A mere hut, log or otherwise, with one similar near by in most instances, ordinarily used as a cooking and eating room - these suffice for their simple views of comfort. I once saw a man and his wife with seventeen children herded together, without thought of change, in one of these shanties. Many of them depend for subsistence, several months of the year, on the spoils of hunting, wild fruits and berries in a great measure, so few acres of land do they choose to plant. If they have cattle (and many of them own and pride themselves in the fact of large herds of cattle), to milk or make butter from them would be as wild a theory to them as to bid us to get cheese from the moon, so entirely out of their calculations is such a mode of proceeding. They assign, when questioned, as a reason for inhabiting that section of the country, that there are lots of lightwood knots, and water "is powerful handy."

Grant also added: "[Yet] there does not exist - for their means and style of life - a more open-hearted or hospitable set of people in the world."

Hunter's surveyors entered Cowhouse Island and camped at the homestead of a "Mr. Short," apparently a composite character constructed by M.B. Grant. Grant wrote:

This gentleman was of the genus Cracker, and a rare specimen of a man not to be outwitted, standing six feet in his wide brogans, stockingless; and the homespun pants might seem to have clung to his lower limbs since boyhood.... All of the [Crackers] ordinarily wear cloth of their own weaving; in some parts of the country a brownish yellow is the prevailing color, as I was told they liked it "to favor the soil."

When the young surveyors arrived, Mr. Short's three daughters, in their late 20s and 30s, changed into their "store clothes," yellow calico. Mr. Short's daughters were not impressed by the visitors or their saxehorn. The women stated that they preferred their neighbor, Stag Morris's, fiddle. One of the daughters reported: "I reckon he kills more bars, makes more bitters and drinks more whiskey, nor ere a man round here, unless it's the old man."

The surveyors attended a Christmas dance or "hop" at the log cabin home of a "Mr. Brown" on the edge of the swamp northwest of Trader's Hill. The dance was managed by a "first fiddle of the company." According to Grant, he was: "the arbiter of good manners, as well as wit and jester. He kept up a sort of ding-dong tune, a ring-dong-diddle, a ring-dang-do, a ring-dong-diddle, a ring-dang-do." Grant noted that the tune "apparently inspired those in whose ears...it was sweet music." Grant was impressed again by the independence and power of the womenfolk. one mother, forcing Grant to dance with her daughter, bragged that her daughters could "roll as many logs, dig as many taters, and dance as long as ere a man in this country."

In contrast to the plantation societies of the Georgia coast and the up-country, the Okefenokee frontier developed as a hunting-stockminding society. Some of the major economic, and social, events of the year were the spring wiregrass burns and cattle roundups, the winter drives to the cowhouses, and periodically, the bear hunts to protect the razorback hogs. Charles R. Pendleton, who grew up on the northern rim of the Okefenokee, recalled the cattle-drive experience in an article in 1900. He wrote:

Forty years ago [in 1860] the Millers, the Hilliards, the McDonalds and other residents of Ware County owned large herds of cattle which browsed on the tender wiregrass on the "burns" during spring and summer. But for winter keeping they were driven to the Okefenokee Swamp where they fed on the canebreaks and other herbs and grasses which were protected from the frost by the dense overgrowth. When the first evidences of rising sap [in the trees] in March heralded the approaching spring, strips of woodland on the borders of the great swamp would be fired and burned over. It was said that the piney woods cow could scent one of these burns ten miles, and ere the tender shoots begin to peek through the ashy carpet left by the forest fire, the cattle would come in great herds out of the swamp to forage on

59

the new-born grass. Driving parties would be organized, and after several days campaign the cattle would be rounded up at a given point, divided according to mark and brand, and driven to their respective summer ranges about the homes of their owners.

He also noted:

These early spring round-ups were interesting occasions for the boys and young men. Each little herd as they divided up for winter had its own male leader which at the spring gathering on the burns was ready and anxious to dispute with all comers the right to lord it over the ridge. The fights were frequent and furious and were greatly enjoyed by the younger set in the drive.

Pendleton also explained:

The "Big Cowhouse" and the "Little Cowhouse" [Chesser Island] are islands in the Okefenokee Swamp. They were so named because certain cattle breeders in Ware and Charlton Counties sheltered their cattle in them in winter as far back as the forties [1840s] and fifties [1850s].

Bear and deer were hunted with dogs, usually from horseback. Several members of the family, often members from several families participated in the hunts. Killing a deer or a bear was often a rite of passage for the young men in these families. It remains so today. Dogs were members of the family. The good bear dog or coon dog was highly valued, and their prowess was the subject of much yarn telling.

Churches and schools were rare on the Okefenokee frontier. Instead, the frontier folk came together for revivals and match-making at summer camp meetings. Only a few places, like Sardis Primitive Baptist Church on Spanish Creek, date prior to the 1870s.

Howell Cobb Jackson described his experience in a frontier church in a letter to the Atlanta Journal in 1890:

The church at Fort Mudge is called the "Pilgrim's Hope," possibly because the pilgrims who worship at this shrine are always hoping for many things which they never get. As a specimen of modern architecture it can scarcely be called imposing. Its ventilation is perfect, and is attained by the means of large cracks through the log walls. Indeed, the entire house is constructed of logs, with abundance of space between them for fresh air and for viewing the surrounding country. We found some fifty or more pilgrims assembled, and two preachers favored us with discourses - the Rev. Richard Lee and Rev. Moses Thrift. If the faith of these pilgrims be measured by the time they spend at their devotions, they all deserve a high place, for services commenced at a little before twelve and wound up a little after four. Each of the ministers opened by saying he had preached out and had nothing to say; yet each

60

occupied about two hours to get rid of that nothing.
The Rev. Moses Thrift devoted a considerable portion of his time to the matters of "Infant Baptism" and "Sunday schools." These he denounced vigorously and warmly. He had the orthodox Baptist drawl at the end of every two or three words, which was doubtless very pleasant to the brethren, but which made his utterances so indistinct that I could understand but a very small part of what he said.
The men and women were separated during the services, and everything was conducted in a very democratic way. Men, women and children would go out and return as often as they desired, the sleepy slept, and the thirsty made repeated trips to the water bucket. Generally, however, the behavior of the congregation was devout, and there were beyond doubt many good people present. [But] the exercises were entirely too long and wearied out everybody.

Jackson also commented on the character of Okefenokee folk in 1890. He was especially impressed by their hospitality and their large families. Following a 25 mile walk on the first day of the survey, he was exhausted when he reached the St. Marys River near Ellicott's Mound. He wrote:

...[here I] met the eye of a certain sympathetic widow who lives on the river, who not only invited [me] to supper, but offered [me] what was infinitely more precious - a feather bed. The house was small, the family [pretty large], there were only eleven children and several of them married, ... but by judicious arrangement, some little scrounging, room was found for all, and I never slept sounder in my life.

Jackson went on:

And now for a few words about the people. Here you see the Georgia cracker uncontaminated and in all of his original perfection. They are generally very poor and very simple, but I can say from personal experience that a kinder, or more hospitable people do not live. Their very errors really seem to arise more from ignorance than from design.

He added:

Many of the houses contain only one room, are built with logs and thatched with clay, and in this room all of the family, including visitors, are stowed away at night, somewhat after the fashion of sardines in a box, but all inconvenience and discomfort disappear when one sees the old-fashioned Georgia kindness with which the owner dispenses his hospitality.

Many families settled and prospered on the Okefenokee rim during the 19th and early 20th century. The Chessers and the Lees lived on islands in the Swamp. They took pride in their ability to live independently and happily in places most people found uninhabitable. Obediah Barber lived on the northern rim of the swamp for six decades. He became a legendary swamp figure in his lifetime - and a symbol of the

Okefenokee frontiersman.

Swamp Families: The Chessers

The Chesser family lived on an island on the eastern edge of the Okefenokee Swamp beginning around 1858. William T. Chesser was the first to move to the swamp. His grandsons Harry and Tom, were some of the last people to leave the Okefenokee. Tom Chesser and his family moved to town in 1958.

The Chesser men were widely known for their hunting and fishing skills in the Okefenokee Swamp. The Chesser's lived by subsistence farming, hunting, and stockminding. William T. Chesser relied very little on goods and markets in other places. Nevertheless, he traded at the stores at nearby Trader's Hill, 15 miles away, as early as 1858-59, purchasing ammunition, cloth, ribbon, shirts, etc. By 1873, he was also selling vegetables and syrup here.

As new jobs developed around the Okefenokee, even the family members that remained on the island took advantage of these opportunities and worked at local sawmills, turpentine stills, and some worked for the Suwanee Canal Company during the 1890s. Others left to work for the Hebard Cypress Company or other lumber companies when they began to log the timber in the Okefenokee between 1910 and 1942. But the Chesser tradition of self-reliance and independence survived in the minds and hearts of the Chesser descendants and other Okefenokee families who knew and loved life in the great swamp.

Today this frontier tradition is preserved in the Tom Chesser Homestead on Chesser Island, a living museum in the Okefenokee National Wildlife Refuge.

Charles R. Pendleton, editor of the Valdosta (GA) Times visited Chesser Island in 1875. The island was called the "Little Cowhouse" or "Chesser's Cowhouse" at that time. Pendleton asked Mr. Chesser about life on the island. Mr. Chesser replied:

...I have always got along. You see I can kill deer, bear, turkey, ducks, geese - can go to Seago [Seagrove] and catch as many fish as I want; besides, as you can see, I have lots of chickens, hogs, and cattle. I get wild honey, too, occasionally, but it is not so plentiful now as it was once. You see the 'serters [Civil War deserters] in the war times cleaned the bees out.

Pendleton went on to record the hunting skill of Mr. Chesser's sons. They usually used their bows and arrows for fishing, but they "showed off" for the explorers:

Our party made their encampment in front of Mr. Chesser's gate, and after a survey of the island, settled to rest for the night. After we had supped on hardtack and potatoes (the latter furnished by Mr. C.) and such other articles of diet as is common to the life we were leading, one of the old man's boys came out and said that he had "roosted" two coveys of partridges, and that if one of us would go with him and another with his brother to hold the lightwood torch they would kill the birds with arrows. The writer and Prof. Locke readily volunteered. The boys had collected some "fat" splinters which made a blazing light, and when the writer and his man approached the spot where the birds had been seen to go to roost, the marksmen advanced cautiously a few steps and beckoned to the writer to stop. He saw them squatting in the grass and he drew his arrows one at a time from the quiver and in seven shots he had killed as many birds - shooting six of the number through the head. When he picked them up he said, "I shoots 'em through the head to keep from spiling the meat."

But on Chesser Island, as elsewhere, life was more than bread and meat. It was often a matter of life and death. Mr. Chesser commented that sickness was rare on the island, but he went on to eloquently recall the death of his son and his wife. His little boy was bitten by a rattlesnake. Wistfully he said: "He died in twenty-four hours. He was kinder pet with the old 'oman, and she commenced to grievin' and pinin' and soon she went away like a pond drying up in the summer, when there was no rain. That is all the sickness I've had."

The Chesser tradition persisted well into the 20th century.

Francis Harper made his first visit to the Chessers on July 12, 1921 after crossing the Swamp from Billys Island with Harry Chesser. He wrote in his diary:

[I found] A primitive and attractive wilderness home, log-built, with separate kitchen and wash-house, barn and cane mill (uncovered). Two or three hounds. About 7 of the 11 children, including Harry, now at home. Eat hominey, tomatoes, peas (field), cane syrup, light biscuits.

The Lees

Across the swamp from the Chessers, Jim Lee, and later his son-in-law, Dan Lee, lived in much greater isolation.

According to family tradition, at least one settler occupied Billys Island before James "Black Jim" Lee, who possessed a massive black beard. James J. Lee was living there by the 1860s. According to tradition, he sold or swapped his claim to the island to "Black Jim" Lee around 1870. Jim Lee had a well-established farmstead there in September 1875 when Charles R. Pendleton and George Haines visited the island. Pendleton and Haines returned a month later with the explorers of the "Constitution Exploring Expedition." His son-in-law, Daniel Lee, moved to the island and by 1884 Dan Lee and his wife Nancy considered the island to be their homestead. Jim Lee died in January 1888.

In September 1875, Pendleton and his local guide, Ben Yarborough, reached Billys Island, and the farmstead of Mr. James Lee. He wrote:

Mr. Lee is almost independent of the world. The only article that he buys beside ammunition, fishing tackle and farming and mechanical implements are coffee and salt. He raises is own bread, beans, sugar, syrup, beef, potatoes and everything else that he consumes save fish, venison and honey, which he gets in great quantities around him. He tans his leather and makes his own shoes, and his industrious wife and daughters spin and weave and sew up every thread of clothing they wear. He lives on government land, is lord of all he surveys, and is happy in his quiet solitude.

The isolation of Billys Island insulated the Lee Family from the cultural changes accompanying the railroads during the 1870s and 1880s. Biologists from Cornell University visited the island during the summer of 1912. They were impressed by the knowledge and unspoiled contentment of this family living in a frontier sanctuary.

Landing at Billys Island at night after a long trip through the swamp from Cowhouse Island in May 1912, Francis Harper recalled the following in an article in 1915:

We trudged up through the cornfield to Dave's home, in the yard of which we were greeted by the deep-throated bearhounds. The folks within the house arose to receive us, and despite our protests set before us food and drink for our refreshment. So true to tradition is Southern hospitality, even in a wilderness home of logs.

Harper reflected:

To look about us in the morning, and to observe unobtrusively the manner of life of the only human inhabitants of the remote interior of the Okefinokee, was a novel and extraordinary pleasure. In the lives of these sober, self-sufficient people is reflected the freedom of the wilderness, no less than its solitude and its privations. Thirty years ago the father and mother established a home on Billy's Island; and they and the ever-increasing numbers of the second and third generations have continued to draw a livelihood from the manifold resources of the swamp.

Harper observed:

The longleaf pines furnished the timbers of their dwelling; the sandy loam of the clearing produces their annual supply of corn, sweet potatoes, and several smaller crops, such as "pinders" (peanuts) and sugar cane; and in the surrounding woods their cattle and razor-backed hogs find sustenance. But no inconsiderable part of their daily fare is derived directly from the wild life about them. Deer, raccoons, opossums, rabbits, squirrels, fish, soft-shelled "cooters" (turtles), Wild Turkeys, Bob-

64

whites, and many of the larger water birds are secured for the table whenever opportunity offers. The bears, whose depredations in some years prevent a suitable increase in the drove of razorbacks, are hunted with hounds and made to compensate with their own flesh for any deficiency in the supply of home-cured bacon. Not only does the family enjoy the product of the tame bees that swarm in upright sections of the hollow cypress logs about the yard, but the young men gather probably an even greater store of wild honey from "bee-gums" in the swamp. They market the skins of the alligator, the bear, the wildcat, and the otter, and get in trade the few necessities of life with which the Okefinokee itself does not furnish them.

The frontier culture gradually gave way to the new industrial world following the Civil War. Although steamboats made their way up to Trader's Hill on the St. Marys River as early as the 1830s, and a steam sawmill was operated at Burnt Fort on the Satilla River by lumbermen from Maine by the 1830s, it was the railroad and commercial society that undermined and supplanted the independence and self-sufficient frontier culture. The Atlantic and Gulf Railroad extended from Savannah to Valdosta by 1860. The Brunswick and Albany Railroad reached Tebeauville just north of the swamp just prior to the war, but it was removed and rebuilt in 1870.

Both railroads were constantly in financial difficulty. The railroad that really altered the landscape and the culture of the Okefenokee was the Waycross and Jacksonville branch of the Savannah Florida and Western, completed along the eastern rim of the swamp in April 1881 as the guns blazed at the O.K. Corral out west.

Obediah Barber

Obediah Barber, who lived on the northern rim of the Okefenokee Swamp, was a larger-than-life character. Physically, he was a big man. His reputation as a successful farmer and herder, fearless hunter, daring explorer, and renowned storyteller lingered long after his death. As often happens, the myth outgrew the man.

Barber was typical and symbolic of the independent, self-sufficient, and self-reliant frontier folk who settled the Okefenokee and its margins during the mid-19th century. His life is representative of the persistence of frontier traditions in some families in the longleaf pine forests prior to the intrusion of the industrial railroad society that began to transform the people and landscape of south Georgia between 1860 and 1900.

Barber was born in Bryan County, Georgia on July 25, 1925. He was the son of Isaac and Frances Barber and a grandson of Moses Barber. He married Nancy Stephens of Tattnall County, Georgia and by 1854 the Barbers had two children. In 1850 Obediah Barber owned a 333-acre farm in Bryan County.

65

The young family moved to the northeastern edge of the Okefenokee Swamp just north of Cowhouse Island on the Blackshear Road in 1854. They bought a 490-acre land lot. Nine more children were born while he lived on this farm. In 1860 Barber cultivated 25 acres; in 1870 he reported 30 acres of improved land. In 1860 he had only two cows; by 1870 he owned 67 head of cattle. In 1860 he owned 130 hogs; he reported 125 hogs in 1870, more than most yeoman farmers of the area. He also produced Indian corn, oats, sweet potatoes, sugar and syrup, a bale of cotton, and sold a little wood, probably firewood.

From 1857 until 1870, Barber served as a Justice of the Peace, first in Ware County, and then in Pierce County when his district was made part of Pierce County in 1859. Barber served as a private in the 24th Battalion, Georgia Cavalry, during the Civil War. In 1862 he served with Capt. T.S. Hopkins' Company of Mounted Partisan Rangers (Mercer's Partisans) at Camp Fort, Georgia.

In 1870, he sold his farm, resigned his public office, and moved with his family six miles across the prairies of the northern Okefenokee to a new farm (a 490-acre land lot) on the northwestern rim of the swamp in Ware County. Here he built a log cabin, a large herd of cattle and hogs, and a reputation as a bear hunter. His new farm was located about seven miles due south of the tiny village of Tebeauville on the Savannah and Gulf Railroad. In 1874 Nancy, Barber's first wife, died.

Barber married Matilda Tatum in 1875. Between 1875 and 1893, they had nine children. By the 1880s he was a prosperous country squire. In 1880 Barber owned 1,520 acres, three horses, and four working oxen. He reported 40 acres of improved land. He had seven children living at home and employed two farm hands, sons of nearby farmers. He owned 76 head of cattle, 150 hogs, and 34 chickens. By the 1890s, Barber's reputation as a skilled woodsman and hunter had made him a living legend.

Obediah Barber was one of the great Okefenokee storytellers. A neighbor, John Craven, noted that he always "made things funny at any cost of the truth."
But time was taking its toll. Matilda died in 1898.

In December 1898, at the age of 73, Barber married 26-year-old Martha Ann Kight. Barber suffered a stroke in 1903. A divorce was acquired in 1907. Barber's health declined, and in October 1907 he was declared a lunatic by a jury. During the next two years E.O. and J.I. Barber served as guardians. Barber died on December 28, 1909. Ironically, there was no obituary.

Obediah Barber witnessed the economic and social changes that gradually transformed the Okefenokee frontier into a railroad society and brought industry and commercial agriculture to the Okefenokee rim. He saw the character of the endless longleaf pine-wiregrass forests change as the demand for naval stores and yellow pine lumber swept the great pines away. He heard stories in the 1890s of logging in the dense cypress bays in the Okefenokee Swamp by the Suwanee Canal Company, but he died just prior to the massive railroad logging operations of the Hebard Cypress Company.

Barber's, and the Okefenokee frontier spirit lives on, however. The Obediah Barber homestead was listed on the national register of historic places in June 1995. The Homestead, located outside of Waycross and called Obediah's Okefenok, has been restored and a living museum developed, catering to school field trips and family reunions of Okefenokee families.
taken from "Moses's Second Family" by Rebecca Clements Barber

Israel Barber

Israel Barber, born about 1770, was of a generation before Moses. His relationship to Moses, if any, isn't known, but he is believed by some family researchers to be his uncle. I heard enough about him from the very old timers, although the little anecdotes they tried to remember were nebulous, to believe he must have been some sort of kin.

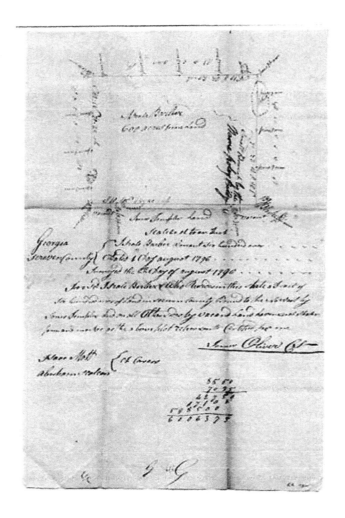

A traditional story about Israel is that he was the first white settler in the area of the great Okefenoke. He moved from Bryan County, Georgia, to the Georgia Bend in 1805 probably in the present Moniac community section.

Israel was in Camden County in the following years, as per public records: 1817 – 1821 and 1830. He was a Justice of the Peace in the 32nd district of Camden from 1817 to 1821.

In 1830, the Camden County census showed Israel as having in his household three males under ten years of age, one male in the 18 to 25 years bracket, himself in the 25 to 44 years category, one female under ten years of age, two females from ten to fifteen years old, and one (? his wife) from 16 to 25 years of age, and 39 slaves.

One of the oral legends about Israel was that President Washington needed his services. What services? Could it be his scouting and guidance for surveyor Henry Washington?

Israel was with the first known US surveying team to map the big swamp. From Ward's HISTORY OF WARE COUNTY, GEORGIA: —...the year of 1831, they [surveying team Henry Washington and George Willis and the Barbers] met near the Okeefeenokee Swamp. Mr. Israel Barber who said he was the first white settler living on the northern border...and had been living in that vicinity for 26 years...Israel and young Obadiah proved to be of great assistance...‖ This passage also stated that the Barbers came to Ware County from Bryan County about 100 years [circa 1825] before being employed as survey guides. Mr. Ward gave Obadiah as a son of Israel, and that disagrees with Obadiah's descendants' record.

Israel died in 1833.

The Okefenokee Swamp

Stretching from Waycross, Georgia to the Georgia-Florida border, the Okefenokee Swamp represented the last of the untamed wilderness in Georgia after the War Between the States. Covering more than 700 square miles of territory, this vast land mass was once thought to be uninhabitable and as such was not distributed by Georgia when it was "acquired" from the Creek Nation. Actually, the Okefenokee was inhabitable and had been extensively settled by early cultures of Moundbuilders, both prehistoric and transitional.

Following the decline of the Moundbuilder civilization, the Okefenokee swamp was the border for three Indian Nations, the Mocama (to the north), the Timucua (to the south and east), and the Apalatchee (to the west). Both the Mocama and the Timucua were members of the Creek Confederacy, possibly descendants of the earlier Moundbuilders. First knowledge of the swamp came during Rene Goulaine De Laudonniere's attempted settlement of the Southeastern coast in 1564.

Later, Spanish missionaries and their armed escorts and English from South Carolina both mention the Okefenokee before 1700. The Spanish called the area Lago Oconi, after a nearby Timucan village. The Spanish established two missions, Santiago de Oconi, on the southern side of the Okefenokee near village and San Lorenzo, further east on the St. Marys. During Queen Anne's war the British drove the Spanish from the coastal islands of Georgia, and for a brief time the Native Indians who inhabited the Okefenokee Swamp lost contact with European settlers.

In 1715 the Yemassee Indians were defeated by South Carolina and traveled south to the St. Mary's River. Decimated by European disease and slaughter the Timucua,

Hitchiti, and Yemassee formed the Seminole Nation. According to Seminole mythology, the Okefenokee Swamp was once an independent kingdom. William Bartram visited the area in the Spring of 1774, although he did not enter the Okefenokee Swamp, he realized the area must be rich and diverse in flora and fauna.

In 1795, in a treaty signed at Traders Hill (Treaty of San Lorenzo or Pinckney's Treaty), not far from the swamp, Spain and the United States agreed that the boundary of Georgia and Florida would run to the start of the St. Mary's river inside the Okefenokee. Andrew Ellicott established the boundary in 1800, entering the Okefenokee from the west and marking a mound at the headwaters.

The Okefenokee Swamp was soon to become one battleground in an ongoing war between the United States Army and the Seminole Nation. In 1814 the Creek Nation agreed to secede some of the land claimed by the Seminoles to Andrew Jackson. When the Seminoles disputed the claim of the Creek Nation to the land, war erupted. In 1818, Jackson, Winfield Scott and 5,000 troops headed south from Fort Hawkins (Macon, Georgia), to settle the dispute with a war. Osceola fought valiantly, but failed the defeat the Army.

A small group of Seminoles led by Billy Bowlegs (Indian name: Bolek) escaped detection by hiding in the Okefenokee Swamp. Over the next twenty years this group grew. It became widely known that Bowleg's Seminole village was a haven for slaves and whites. The Wildes Family massacre occurred on June 22, 1838 on the perimeter of the swamp. It is the last Indian attack in present-day Georgia, and came during the Second Seminole War.

Other spellings of Okefenokee

Spelling	Year
Ekanfinaka	1790
Akenfonoga	1796
Eckenfinooka	1810
Okefinoka	1813
Oquafanaoka	1818
Oke-fin-a-cau	1818
E-fi-no-cau	1854

In October, 1838 the United States Army attempted to force the Seminoles remaining in the Okefenokee Swamp to submit to a law passed in Washington called the Indian

Removal Act of 1830.

General John Floyd built a string of forts (one of which was called Fort Mudge) surrounding the swamp to prevent the escape of the Seminoles. General John Floyd engaged the Indians on the outskirts of the Okefenokee Swamp that October. Following the battle, General Charles Floyd (John's son) moved into the swamp in pursuit of the Seminoles. He discovered Floyd's Island, largest in the swamp, which held an Indian village and one Indian. After a couple of skirmishes, Billy Bowleg's Indians escaped Floyd's dragnet and headed south to the Everglades.

Ware County courthouse was the site of the first sale of the land in the Okefenokee in 1852. The following year Daniel Lee entered the swamp and laid claim to Billy's Island (named for the Chief Billy Bowlegs). For fifty years Dan Lee, his wife and family, lived deep in the swamp. In 1854 Doctor George White gave the commonly accepted meaning of the term "Okefenokee," as Ecunnau or "earth" and finocau or "quivering." In today's literature it is still known as the "Land of the Trembling Earth." This is not a reference to earthquakes, but to the unstable earth that would shake from something as light as a footfall. Another early settler was William Chesser, who moved to Chesser Island in 1858 to escape a manslaughter charge.

After the War Between the States, settlers began to claim the land around the edge of the Okefenokee Swamp. The State of Georgia still claimed the swamp itself, which it classified as *unsurveyed land*. In 1871 Obediah Barber, who had lived near the swamp since 1854, established a homesite within the boundaries of the Okefenokee. His homestead, which still stands, is the best preserved of all early settler cabins and is the centerpiece of Obediah's Okefenok.

He would live in the swamp for the next 35 years, outliving two of his three wives. When surveys were done people sought Obediah to guide them through the Land of the Trembling Earth. His exploits earned him the title "King of the Okefenokee".

The Atlanta (Daily) Constitution sent a team to explore the swamp in 1875, and both Obediah Barber and Dan Lee became famous. In 1881, with the completion of the Waycross and Florida Railroad (later part of the Savannah, Florida and Western), railroads began to encroach on the Okefenokee. This line passed on the eastern edge of the swamp.

In 1889 the Georgia legislature approved the sale of the remaining land of the swamp. A group of investors headed by Captain Henry Jackson and consisting almost entirely of friends of then governor John B. Gordon, purchased almost 240,000 remaining acres in 1891. They moved huge dredges into the swamp, building the canal at a rate of 44 feet per day. Over the next two years the group constructed 12 miles of canals, but were forced to abandon the swamp because of financial problems, entering receivership in 1897.

Railroads entered the swamp in 1897, with the construction of the Atlantic, Valdosta & Western Railway (called the Jacksonville Short Line). The line was completed the following year. In 1901 Charles Hebard began a logging operation in the Okefenokee. Hebard's company laid a railroad track 35 miles to Billy's Island. It grew to the point of having a church, movie theater and a school for the children of the workers. By 1928, operations were scaled back and soon the village was a ghost town. The cut and leave policies of the lumber company left untold thousands of acres of habitat destroyed. Scaled-down logging operations did continue in the Okefenokee Swamp through 1942.

Francis Harper, who visited the swamp as student at Cornell, wrote in the U. S. Biological Survey, 1917, "It is a refuge for some especially rare or interesting forms of animal life. It is a winter resort for large numbers of migratory waterfowl. It still contains...500 square miles of diversified territory in an absolutely primeval state." Harper liked the Okefenokee Swamp so much that he moved there, building a house on Chesser Island.

A major fire destroyed a significant amount of habitat in 1925. Later fires, in 1931, 1932, 1954 and 1955 also struck the swamp.

In 1931 a proposal was made for the federal government to purchase the Okefenokee Swamp with the intention of preserving the area as a "wild-life" sanctuary. The Special Committee on Conservation of Wild-life Resources visited from March 9 to March 14, 1931. Their conclusion was that the swamp was not of value as a migratory bird refuge, but it would make an "attractive and valuable sanctuary" for indigenous species. The report notes that the habitat of the ivory-billed woodpecker was slated for destruction the following year.

Francis Harper wanted to save the swamp he knew and loved. Jean Sherwood had tutored Franklin Roosevelt's children before she married Francis Harper, so she decided to write her former employer. Her first letter, dated Noverber 25, 1933 implored the President to withhold funds from a canal project slated to cross the Okefenokee. While he deferred, saying the time was not right, the proposal was deemed unfeasible. Jean Harper, however, continued to write President Roosevelt, who created the Okefenokee Wildlife Refuge on March 30, 1937 when he issued Executive Order 7593.

Francis and Jean had won the protection of their beloved swamp. Or so they thought. With the swamp under federal management, Harper's farming friends found they could no longer kill bear or bobcats that attacked their animals. Over a short period, many left to seek work outside the Okefenokee.

In 1996 controversy flaired over Dupont's attempt to mine titanium from Trail Ridge. Although not techinically in the protected swamp, it is Trail Ridge that impounds the waters creating the swamp. Environmentalists strongly objected to the mining, and Dupont ended up donating the 16,000 acres to the Georgia Wildlife Foundation, the largest single gift in their history.

Henry Obediah Barber

July 25, 1825   Henry "Obediah" Barber born, Bryan County, Georgia

Bryan County, Georgia
Henry Obediah Barber

December 28, 1909

Henry "Obediah" Barber dies at his home in the Okefenokee Swamp

Okefenokee Swamp

Henry Obediah Barber

A towering figure at 6' 6", Henry Barber was perhaps as unique as the place he lived, the northwest rim of the Okefenokee Swamp. His home is today on the National Register of Historic Places, and according to the folks who have developed the homestead as an Okefenokee attraction, it is the oldest settler's cabin in the area.

On three occasions attempts were made to map the local area and Obediah was the man chosen to guide the explorers into the swamp from his home just a few miles south of Waycross. Barber was father to 20 children from three wives.

Okefenokee Swamp's

Obediah's Okefenok

Waycross, Georgia's Favorite Family Fun Spot

The 1800's Restored Homestead of Obediah Barber (1825-1909)

Legendary "King-of-the-Okefenokee"

NATIONAL REGISTER OF HISTORIC PLACES

A homestead representing the frontier agricultural lifestyle maintained by an early settler at a time when industry and commercial growth was a concern. The park also displays zoological and biological knowledge obtained by this great swamper. He knew every plant and animal by name, sometimes only by given "swamp names." Serving as an educational reminder that every living thing has a place on earth, even the strangest of swamp creatures, the employees of Obediah's Okefenok share a respect for these animals and their habitats as shown and demonstrated throughout the exhibits therein.

http://www.okefenokeeswamp.com - email: **obediahs@okefenokeeswamp.com**.
Registered. All rights reserved.

Historical Information

THE HOMESTEAD

Obediah's Okefenok began in 1989 after the restoration of the 127 year old cabin built by swamp legend, Henry Obediah Barber. Named *Obediah's Okefenok* by the property owner, to simply imply that Obediah would have called his home "Okefenok" ('ok fi' nok) instead of "Okefenokee", because swampers often left out extra syllables as they spoke the territorial slang.

The log home is the oldest swamp settler's home to remain in and around the swamp, constructed by the hands of a renowned farmer, hunter and explorer. Obediah lived on the northwestern rim of the Okefenokee, and was a larger-than-life character at 6 1/2 feet tall. He served as guide for surveying parties exploring and mapping the swamp in 1857, 1875 and 1890. By the 1890's his reputation and knowledge had made him a living legend. A centerpiece of this historical park now known as *Obediah's Okefenok*, the cabin is located 7 1/2 miles south from downtown

Waycross, Georgia, on Swamp Road.

THE LIFE, - THE LEGEND, - THE KING

Henry "Obediah" Barber was born in Bryan County, Georgia on July 25, 1825. He was the son of Isaac and Frances Barber and a Grandson of Moses Barber. He married Nancy Stephens of Tattnall County, Georgia, and by 1854 the Barbers had two children. The young family moved to the northeastern edge of the Okefenokee Swamp north of Cowhouse Island on the Blackshear Road in 1854. They bought a 490 acre lot. Nine more children were born while he lived on this farm.
From 1857 until 1870, Barber served as a Justice of the Peace, the first in Ware County, and then in Pierce County when his district was made part of Pierce County in 1859.

He also served as a Private in the 24th Battalion, Georgia Calvary, during the Civil War. In 1862 his service was with Capt. T.S. Hopkin's Company of Mounted Partisans Rangers (Mercer's Partisans) at Camp Fort, Georgia.
In 1870, he sold his farm, resigned his public office, and move with his family six miles across the prairies of the northern Okefenokee to a new farm (a 490-acre land lot) on the northwestern edge of the swamp in Ware County. Here he built a log home, a large herd of cattle and hogs, and a reputation as a brave bear hunter. At that time the location was about seven miles due south of the tiny village of Tebeauville on the Savannah and Gulf Railroad (S&G R/R). Just north of Tebeauville where the Brunswick and Western Railroad crossed paths with the S&G R/R, a new town was developing. The year was 1874, the town is now known as Waycross.
Barber's first wife, Nancy, died in 1874. He then married Matilda Tatum in 1875. Between 1875 and 1893, they had nine children. Which now totaled 20. With approximately 40 years between the first and last child's birthdate, Obediah became a father for the last time at age 66. By the 1880's he was a prosperous country squire.
In 1880 Obediah owned 1,520 acres, three horses, and four working oxen. He reported 40 acres of improved land. He had owned 76 head of cattle, 150 hogs and 34 chickens. He devoted four acres of his farm to rice growing, producing 3,875 lbs. of rice in 1879. Corn was grown on 24 acres, four acres were devoted to oats, two acres to sugar cane, and sweet potatoes were grown on two acres. His bees produced 110 lbs. of honey and 12 lbs. of wax in 1879. He estimated that he sold $300.00 worth of farm products in 1879.
Matilda died in 1898. In December 1898, at the age of 73, Barber married for the third time, to 26 year old Martha Ann Kight. Barber suffered a stroke in 1903. A divorce was acquired in 1907. In 1908 Obediah was listed as a contestant in a Fiddling contest, held in Waycross. Barber's health declined in 1907, during the next two years E.O. and J.I. Barber served as guardians. Barber died on December 28, 1909. Ironically, there was no obituary. He was buried in Kettle Creek Cemetery, about 10 miles northwest of his home.
Although Obediah saw the beginning of the end of the wilderness and the frontier tradition in the Okefenokee Swamp, he was valued as a source of wit and wisdom.

The great Swamp that Barber explored was designated as the Okefenokee National Wildlife Refuge and a Georgia State Forest, the largest in the state, and later as a National Natural Landmark, and a Wetland of International Importance.

The Log Cabin of Obediah Barber is no architectural masterpiece. It is typical of log homes in and around the Okefenokee Swamp that were described and sometimes photographed by surveyors, writers, and scientists between 1875 and 1915. Because of its rustic character, the cabin was used for a movie set for the film "Swamp Girl" in the early 1970's. Today, the house is the material core for a historical park that interprets life in and around the Okefenokee during the period 1850-1910.

This information and more is now on file with the United States Department of Interior, National Parks Service, and has listed the Obediah Barber Homestead on the National Register of Historic Places as of the date, June 20th, 1995. A bronze marker has been placed in front of the cabin to commemorate this listing. Placed, March 23, 1996.

MOSES EDWARD BARBER

"The Way It Was" newspaper column from 1978
The information contained in this article was given the writer [Tate Powell, Sr.] by the late Mrs. A. W. Barber Rowe, Macclenny, and was published in the Press on December 2nd, 1938.

In 1978, I wrote a four-part story on Moses Barber for THE BAKER COUNTY PRESS (published at Macclenny, Florida) under the column heading —The Way It Was.⌐ The story was based on inadequate research (records were not as available in olden days as they are now) and on oral history that came from oral historians who were somewhat shy of being 100% trustworthy. Later research and much scrutiny has prompted me to re-write parts and to clear up some obvious errors. For those who read the newspaper account and the several stories borrowed liberally from it, this writing should be accepted as a more correct narrative - but it is still far from complete and, barring miracles, the story of Moses Barber will probably never be completed by anyone. For those who copied from my story and unwittingly assisted me in promulgating a false history of our ancestors, I can do no more than apologize and offer this corrected narrative.

Ancestry and almost total confusion

Moses Edward Barber was born in Georgia in or about 1800 and probably died in Florida (maybe southern Georgia) in 1870 or after. There are legitimate questions about his death circumstances and date. His parentage is still not satisfactorily determined for my self as of July, 2002, in spite of several genealogies given for him, including some that seem transparently fabricated. Sadly, two lineages I had pieced together in the 1950's and 60's as conjecture only (after a couple bottles of wine and the company of a charming female distant [I said DISTANT cousin), and plainly marked as such (the wine and companion, however, were not mentioned), have entered into many accounts of G-g-g-grandpa Moses's life. Because of their thorough and professional investigation, I once thought the pedigree given for him by Mrs. Sabina (nee James) Murray of Jacksonville and Bobby Tatum and Luther Thrift of Georgia to be the most acceptable to date even though there were inconsistent dates involved in that line.

Their accepted background of Moses Barber is that he was a son of Moses and Mary (nee Wesley) Barber of Montgomery County, Georgia. However, recent information from Helen Fertic and Margaret Taylor shows, almost without a doubt, that the aforementioned Moses and Mary's children did not match the siblings of the subject of this writing. A Moses and Mary who appear to be the same as the above are found in Alabama as late as 1850.

It is interesting to note that a Moses Barber of a generation before the subject of these notes had a sister Susannah who married Peter Yates, and that the alleged gunman for Moses Edward Barber in the ambush of Sheriff Dave Mizell in central Florida many years later was Needham Yates, and Needham was said to be a cousin of Moses.

Some family members of a few generations back, including Thomas McDuffy Barber, claimed that Moses and his wife Mary Leah were born near Augusta, Georgia, on Moody's farm (never located). Since Moses spent much of his supposed last days at the farmstead of his Moody relatives (don't know how they were related, but I recall coming across a marriage of a Moody with one of the Barber girls in

Georgia around the end of the 18th or the beginning of the 19th century) and with John and Holden Barber near Hazelhurst Plantation (according to his grandson Moses Edward Barber of Suwannee County...personal interview), it seems very probable that the older generations got birth and death places confused. However, it is believed by several Barber researchers that most of our Barbers came to southern Georgia from old Bryan County, Georgia.

Still others were adamant that Moses and Mary Leah came from the area of Rome, Georgia, and one said the birthplace was near Athens (examples of how oral history can lead to confusion).

Some have given Moses Edward's paternal grandfather as William Barber of Orange County, North Carolina. William's known wife (he was married twice it seems) was named Sythia (sometimes given as Sythe and Sythia Pearl in oral histories). An incomplete list of children by one or both wives were Moses (see above), Samuel (youngest), Richard, William, Aaron, Susannah (married Peter Yates), Nancy (married Stephen Stanford), Mary (married a Taylor), Ruth (married a Bishop), and Tamar (married a Roberts). William was born c. 1744 and died c. 1799 in Georgia.

William entered the North Carolina Line during the War of Independence as a lieutenant. He was captured by the British and exchanged. He re-entered the colonial army as a sergeant and again was captured. He was exchanged and returned to service as a slick sleeve private. In spite of his less than illustrious military career, he was awarded land in Georgia for his service.

William drew land in the 1803 lottery when he was a resident of Bryan County, Georgia (actually his legal heir drew for him...he had been dead for a few years). His wife Sythia made out her will in 1799 leaving all her estate to her daughter Mary Taylor except one shilling each to her late husband's children, Tamar Roberts, William Barber, and Moses Barber, and a featherbed to her husband's youngest son Sam Barber (wasn't she generous? Sounds like a classic stepfamily thing). Most of the children lived for a while in a broad area west and south of Augusta before scattering out to south Georgia and other parts.

William of North Carolina had sisters Keziah and Cassandra Barber. Keziah married Col. William Cone, the famed Indian fighter and politician of the Carolinas and Georgia (see WILLIAM CONE later in narrative). A descendent was Fred Cone, a governor of Florida. Cassandra married Matthew Carter and is reputed (reputed only I must emphasize) to be an ancestress of the Carters of Plains, Georgia.

William's father was also a William Barber. He was born c. 1700 in Virginia of old Maryland stock. Whether or not he is truly descended from Dr. Luke Barber of Maryland is not known even though some tracers in the Barber family made the tenuous claim based on amateur genealogical sleuthing with no documented connections (inventing pedigrees is not limited to Barbers, it must be noted). The

Luke Barber connection is tempting because of the man's colorful nature. He entered the Maryland colony as a Church of England priest and soon sent for a boatload of —ladies with which he provided entertainment and relief to gentleman of the colony for certain fees. Supposedly, his behavior and business venture were severely criticized by the Lord Protector Oliver Cromwell. How much of this is fantasy and how much is truth has not been ascertained.

Other names mentioned in some Moses Edward Barber's genealogies are Edward Barber of Virginia and James Barber of North Carolina. This must not be automatically entered into the Barber lineage; it is added because I'm a firm believer in reporting everything heard or seen in my family searching and thus providing clues for further study by more able researchers in the future. Most would prefer not to include one James Barber because he came over as an indentured servant.

On the other hand, Helen Fertic, an in-law of Isaac J.'s branch and who lives in Oklahoma, has offered substantial material that suggests Moses's father was William of Liberty County, Georgia (I once surmised the same…but then, I have given poor ol' G-g-g-grandpa Moses so many daddy's over the course of my studies that I'm certain he is confused himself…wherever he is spending eternity). In fact, her material fits so well into a possible ancestry that the only factor standing in my way of readily accepting it, as it did several years ago, is that it shows one who could be our Moses still in Georgia in 1830 whereas the family insists Moses was in Florida at that time…but oral history, like documents, can be incorrect also. I went over these same census notes back in the 60's and tempting as they were, I allowed oral history prevent me from seeing it as well as Helen.

Here are the census data: a Moses Barber and a female (? wife) are listed in the 1830 Liberty County census as being in the 20 – 30 years old bracket with a son and daughter under five (? Isaiah and Mary Ellen). In the same census are Samuel and William in the same age bracket. A William, old enough to be their father is also in Liberty County in 1830. The elder William had a son and daughter presumably by his second wife the former Mrs. Elizabeth Horn Denison. This could explain some of the half brothers and sisters attributed to Moses.

We still have no inconclusive proof of any of the pedigrees given for Moses Edward Barber.

It would be amusing if it were not absolutely ludicrous that one of the well-prepared genealogies for Moses is exactly the same that Norma Barber Payne and I pieced together in the early 1960's as conjecture only. She worked from Washington, D. C. downward and I worked from Florida northward, and we put the pieces together with a little fudging here and there on my part to create for ourselves a good looking pedigree with an eye on disproving or proving ourselves at a later date…which never arrived.

I made the serious mistake of distributing it to other family amateur researchers. Alas, although it was conjecture only it has entered the realm of legitimacy.

I had voluminous loose notes on Barbers from the British Isles and the entire eastern United States seaboard, but they disappeared along with the books of family record sheets and pedigrees I had worked on for decades, first, when vandals destroyed most of my research in 1979 and, second, when a relative took the remaining material away from a family re-union in the mid-90's with no one's permission. He did not return the material and claimed not to have known what we were talking about. This is unfortunately one of the less desirable traits in some Barbers. He has since died. Rest his soul.

Incidentally, these episodes, plus going broke and the importunate and rude attitudes of some amateur genealogists soured me on family history for several years (I do not consider myself as ever having been a genealogist).

Moses's physical characteristics

Physically, Moses Barber was not tall like several of his children and grandchildren (male and female, six feet and over). From what could be ascertained from several sundry sources, he must have been well under six feet tall, even tending to be of short stature. All who knew him or had heard of him were in agreement that he cut an imposing figure nevertheless and that combined with his charm turned the heads of ladies wherever he went.

His daughter Meddie Barber Wilson recorded in a letter to her kinswoman Mrs. Ola Barber Pittman that her maternal grandmother often remarked how handsome Moses was (good looks is just one of the many crosses some of us Barber men have had to bear through life).

He was of fair complexion, had very blue eyes, and his hair was either reddish or dark brown (both descriptions by descendents have been given, but most claim his hair was reddish or —sandy). He was possessed of a prominent aquiline nose (a strong Barber trait). He sported an enormous handlebar mustache that he blackened with fireplace smut whenever he was to attend church or was —goin' out amongst Them. He wore a broad brimmed black hat and, as was the fashion of his day, always dressed in a black frock coat.

He suffered from arthritis, especially in the shoulder (? Which one) that either had been shot or dislocated when attacked by Indians in the Second Seminole War (see the story later).

Marriage - Mary Leah (? nee Davis) Barber

G-g-g-grandmother Mary Leah Barber, born c. 1800 in the vicinity of her husband's birthplace (according to some of her grandchildren), was described as being very beautiful. She was possessed of pale skin and blue eyes. Her jet-black hair might have helped give rise to the myth that she was Minorcan or Spanish (added to the description of black hair was the couple of times she was listed in contemporary accounts as —Marial). It is my belief that she was a daughter or granddaughter (different ages given for them make it difficult to decide) of Jonothan H. and Nancy Davis and probably was of old Welsh stock. Please note the word —beliefl in the previous sentence; I had not one tiny datum to base it on…gut feeling only.

She was known to be a shrewd businesswoman, was capable of operating the plantation in her husband's absence, and was reputed to be the best shot in the area. Her cause of death has not been learned. She died in the late years of the 1850's. Regarding the few times G-g-g-grandmother Barber was listed as Maria, it should be noted that some 19th century records keepers seemed to think that any name ending in an —eel sound was surely a diminutive or nick name and therefore should be more formally entered into records with an —ial ending. Thus Mary became Maria. I've seen Pollia for Polly and Mollia for Molly. And some were determined that all Johns had to be Jonothans and all Harrys were actually Henrys, Harolds, or Harveys (let's hear it for all those genealogists who believe anything written down by anybody of an official nature of a generation before them is beyond question!).

The Minorcan-Spanish myth

That G-g-g-grandmother Barber was of Minorcan-Spanish descent came about when a cousin Carmeta Barber Ray of Sanford theorized in the early 1960's from flimsy and non-data as given above that Mary Leah might be Spanish. It was total fabrication, but it sounded good to me. It sounded like something I'd want to have in my background. I wrote it down and discussed it with another cousin Anna Fertic Warr of Augusta. Ann liked it even more than I, and from there a totally untrue pedigree grew…but with nothing less, I suppose, than good intentions. With all due respects to both Carmeta and Anna (both personable company), their imaginations were as capable of running amok as mine. In time a complicated story of adoption, previous marriage, and even international intrigue was invented to cover the obvious contradictions in poor ol' G-g-g-grandma's story (sorry, kinfolk, facts have been faced).

I thought it prudent to delay publishing the revised and truer story of Moses and Mary Leah until after the two ladies mentioned in the preceding paragraph had gone on to their rewards happy in the notion they were descended from the unlikely pairing of a sultry Latin beauty and a backwoods land and cattle baron.
Carmeta promised to let me see her grandfather's Bible that proved Mary Leah was Spanish. When I was finally able to check out the record page, it listed —Mary Leah

Barber!...there was no maiden name given, and it was mostly in Uncle Duff's typical poor Barber men's penmanship with wandering notes over the family record page. My grandfather Rowe Barber had accompanied me on that visit, and he was firm that it was, in fact, Uncle Duff's Bible and handwriting. On the way home, he chuckled and thought it amusing that Duff had —pulled another one.‖ Uncle Duff's mother's Bible, as mentioned later in this narrative, said nothing at all about her mother-in-law (the Bible is still in our north Florida family).

From Travis Alvarez of Houston, Texas, and formerly of Starke, Florida: I have researched my Alvarez family for over twenty years and I can't place Maria Alvarez in any of the Alvarez families.‖ Mr. Alvarez couldn't place her on account of she just ain't there.

I might add that the Minorcan-Spanish myth was born under the influence of some fairly good wine though of questionable vintage and label (I haven't always been good, you know).

As long as we hold the Spanish-Minorcan myth dear we are not free to pursue correct genealogical research and discover the true background of Mary Leah Barber. I wonder how many clues deteriorated...lost forever...as we contentedly clung to our Spanish lady myth.

I was in on the making up of the false pedigree, and I can Claim the privilege of refuting it. We must erase the Minorcan-Spanish myth.

I offer my abject apology to all of Moses Barber's descendents for my part in the creation and promulgation of this myth, and I beg that all my previous writings, queries, and answers containing this myth in their possessions be erased.

Children of Moses and Mary Leah

· ? John (no data and not documented. ? Perhaps a son by a previous marriage or even a half brother)
· ? Joseph Andrew "Big Joe" "General": born c. 1820; died after 1905; married (1) Mary Smith (2) Mrs. Ruthie nee Spears Ellison (still not certain if he was a son or brother of Moses)
· ? perhaps a daughter who married a Surles of Volusia County and died in Saint Augustine (based on a recollection of the late Sen. Surles, the Lion of Saint Augustine)
· Mary Ellen "Nellie" "Nell": born 1827 or '28, Georgia; died_____,
Bradford (the present Union) County, Florida; married Joseph Hale about 1845
· Isaiah: born 1829, Georgia; died 1865, South Carolina; married (1)_____

Alexander about 1850, (2) Elizabeth Ann Thompson about 1855
· Archibald Aaron "Arch" (name sometimes listed as Archibald E. or Archibald

Edward): born 1830, Alachua (the present Baker) County, Florida; died 1903, Lafayette County, Florida; married Martha Belle Geiger about 1851

· Margaret/Margaretta/Margrethe: born 1831, Alachua (the present Baker) County, Florida; died_____, Bradford (the present Union) County, Florida; married Durham Hancock in the late 1840's

· James Edward "Ed" "Edderd": born 1833, Columbia (the present Baker) County, Florida, died 1868, Baker County, Florida, married Victoria Eugenia (or Uceney) Regina Thompson about 1858

· Moses Edward "Little Moses": born 1834, Columbia (the present Baker) County, Florida; died 21 March, 1870, Orange County, Florida; married Penelope Alexander about 1855 (said to have fathered several children out of wedlock)

· Isaac Joseph: born 29 July, 1835, Columbia (the present Baker) County, Florida; died 20 March, 1870, Brevard or Orange County, Florida; married Harriett Christina Geiger about 1855

· George William "Bill" "Mean Bill": born 1836, Columbia (the present Baker) County, Florida; died after 1890; married Sarah (? Alexander) and perhaps (2) Mary, last name unknown about 1855

· Elizabeth E. "Betty": born 1837, Columbia (the present Baker) County, Florida; died c. 1870 in Jacksonville; md. Alexander Blum. Believed to have had a child by Belone Robert Dinkins.

Some general notes and questions on Moses and Leah's marriage and on the above offspring and on some children who might or might not have existed

Two dates have been given for Moses and Leah's marriage, six years apart. Uncle Duff Barber said his grandparents Barber were wed in 1820 and somebody else came up with the date of 1826. Uncle Duff said his date was in his parents' Bible (never seen by me although his daughter Carmeta reluctantly let me see Uncle Duff and Aunt Dona's Bible [see The Minorcan-Spanish myth above). I had Uncle Duff's mother's Bible (now in the possession of younger relatives), and there were no dates of her parents-in-law entered.

If Moses and Leah were married in 1826, perhaps Moses was married previously (and Mary Leah too; 26 was getting up in years for someone, in particular a woman, to remain single in those days). Could this be where Joseph Andrew —General came from and perhaps was not Moses's brother? Could the John H. Barber of Barberville be a son rather than a nephew?

Perhaps the John W. and Holden Barber of Hazelhurst and Valdosta, Georgia, were sons by a previous marriage since he spent quite a bit of time with them (Mrs. Ola Barber Pittman of Valdosta said they were close kin but she didn't know the exact relationship…she thought they were either cousins or nephews). This is a dangerous paragraph, and it is questions such as these that so easily transform into —facts.

These are mysteries I wish a better prepared and more knowledgeable researcher would tackle, and I do mean better prepared and more knowledgeable than my self and some of my contemporaries (though now passed on) who seem to have chosen to force bits and pieces into the jigsaw puzzle of our family history when the pieces didn't actually fit.

Family tradition held that Moses was the father of 13 sons and 6 girls, legitimate-wise.

Uncle John Barber of Palatka remembered hearing his grandmother Barber tell of one of Moses's sons killing another son in a fistfight in Baldwin, but their names were not recalled. This sounds more like a couple of Moses's adopted nephews than his sons for whose endings we have fairly good accounts.

The trip to Florida

All the old timers I interviewed gave the same story, but without details, why Moses moved to Florida; they claimed there had been a big split up among the family in Georgia in the late 1820's. This is not an uncommon tale among descendents of early Florida pioneers. Not to discredit the tale – among the quarrelsome Barbers such a reason would not be unheard of – we must bear in mind that the promise of vast acreage free for the taking must have sounded good to those folks among our antecedents and that would have been sufficient reason for moving south.

The train of ox drawn wagons and carts departed Fort Alert near Traders Hill on the Saint Mary's River. In the train were the Barber brothers Moses Edward, Samuel, William W. (? Wright or Warren), and possibly John and Joseph Andrew (aka General); William —Bill Driggers; Daniel Green; Elisha Green; Daniel John —Dan Mann; William —Bill Richardson; William (? Elias) Wester; Elisha Wilkerson the elder; Elisha Wilkerson the younger; and maybe Joshua Geiger (pronounced —Gigger in olden times among Crackers).

Each married man had his family with him. Some think William was already in Florida and John and Joseph Andrew came later. As noted under the heading Moses's siblings (see later in narrative), some older heads told me Joseph Andrew and John might have been sons of Moses rather than his brothers (see earlier discussion…Don't you like this confusion?).

All the pioneers listed above were living in southeast Georgia when they decided to move to Florida. It is almost certain some were familiar with this section of the territory. Some of the family said that William W. had been down earlier to scout around the northeast Florida country and had applied for a grant of land (they confused him with a William Barber who applied for land in Gadsden County in the late 1820's). Elisha Green and others supposedly had served in this section of Florida during the First Seminole War (Mr. Green was a veteran of that war and the Creek War [he served under Gen. Andrew Jackson], but his service in northeast

Florida is a moot question), and this adds some validity to Dr. Samuel Proctor's theory that this area saw action during that conflict (see later under —The Early Years in Florida.

Be advised there were probably no slaves brought down. From what was heard about the trip and who was on it, all slaves were purchased after the pioneers had settled.

I was told there were sheep, swine, horses, and herds of cattle (never heard of mules being with them but surely there were some) to control and drive. Aunt Cissy Barber Rowe, granddaughter of Moses and Mary Leah, said chickens and geese were transported in wicker cages. Mary Leah set the cages in the shallow creek water they forded to clean out the droppings and, after the water cleared, to give the fowl a drink. One only has to use the imagination to make a list of all the items they brought. Doubtless, they carried nothing useless.

The travelers camped first at Fence Pond, now known as Toledo (nothing there today). The second night was spent atop Trail Ridge. They traveled 10 miles the third day and spent their last night in Georgia near the present Stokesville community. The wagons and wooden axle carts floated across the Saint Mary's (known to them as —Big River), the animals and foot traffic forded or swam, and just east of the confluence of the Big Saint Mary's and its South Prong (—Little River) the intrepid band of pioneers set foot on Florida sand and began a new life. This would be where William would settle later.

They then followed the river and its south prong upstream. Moses had announced to the train that he was stopping and making his home at the first good-sized spring he found on the Florida side. He was as good as his word. On the east bank of the Little Saint Mary's River near the presently named Dick White Branch they came upon such a spring. Moses halted his oxen and began unpacking in spite of warnings by his brother William and Mr. Elisha Green that he was —smack kadabl in the middle of an Indian trail.

He was called a fool to set up his household on a route that was used by Indians who were hinting at belligerency, but within thirty years Moses Barber had carved out, whipped, shot, sweated, and loved his way into an empire that stretched loosely from his headquarters near the present Macclenny down to the Everglades.
Mary Leah told the parents (Moses and Mary Thompson) of her daughters-in-law Lizzie and Vic while they were her neighbors that the wagon train arrived on the site of the future Barber Plantation in July of 1829 after a four days journey from Fort Alert. Moses also gave that date when relating the tale to his grandchildren and new neighbors. We once used the date of 1833 in our Moses stories because of census data, but this could be incorrect when weighed against the date given by the travelers themselves (there are many times I will accept oral history over shoddy documents such as the 1850 census). The arrival date continues to be a moot point.

The most overworked word in an amateur genealogist"s vocabulary is documentation. Whatever one of them has to say about his/her forebears has "documentation" regardless of where it came from, and they demand "documentation" for whatever another has to say on the same subject. They often pooh-pooh oral history despite the fact that is where they began their searching. We begin life with oral history. When that big warm thing picks us up, cuddles us, and puts something satisfying to our tum-tums in our mouths and says, "Mama loves her „ittle punkin" pie", we have received our first bit of oral history...she didn"t hold a birth certificate and census record behind the bottle (or whatever) to "prove" the relationship. Oral history can be twisted and confused in its passing down from generation to generation, because it is the product of human beings. Documents are also the product of human beings and can be just as incorrect. When no documentation ever turns up, we have little choice but to go with what grandma told us.

All the pioneers stopped with Moses for a while, some for as long as a year, before heading off in their respective directions.

Members of that wagon/cart train into what was to become Baker County all agreed there were only three families in the area when they arrived. Archibald Hogans near the present Baxter was the only one named. Some old timers said they think they remembered their older kin telling about a family of free blacks named Locklear living on the Saint Mary's. Perhaps one of the three families was that of James M. Burnsed who lived just south of the Hogans place.

The country

Most of us writing on Florida's territorial days like to dwell on the word "untamed" as if the pioneers forged into an unknown and totally inhospitable country. That was partly true for much of the land and almost totally true for other parts, but we must be advised the human race had been traversing, dwelling in, and to some extent developing what the Spanish named La Florida for millennia. And knowledge of La Florida had been rippling out to interested people for a long time.
There were routes through north Florida begun by animal migrations; followed by proto-Indians; and used by later Indians, explorers, and traders intermittently. These trails amounted to no more, according to early reports, than beat-out paths through the woods. The roads would soon be broadened by droves of livestock and rutted by pioneers' and traders' wheeled vehicles. Whenever a route was impassible for wheeled vehicles due to deep dry sand or mud, a new path was taken. Thus in several stretches there were few to several more or less parallel trails.

Small to large patches of cleared land dotting the landscape evinced ancient farms of aboriginal and later Indian settlers, and these were often utilized by the earliest Anglo-American pioneers until they could clear larger tracts or find more fertile land elsewhere. Grandison Barber (relationship to Moses unknown) was one of the opportunists who settled old Indian fields, and that would include the site where the Burnsed Blockhouse/Coll Brown house stood in the northeast of the present Baker County for the greater part of two centuries.

The topography of most of the land where the first train of settlers stopped was rolling with some stretches of very flat land. The low hills were mostly aligned north and south with small swamps, called ponds, bays, and heads in between (twentieth century clear cutting, bulldozing, and reforestation efforts have leveled much of the landscape and filled many of the small low wet places). Along the route of the present CSX railroad from Trail Ridge west through Olustee was a series of swamps and open marshes. Some of the swamps were known as ―open‖ and others labeled ―tight-eye‖, ―impossible‖, or ―impassable.

Giant pines, mostly of the long leaf variety stood in wiregrass flats. The pines were interspersed with black jack (called turkey oaks elsewhere) and red oak on sandy hills. Great stands of red cedar, sometimes referred to as junipers, were especially abundant along the hilly area through the mid section of the present county.

Cypresses several feet thick stood in the waterways and few lakes. On the edges of the river and creek swamps grew yellow poplars some reportedly over 150 feet tall. Some of the old fields of the Indians had been taken over by oak, hickory, sassafras, maple, etc. to form hardwood hammocks. Cabbage palms, never plentiful and then absent from the county for many years after the first Anglo-American pioneers settled in, once dotted the wet and dry landscapes, and particularly so along the streams. Cabbage palms soon disappeared due to the new comer's taste for swamp cabbage and for the comparative ease of cutting the trunks for habitations and fortifications.

There were no brushy areas beyond the swamps. Annual burns by nature and Indians kept the undergrowth down, emended the sandy acid soil a bit, and provided fresh pasturage for cattle and wildlife. The Crackers continued the practice.

The Florida first witnessed by the pioneers was not the Florida we see today. Beyond the swampy areas the land was clean. The socio-political agendas of self-styled environmentalists (and, unfortunately, some sincere but unwitting environmentalists) were espoused by lawmakers in the late years of the 20th century, and the annual winter burns of the aboriginal peoples and Crackers were banned. As a result, jungle like brush began to crowd out the habitats of certain flora and fauna such as wiregrass and fox squirrels. In times of drought, the brush becomes explosive tinder and nothing is safe when either mankind or nature strikes fire to it. Florida pinelands ecosystems, depending on burns, are disappearing almost as rapidly from so-called conservation efforts as from development. Nature is going to have her burns – she knows burns are necessary – and it would be much more sane to return to annual winter controlled woods burning than to turn the responsibility back to her or over to criminal firebugs.

Game was plentiful. Venison, gator tail, turkey, quail, and wild swine sustained the early settlers. Catfish from Big River were up to five feet long (rather large catfish were still being caught in the 1940's).

Rivers and creeks were clear, pure, and stained tea brown. Most waterways of any size could support floating traffic, and the Big River and its tributaries were soon utilized by the Crackers for market travel. Sea-going craft came up the Saint Mary's as far as Traders Hill and were met by the pioneers' cotton, timber, and pelts. Four major routes from Georgia converged on their ways south, east, and west near the Barber Plantation. Through the Soakum section came a route toward Barber's Station from old Indian territory of middle and west Georgia. This was used often by the US Militia during the Second Seminole War. Along a slightly higher strip of land between the Okefenoke and Pinhook was a trail sometimes referred to as the Old Train Road, Old Yarborough Train Trail, and some other names not much different from the two just mentioned (the Old Train Road joined the Yelvington Trail that came down the west side of the Saint Mary's River). From the present Moniac, a road came south along the east side of the Saint Mary's, and several miles to the east was Trail Ridge.

There were three east west routes. The Jacksonville-Tallahassee Post Road was the main one, and it was often several miles north of the present US 90 (some sections near the Turner Cemetery could still be made out in the 1950's). Another went from Jacksonville and the present Clay County to old Alligator/Lake City approximately along and sometimes far south of the present I - 10. Along the present CSX railroad was the turnpike. Property owners along the route literally kept a pike (pole) across the road and turned it for traffic after a toll was paid. It was said Moses and others were permitted the pike concession by the territory in return for their keeping up the stretch that lay in their property, but I haven't found anything official on this. Older heads claimed Moses began making his fortune with the money that came from his pike concession. This has not been researched.

the people "the crackers"

The people who traveled in that first settler train into the present Baker County were of Anglo-Celtic-Amer-Indian background...simple folk with few worldly possessions. Some of them lived not much above an animal like subsistence. Dying and procreating were undeniable accepted facts of the life inside their simple cabins. Women were tough, but some evidently died an early death due to the rigors of frequent childbirth and hard labor. Infant deaths were not uncommon. But contrary to today's myth, most of those folks of olden days, if they survived childhood, lived a long and productive life.

They were Crackers.

For most of its history the word "cracker" has been used as a derogatory appellation among English speaking people. As events and people came and went it was applied to various groups and always to the unsophisticated and boisterous...the equivalent of today"s "good ol" boys". English writers mentioned cracks over four hundred years ago. In the mid 18th century when poorer classes of white Georgians and Carolinians stole across the Florida border and spirited away cattle, horses, and slaves from the Spanish and Indians, it was said the Spanish spat out an epithet that sounded much like "Quaqueros." During the American Revolution, when loyal or conscription dodging families fled to Florida, the British born citizens of the colony referred to the greatly resented newcomers as "Crackers"...and British governor James Grant called them, "those damned Crackers." As is the wont of so many amateur historians of our day, a story just had to be invented to give an origin to an unusual label from the past. In the case of a theory becoming a fact and perpetuated myth, those well meaning but benighted souls decided that Georgians driving their cattle down into Florida while cracking their cow whips gave rise to the term "Cracker." Crackers were Crackers in Great Britain at least a couple hundred years before the common use of the cow whip by Crackers in America. Most early Cracker pioneers were too poor to own enough cattle to necessitate the use of a whip. And to cap it off, Cracker cow hunters "popped" a cow whip rather than "cracked" it. Let us lay the whip cracking origin of the label of Cracker to rest...once and for all.

The Early Years in Florida

Moses and Mary Leah (pronounced "Leer" by some and "Lee" by others) stretched a tent among giant pines and ancient live oaks and settled in with their two small children. The other families decided to camp on the hill also, at least for the remainder of the summer.

Moses and Mary Leah's original home, a simple dirt-floored one-room structure of logs called a —single Pen, was erected on the highest point of the settlement (see newspaper article below for an almost exact location of the house). There was but one entrance. After having lived in cowhide and canvas covered wagons for a few weeks, the little hut probably was a welcome relief. Because of impending Indian troubles, Moses is said to have partially sawed out notches in some of the logs for a rifle butt to be used to knock them out for loop holes, loop holes being convenient for pushing rifle barrels through. I was told his first loopholes were on either side of the one door. My questions were. —Why just beside the door?‖ —Why just one door?‖ I never received answers; the tellers of the tales didn't know.

Later Moses had pine logs cut, sharpened at both ends, and driven into the ground to create a closed in yard in front of the cabin. I was told that at first the stockade was attached to the ever-being-enlarged cabin but that the stockade didn't surround the entire house, just a small front yard. I never learned the reason for this arrangement. The thinner ends of the peeled logs alternated with the thicker ends. The solid fence, except for firing holes, was 10 – 12 feet high, tied together stoutly with braces and a firing platform attached. When the Indian raids began, Mary Leah stood on the firing platform and did most of the shooting; Moses was not a good shot (? vision problems). Mary Leah told her neighbors the Moses Thompsons that she had loaded many a muzzle-loading blunderbuss and killed Indians.

Ironically, Moses told his descendents that when he arrived at the spring on the sand hill above the South Prong, the site had been a —fortified place‖ at some time in the past. When I discussed this with Dr. Samuel Proctor of the University of Florida in 1975, he said his and other's findings made them believe the area might have seen some activity during the First Seminole War. He said our county probably had a site of the most easterly activity of that conflict. He further stated that he was of the opinion that Gen. Andrew Jackson and his Cherokee allies had crossed the Suwannee and had been quite near our section of Florida. If Cherokees were indeed in the area and some might have remained, I will have to re-think my stand that all Crackers with a claim to Indian blood are actually of partial Creek stock and that none had Cherokee in them (this would not be the sole time I've had to re-track and retract).

I lost touch with Dr. Proctor soon after; his housekeeper refused to allow me to disturb him. I reckon he has moved on to that great historical research site in the sky. I was fascinated by his informal presentation and wish I could have been privy to his research papers.

Dicky Ferry (without a doubt this country's foremost historian of the War Between the States and especially of the action of that war in Florida), Prof. W. Harold Milton, and Leonard —Shakey‖ Waldron found military artifacts and coins of the early 1800's in and around the ridge above Dick White Branch on the old Barber Plantation site. Perhaps Dr. Proctor knew for certain whereof he spoke. I, for one, would not argue with that most respected Florida historian of our time.
Since this writing was begun, Leonard "Shakey" Waldron, a man with an abiding enthusiasm for local history and searching for artifacts, died. His home was situated on the old Barber Plantation and probably on a US Militia camp or entrenchment site of the First Seminole War.

Moses had also related to neighbors and descendents how he and his brothers had seen signs of a fortified place on the south bank of Big River (old timers called the Saint Mary's and Little Saint Mary's, respectively, Big River and Little River) north of the present Oak Grove/Burnsed Church. This seems to fit an account I read once (? In a Florida Historical Society quarterly) that the Spanish maintained a fort on their side of the river at this crossing place during the Patriots' War (War of 1812). When one thinks of a fort today, one envisions something like Ft. Marion/Castillo de San Marcos in St. Augustine, but the great majority of Florida forts were little more than logs and dirt that fronted trenches. To my knowledge none has ever investigated the site.

Sam Barber made his way along a major (for that time) Jacksonville-Pensacola route and set up housekeeping for a few years in what we know today as Soakum. William retraced the trail from Georgia and settled on Trail Ridge on the Florida side of the Saint Mary's River. The other Barber boys erected their cabins near Moses. The Manns traveled west along the Jacksonville-Pensacola Road and settled a few miles north of the present US 90 between Glen Saint Mary and Sanderson (see more of the Manns later in the narrative). Elisha Green continued farther up the South Prong to its headwaters. Daniel Green went east into the Georgia Bend and the present Nassau County. The Westers and Richardsons moved west and south, respectively, to Olustee and Mud Lake. The Wilkersons went first along the route west with Sam, but returned to Big River. Later some of their offspring took the Yelvington Trail and scattered along the route into the present Clay and Putnam Counties.

Whether or not Joshua Geiger came with the pioneer train is still not determined, but soon after the arrival of the families listed above, he had set up housekeeping in the vicinity of the Manns (see above). A good description was given by my granddaddy Barber, which he got from his father: the old Geiger (and Mott) place was 6 miles east of Sanderson and one mile north of the railroad on the west bank of the Little Saint Mary's River (six miles was a bit shy of the actual distance…but miles seemed to be considerably —longer in those days). He later removed to the Georgia Bend and then to Nassau County.

Sundry Notes on the Plantation

When the Indians began to attack in larger numbers and with increasing frequency, Moses had the stockade expanded to enclose a large area that included his barns and slave quarters. Most area families referred to the Barber place as a fort. During the Seminole War the Barber place was designated a blockhouse, i. e. a fortified structure within a block of twenty miles square in the zone of belligerency.

Most of Moses's original north Florida plantation and much of the lower Georgia Bend comprised Military Defense Square #6 as specified in an act approved on the 23rd of January, 1839. It was to be manned with 20 members of the militia, ½ of them mounted. I never heard any of the older members of the family talk about soldiers at the plantation during Indian troubles, although they often talked of settlers from the extensive surrounding vicinity coming to the fort for protection during several raid alerts. I've been told that digging at the site has produced military artifacts decades prior to Civil War vintage and thus might be from the period of the Second Seminole War (some are contemporary with the First Seminole War).

As his family grew & orphans and relatives were taken in, Moses erected 2 huge log rooms under a roof in common. A single log structure was called a single pen and two side by side joined by a single roof was a double pen. The pens were divided by a broad un-floored breezeway. The breezeway was large enough to permit wheeled traffic and horses to pass through. Eventually, the traffic was made to be pedestrian type when Moses had the breezeway floored with the same eight-inch thick puncheons as he had used in the house.

The original cabin was then utilized as a kitchen and was separated far from the main dwelling. Later Moses had it connected to the house by a covered walk, and eventually he added a boardwalk to create a dogtrot. The kitchen floor was packed dirt covered with white river sand.

Both the dwelling house and kitchen were furnished with "mud" chimneys, giant fireplaces constructed of clay, sticks, and Spanish moss that had to be rebuilt every few to several years in the wet Florida climate.

At first, water was brought from the spring near the river, and later wells were dug. One, of a vintage around the War Between the States period and cased in with brick, was visible on the property until well into the later half of the twentieth century. Moses had the land on the west side of the river cleared for cotton growing (that land has been in cultivation by various owners until the new county high school was erected there in the late 20th century). When that land wore out, he moved the cotton planting to where the community of Sanderson is now. Where leisurely groups play a round of golf in Macclenny today was once Moses's cornfields and vegetable gardens. These plots would lie fallow every three years to be host land for stock herds for the purpose of emending the worn-out dirt.

What is now Glen Saint Mary and Pinetop was his swine territory. Sheep were kept closer to the main farmstead tended by armed herders constantly on the alert for red wolves. His cattle roamed throughout the present Baker County and into parts of the present Columbia, Duval, Nassau, and Union Counties. Later the cow country was extended into other parts of the peninsula, particularly Gulf Hammock south-southwest of the plantation on the Gulf of Mexico and the eastern side of the wide Kissimmee prairie and marshes, and that much land was needed because by the beginning of the War Between the States he is reported to have had hundreds of thousands of head of cattle in the state.

Soon after the Barbers arrived in Florida a short-lived horse and rider mail delivery was instituted. It was succeeded in 1835 with a stagecoach mail and passenger service run by James S. Harris. The route which began at Garey's Ferry/Fort Heileman (Middleburg) ran to Cracker Swamp (between the present White House and Baldwin), Brandy Branch, Deep Creek, Trail Ridge, Barber Bay, Barber's stockade, Lake Spaulding (Ocean Pond)/Olustee, and ended at Alligator (the present Lake City). From Barber's, the route extended north into the Georgia Bend and on to Traders Hill. Its southerly route was to Trail Ridge whence it divided, one fork to

Green Cove Springs and the other toward Newnansville/Gainesville. I don't think Green Cove Springs and Gainesville were named when the stage service began. The reader is referred to a description of roadways earlier in the narrative.

The federal census of 1840 showed Moses and Leah with eight children and eleven slaves. Ten years later, another child had been born and several blacks added to the slave quarters. In addition, four white laborers, a clerk (cleric/minister) and his wife lived at Barber's Station. In the 1840's and through the following two decades Moses Barber served his area of Columbia and New River Counties as Justice of the Peace and postmaster. His descendents were told that he was elected as a representative from Columbia County to Tallahassee, but this has not been found in records.

At the cessation of Indian hostilities, Moses moved his slave quarters farther from the house. If they were standing today they would be about where the Pine View country club sits and would range south for about a hundred yards. The foundations could be made out in the 1920's in the field behind the Ab and Eula Kirkland house (now the home of Mr. and Mrs. Emory Kirkland). A white overseer with dogs and shifts of handlers prevented runaways.

By 1860, there were 54 slaves on Moses's New River County plantation (the present Baker Co.) and, as per the stories of the older folks, about the same number scattered elsewhere on his other holdings (not borne out by records of the time). The Barber Plantation group was broken down into 30 males and 24 females. Their ages ranged from one year to fifty-five. Among the slaves were seven mulattos. By the time Moses had no choice but to watch his slaves escape prior to the Yankee invasion, he was said to have had over 100 human chattel.

MOSES BARBER PLACE IS MOST INTERESTING.

The information contained in this article was given the writer [Tate Powell, Sr.] by the late Mrs. A. W. Barber Rowe, Macclenny, and was published in the Press on December 2nd, 1938.

The Moses Barber place northwest of Macclenny and near the South Prong River is one of the most interesting old homesites in the state in historical value (it's location is near the present home of Prof. And Mrs. W. H. Milton).

Moses Barber was one of the early settlers of Baker County and one of its outstanding citizens. He was possibly the largest cattle owner in Florida about the time of the outbreak of the Civil War.

The Barbers and many of the Rowes now living in Baker County and elsewhere are his direct descendents and most of them are living up to the cattle owning tradition of the family.

During the Indian Wars in this section the old Barber place was one of the strongholds of the early settlers. The place was surrounded by a log barricade with portholes thru which riflemen did their part in subduing the Indians.
In the last fights with the Indians just before they were compelled to leave their headquarters in and near the great Okefenokee Swamp, seven different raids were made on the Barber place in one day and all were repulsed with heavy loss to the Indians.

During a lull in fighting that day Mr. Barber had to go outside the stockade to look after some hogs and was shot in the shoulder by an Indian hid behind a stump. The wound was not so serious but that Moses Barber was able to return the fire and make his way back to his fortified home.

It was shortly after this incident that the Indians were forced to move to the Everglades and it is said that none of them have ever been seen in this section again.

While nothing is left of the old buildings of the Moses Barber place its location can be found just north of the former home of Paul Crews – now the home of Mr. and Mrs. I. D. Burnsed – and many people believe that large sums of money and gold were buried on the place – a rumor that has been handed down for generations.

The site of the old place has been dug over and is filled with holes by those who believed this story of buried wealth.

Some heavy fighting incident to the Battle of Olustee during the Civil War was fought near this place and the breast works that were thrown up can still be plainly seen on both sides of the river within sight of those traveling on U. S. 90. The breast works are on the north side of the river.|

The famous bulldogs and the Indian attacks

For protection of his sheep and other stock against wolves, whompus cats (panthers), and bears, Moses needed dogs, many dogs. Moses had so many dogs it took a beef a day to feed them. A youngster named Starling (Jeff and Manning's father Abraham or grandfather_____) from the Georgia Bend was a hired hand at the Barber Plantation and was in charge of the feeding.

In addition to discouraging predators, the large dog pack was to keep the Indians away and warn of any brave enough to approach the plantation house. It was said the Indians were very fearful of the dogs and tried to kill them with arrows from an upwind position so as not to give their presence away. A few of the animals fell victims to the arrows. However, the attack on the dogs set them a'howling and barking, and the Indians were foiled again. This was info from Mr. Manning Starling of Macclenny.

Moses decided to add seven vicious bulldogs to his already great dog population at the plantation after an Indian almost killed his boss slave Jason (see this story under the heading Mary Ellen Barber Hale). The bulldogs were also used for the purpose of keeping slaves in line and for hunting those who dared try to escape. He trained his dogs by sending a slave into the woods and then setting the dogs loose on the trail. Knowing what would happen to him if he were caught, no slave was careless enough to allow him self to be a victim of the dogs. Some of the slaves seemed to relish the training as if it were a game. It was probably the nearest they came to feeling even a hint of freedom. It was said that one in particular often asked if he could be the fake prey, and he devised different creative ruses to throw the dogs off his trail. His slaves were too valuable to be damaged, so Moses made certain that none was caught...just treed. However he once sic-ed the dogs too soon and a slave was badly bitten on the heel as he was climbing an oak. Moses saw that the wounded heel was medicated and caused to heal. I heard that slave became the fastest runner in the quarters, notwithstanding he had suffered a badly damaged heel.

Moses was evidently fond of his pack of dogs, but he never brooked lack of discipline from them. He used his cow whip to keep them in line, especially at mealtime. The bulldogs ate first, then the pregnant and nursing bitches, and finally the remainder of the pack. Each went to its assigned place at the feeding trough. Any dog getting out of place, dashing for the feeding trough, or tying up for a fight felt Moses's cow whip.

For many years Moses kept a small cur with him at all times. The little dog was an —Indian smeller‖ that warned its master of Indians in the neighborhood. It (never heard anyone mention the cur's gender) was with its master at all times and was said to be able to detect Indians even upwind. When Moses was horseback the cur sat in the saddle in front of him, and when he was in a wagon or other wheeled vehicle, the little dog was in the seat next to him. Its first alert was the hair on its nape standing on end. The second alert was an almost inaudible low growl. I was told the little dog never growled or raised its hair unless it smelled Indians.

. Once during a lull between Indian attacks, there were seven that day according to his granddaughter Mary Leah —Cissy Barber Rowe, Moses, with his cur, and his boss slave Jason were trying to gather their hogs before the Indians gained an opportunity to kill them. A missing shoat of exceptional quality gave them reason to search in the acorn rich groves in the vicinity of the present Glen Saint Mary/Pine Top (or as said by some to be about five miles from the stockade).

The dog gave him a warning. Jason was getting nervous. He begged his master to return home immediately. Moses later said it was the only time his cur had given him such a short notice of Indians. Almost as soon as the dog began growling an

95

Indian hiding behind a stump shot. Moses wheeled his horse around to head for the stockade, and in doing so the horse lost footing and threw him to the ground. As Moses fell he received an Indian rifle ball in his shoulder and his over and under shotgun/rifle combination dropped, hit a root, and split the barrels apart. He quickly retrieved his firearm and swung back onto his mount. He raced toward the stockade. Jason saw the shoat and grabbed it up onto his horse before following his master even though Moses hollered back to forget the pig. He is reported to have said, —I can replace a shoat easier'n I can a nigger, damnit. So come on!‖ Some connected this incident to the May 1841 raid in which his brother Bill/Will was killed a few miles east of Moses's stockade (see William W. Barber).

The Indians, on very fast ponies, almost overtook them, but they made it to safety. The fighting continued all night with heavy losses by the Indians, but when the morning mists and gun smoke had lifted, every Indian, alive and dead, had disappeared.

Indian raids seemed to be almost always just before daybreak, but nighttime and daytime attacks were not unheard of. If the raiders could do nothing else, they would set fire to the haystacks. Neighbors described seeing the brilliant glow of Moses's burning haystacks even as late as the Third Seminole War (said by the history experts not to have reached north Florida…the Crackers knew differently).
When attacking in the early years of the war the Indians approached singly, fired a flame-tipped arrow and then retreated. The fiery arrows seemed never to catch on the peeled green stockade logs, so they changed tactics; they then crawled on their bellies from the west along the river toward the fort with lighted splinters in their mouths. This made them easy targets, and they never seemed to learn how to attack without making themselves so obvious. When Jason's shot from the Barber stockade resulted in the flaming splinter being dropped and a loud —Wah‖ coming from the struck attacker, Moses would holler, "Jason, you ol' son of a bitch, you got another'n."

The slain Indian's companions would rush out to drag the body back into the woods. Although a vengeful Indian fighter, Moses commanded that the body retrievers not be fired on. No bodies were found after the battle had ended; the Indians took their dead and wounded with them. It was said they feared bad luck if the bodies of their dead fell into the hands of the whites.

Whether Moses's insistence that the body-recoverers not be fired on was due to altruism (doubtful), superstition, religious beliefs, or to an undiscovered practicality is a moot subject. His attitude was strange for one who had once ordered an Indian to be skinned alive and left hanging in the middle of the trail as a warning for no others to mess with Moses Barber.

Old timers claimed the dead Indians were buried in great mounds nearby. This was a case of oral history being totally incorrect; first, the mounds in this area were from pre-historic times, and, second, Moses wouldn't give them time to perform such a feat.

The Second Seminole War dragged on for seven miserable years. Moses lost kin and much valuable livestock and crops before Bolech (or Ecochattee or whoever) and his warriors retreated south. He and Leah took in some of the orphaned related and unrelated kids and added them to their family.

The last raid was by a large band of Indians that was passing through from the Okefenoke. Moses and his crew chased them south along the Alachua Trail (partially and approximately along the route of SR 228). They saw a thin trail of smoke in the sky above a small dense pond thicket. Moses said, —Boys, ain't no use in us a'thinkin' we c'n git to'm in _at _air pond. They got th' _vantage. Let _em go. Mayhaps we seen the last uv'um.‖ Now, whether or not G-g-g-Granddaddy Moses spoke exactly this way, I don't know; I just recorded it as best I could when hearing it repeated from older heads fifty years ago.

Capt. Ben Miller and his Georgia Militia were also given credit for this incident. Perhaps (or as Moses would say…Mayhaps) the Barbers and Capt. Miller's unit were together on this campaign. Capt. Miller's report of the last hostilities gave a more easterly route of chasing the Indians through the present Baker County. Most old Crackers named the leader of the Okefenoke Creeks Billie Bowlegs. He might have been Bolech or he might have carried the Crackers' favorite label for any Indian whose name he did not know or could not pronounce (as per several old time folks in this area).

Jason and the slaves

Moses bought Jason soon after moving to Florida (some said it was just prior to the Second Seminole War). Three different auction sites been given by descendents – St. Augustine, Jacksonville, and Savannah. Uncle Duff Barber via his daughter Carmeta claimed Jason was purchased in the late summer of 1829 in Saint Augustine and that his papers stated he was born on Alimicani Island, part of the Zephaniah Kingsley slave property. I never saw the —papers, and I am beginning to have doubts about the family being in Florida in 1829. After mulling this tale over for the past several years I am convinced we have another Uncle Duff type made-up story on our hands. I can't help but be incredulous about Uncle Duff knowing much about Kingsley and Alimicani; Carmeta, however, was well read and knew her Florida history.

Jason was a powerful intelligent man who quickly learned to handle a musket and almost matched his mistress as a sharpshooter. Jason's eventual position was boss slave. He was accused of being a harsh taskmaster over his subordinates. Jason and his mistress were the main defenders of the stockade when Moses was away. The other slaves were assigned the job of loading and re-loading firearms. It is worthy of note that there was never a mention of a slave taking advantage while holding a loaded rifle to turn it on his master, mistress, or black overseer.

After Mary Leah died sometime in the late 1850's, Moses took up with the young Rebecca Clements of Columbia County (see Moses's second family later in the narrative). She had been living in the household of his brother Sam, and Moses brought her to his plantation as a housekeeper. It was thought by some that she and a brother were orphaned by an Indian attack and were reared by Sam and Mary Barber. Jason had been devoted to his mistress and resented the relationship (unmarried) of Moses and Rebecca. He sulled (sulked) and said he would work for Mr. Isaac (his owner's son), but not for Mr. Moses.

Moses took Jason to the barn and gave him a sound whipping and gave him to his son Isaac. Some of the family said that was the only time Moses whipped a slave; they said Moses was bitter that Jason, who had become more than a slave in the Barber household, dared damage the special tie by being impudent. Still others said it was Moses's wont prior to taking one of his many trips away to always whip his boss slave. I recall some branches of the family giving the story about Moses taking his boss slave to a shed and caning him before leaving for a period of several weeks, evidently thinking it would keep the boss slave, and therefore the underling slaves, in line in his absence. We have no way of discovering the truth.

There are three stories regarding Jason's end. He was said by some to have gone to central Florida with his new master and died there, but Isaac didn't go to the Kissimmee territory until after the war's end and, therefore, until after emancipation (of course, Jason could have gone as a freedman). Some said he ran away and disappeared. Others claim he went to Jacksonville after the war and died there in dissipation near Aunt Penny Barber in the West Ashley/Church Streets neighborhood.

There was a story that in the late 1880's an elderly, large framed Negro came to Macclenny and spent a few days camped near Dick White Branch on the present golf course. He poked around the soil, raked leaves off a small patch of ground, and brought some wild flowers to that cleared spot. When asked by some of the old timers what his business was there, he answered, —Jes' looking for a little bit a' happiness that once stood on this ground...jes' a little bit a' happiness.‖

Of the more than 100 slaves reputed to be on the Barber Plantations, only two names other than Jason have come down through history – Dick White and Willis Rawls. Mr. White was able to purchase, with help from the Freedmen's Bureau, a large part of the old Barber plantation home site after the War Between the States (he did not receive a deed). It is ironic that he was then master where he had once been in servitude. The little stream that runs through the original property is today called

Dick White Branch. He is reported to have given work to any who came by regardless of color or previous allegiance. To some of the now landless Barbers he offered a little piece of land to till. Some politely refused (pride), and others suggested a certain anatomical repository of Mr. White where he could insert the land offer and the land.

Uncle Willis Rawls, unlike the majority of the freed people, remained in Baker County and made a meager living chopping and splitting wood for white folk. He moved from family to family, staying 3 to 4 days at a time. As he aged into being totally dependent, Uncle Rob Rowe, a Confederate veteran, built the old gentleman a small house in a back corner of his yard. Another kinfolk of mine claimed it was Uncle Ben Rowe who took the old fellow in. It was said that when Uncle Ben built himself a new kitchen he moved the old one to a corner of his yard for Uncle Willis' modest little home. Whichever is correct, he lived out his last years in relative ease. He had humbly requested that his remains be placed in the old Barber slave cemetery, and at his death, Uncle Rob (or Uncle Ben, if he were the benefactor) complied. Within the same week in 1898, Uncle Willis Rawls, a former slave, and his former master's nephew (and former Confederate soldier), Moses B. F. —Ben Barber, were the last interments in the cemetery. It soon went untended, and forty years later when the US Government sought out the graves of veterans buried there, it was barely distinguishable as a burying ground.

The reader is asked to ignore the so-called history that comes from made-for-TV movies and miniseries, historical novels, and revised school history texts of the late 20th century and instead apply some logic to the subject of slavery. From our perspective we see slavery as a heinous act of humankind against itself, but in the last centuries prior to the emancipation of American slaves, the institution of slavery was considered by most people living at the time to be a part of the overall scheme of life, if for no other reason than it had existed from earliest history and had received little negative press in the Old Testament. A unit of human being property was expensive in America, and despite today's popular conceptions, physical mistreatment was surely not a frequent, regular, and widespread practice. Research has proved there were overseers with no money invested in the slaves who probably enjoyed beating down another human element in subconscious effort to elevate their own sorry states. Doubtless there were neurotic and psychotic owners who were cruel. But the reader is asked to recall the money he invested in his vehicle sitting under his carport and ask himself if he would make a habit of taking a 2 X 4 to it with the distinct possibility of damaging it. My case rests. It's time for us to accept that the horrendous practice of slavery existed, that it is now over, and that we must get on with life...we are all free now. Its use as an excuse is wearing thin.

The Cemetery

In our branch of the family, the burial ground on the plantation was called "the slave cemetery." Members of the Barber family were interred there also. Mother Vic Barber said her husband James Edward and her mother-in-law Mary Leah were laid to rest in the little cemetery. Moses B. F. —Ben‖ Barber expressed a wish to be buried there beside his parents. His wish was honored in 1898 (see MOSES B. F. BARBER). From rather murky oral history, a brother of Moses (? John) was the first to be buried there soon after the Barbers arrived on the banks of the Little Saint Mary's River.

There were between 60 and 70 interments in the approximately ¾'s of an acre rectangular cemetery.

Others in the cemetery are Herndons, Daughartys, and Jonothan Davis and his wife Nancy.

See my PRESS column titled The Black Pioneer and the Wood Chopper for another story on the burials.

Miss Nettie Rowe told me her mother and grandmother said that soon after the war, they were sitting on the porch of the old Barber house one night when they saw what they perceived to be ghosts wandering among the graves - will-o-the-wisps or traveling lights. The women armed themselves with axes (don't know what danger an ax would be to a specter) and slipped down to the cemetery to investigate, wondering if the ghosts of the Yankee soldiers had returned. They discovered the —ghosts‖ were pale colored cows that had entered the cemetery to graze during the moonlit night. From the women's description of the experience, it seems the cemetery lay at the foot of the rise the house sat on and to its east-southeast. This would be about where Miltondale Road separates the present golf course from a residential development. If I remember correctly (the mind is getting fuzzy with age), according to Dicky Ferry's metal detecting, we think part of the cemetery lies under Denny Wells' house. When Dicky searched the area, his metal detector almost always stopped giving signals at the perimeter of an approximate three quarters acre rectangular area that included Mr. Wells home site (I repeat, the mind is getting fuzzy these days, and I could be wrong on this).

Soon after the last interments, G-grandpa Charley Barber, his cousin Duff Barber, and brother-in-law Dave Rowe attempted to locate more graves in the old cemetery. G-grandpa was hoping to locate his father's burial spot. They used his mother's memory and a long steel rod probe, but found nothing.

The cow whip

Moses was an expert with the cow whip. He taught his boys to do as well as he. Among the activities at rests on the cattle drives was whip practice. Moses could adeptly prune a small pine tree with his whip. To test his boys' ability, he would cut down a pine sapling with his cow whip, then the boys were lined up and each had to cut a pine sapling of equal size with his own. When one failed, he felt his father's whip on his butt (as per the late Mr. Barney Dillard of Astor, Florida, and he didn't say—butt).

My father, William Monroe "Dub" Barber, was the last expert cow whip maker in this county...maybe in this area of Florida. Others later touted themselves as plaiters of whips before audiences at some of the soi disant folk fests, but the work of most I saw seemed to be based on how they thought a whip might look like rather than having learned it from older experts and, therefore, from uncounted generations. Pop used good cowhide leather and a variety of plaiting patterns and different numbers of leather strips, including a square plait for riding quirts. The tail ends were plaited of buckskin, and the crackers or poppers were also of fine buckskin (they didn't last long when the whip was frequently popped). When he finished, it was either my mother's or my duty to —roll the whip by laying it on the wood board floor of our porch, putting a stout plank on it and then, perched on the plank with our full weight, roll the whip back and forth from top to tail. This was necessary to even out the plait and make the whip more pliable. A rubbing down with neatsfoot oil facilitated the process. Mother Pearle often complained about the oil that got into the grain of her porch floor from rolling the whip, but she would get out the lye soap, scalding water, and corn shucks floor scrub brush and —go to town on the stains. Pop whittled out his handles from oak or hickory and shaved them down slick with a piece of broken glass.

the cattle drives, and Moses moves south

I was informed that Moses took advantage of the Armed Occupation Act of 1842 that opened former Seminole territory to any white settler who would take, improve, and defend a certain number of acres for each adult member of his family. I was further told that Moses counted up his kids, upped the ages of some, added his wife, included his adopted nephews and nieces, and tried to slip some slaves in too. As a result he supposedly wound up with some sizable separate tracts of land that stretched from Fort Christmas on the Saint John's River to the marshes of lower Brevard County and over into Hernando County and as far south as Fort Bassinger in the upper Everglades, so we were told.
Records of the Armed Occupation Act do not bear this out (are we beginning to see the legend has truly outgrown the man?). In fact, this presaged a fault among many latter day Barbers...they are forever passing up marvelous opportunities for acquiring valuable land for almost nothing and therefore opening the way for others to take the advantage.

Some of the land Moses claimed and much of the land attributed to him was never actually granted to him, but, at first, that was no problem in the wilds of central and south Florida; ranges were open to all. That eventually created a problem however when cattle owners either inadvertently or purposely added other cattlemen's stray stock to their own. Such actions were the forerunner of the infamous Barber-Mizell Feud of 1870.

Some of the huge land grants and land purchases said to be Moses's are simply not found on record and probably did not exist. This is a proper place to insert that there is no documentation that Moses, his father, his grandfather, or his siblings received Spanish land grants in Florida. That was another wild tale given me that I foolishly included in my early narratives of Moses (and for which I am embarrassed and abjectly apologetic).

For several years, late 1840's to 1870 (erratic during the war) - Moses, his sons, and employees made cattle drives each year to the Kissimmee territory and upper Saint John's marshes for the winter and back to the plantation lands on the Saint Mary's in early spring. Small herds were kept at both sites for sustenance for family, slaves, and employees after the main herds were driven away. In north Florida the stock was shipped out to markets from Jacksonville, and from south Florida the shipments went from Punta Rassa to Cuba and up the Mississippi River. After the rails came through in north Florida, Baldwin became shipping headquarters for that part of the state.

From the many and often conflicting reports heard about the drive routes, it is difficult to state with certainty where they lay. Some overnight camping sites, trails, and cow pens locations mentioned by old timers were the south end of Trail Ridge, Lake Geneva, Hollister, between Lakes George and Kerr, Astor, and Fort Christmas. It was said that although a horseback trip to central Florida might take as little as three days on a very fast gaited horse (nine to ten hours a day), the cow drives took ten to fourteen days with a cow pen at the end of each second day. I was not privileged to know why the pens were situated only every second day on the route. Neither did I learn details of rivers crossings or of problems met with in inclement weather, but there is no doubt the drives were a struggle for men and beasts.

The young men and boys along the drive trails enjoyed going down to the Barber camps to hear the fireside tales and to watch the cow whip practice (see the Cow whip). Moses would usually give them a coin or two for running errands and spelling the drivers at night keeping wolves and other predators from his stock.
Other drives, especially after the War, were to Savannah and Charleston markets. It was on a return from one of these drives to Charleston that Moses's son James Edward died (see james Edward barber). After he was widowered, Moses met a number of ladies along the cow drives who were agreeable to keeping him company in an intimate fashion. It was rumored that he kept a female companion at each cow pen.

"Cowboy" is a term created by 19th century eastern newsmen. In Florida he was a —cow hunter‖ (later also called a —cow puncher), and the stockowner or dealer was a —cow man‖ or —cattleman. Florida was the first cow country in what is now the

United States, and the Diego Plains, now the general area of Ponte Vedra and Palm Valley in Saint Johns County, was the first Florida cattle range. From the early Spanish vaqueros along the Guano River almost 400 years ago, through the English herdsmen on the lower Saint Johns and the Anglo-Celtic-American cow hunters of territorial days, down to the modern beef industry of Florida (especially the central part), the state has remained among the country's top beef producers. The descendents of the original Spanish cattle were tough, long horned, and known to the Crackers as —scrub cattle‖ or —piney woodsers‖ and were important in combining with later introduced breeds to create the perfect animal on the hoof for the often unfriendly Florida climate and habitats. Cow dogs, wiry mongrels with a strong serving of bull dog in them, were indispensable in bringing cows out of the scrubs and swamps. Old time Florida cows were wild and the cowpuncher often had to sic the dogs on the meaner ones to hold them until the roper arrived. As the red wolf disappeared from the Florida woods in the first decades of the 20th century, the scrub cows' long horns of defense were bred out…so were the gores of accident and battle that gave opportunity to the screwworm fly.

When not driving cattle, Moses often availed himself and his mount of water transportation on the Saint John's to and from central Florida. He saved wear and tear on his horse and rear as well as some time. I was told he sometimes went by horseback or buggy downstate and took a boat back to Jacksonville and that he necessarily utilized the ferries on the river for horse and buggy when visiting Saint Augustine and New Smyrna. Uncle Carl Barber of Fort Christmas and Uncle John Barber of Palatka said they heard that Moses often took down a wagonload of merchandise from Jacksonville to sell to the settlers in Brevard and Orange Counties and returned to the plantation in north Florida with a double handful of gold. —He never missed a beat‖, was the way one descendent described Moses's ability to take advantage of every move and event. Another said, —Moses never made a trip empty handed.

Mr. William I. Barber of Kissimmee said Moses's Kissimmee farm was known to old timers as the Ed Newton place, now Osceola Memory Gardens. According to Mr. Barber's daughter-in-law Mary Ida (nee Bass) Barber Shearheart, Moses's slaves farmed the present Rose Hill in Osceola County. Moses's center of operations was in Brevard near the Orange County line. I often heard Lake Hell'n Blazes mentioned as being in his territory.

Moses told his daughters-in-law in Baker County that it was never his intention to set up permanent housekeeping in central Florida. None of his children were known to permanently settle there except Isaac. Most, if not all, his nephews and nieces (William's children) remained in the center of the state.

The Barbers' religion and Moses' morals

Jonothan H. Davis, a cleric (listed as "clerk" in the census) was believed to be a Baptist elder (an elder would later be known as a pastor among the progressive or missionary sect of the Baptists). He and his wife Nancy lived on the plantation. Information from non-related families in the area support the belief that Mr. Davis was a local elder and that he might have conducted services in Nassau and Columbia Counties and perhaps in the Georgia Bend.

Moses had two daughters-in-law who were strong Baptists. Arch's wife Martha (nee Geiger) was a schoolteacher who operated a Sunday school (sometimes meeting on Saturday evening) in the original Barber area of northeast Florida and later at her home at Horse Prairie (the present Dixie County). She is supposed to have been the prime mover in the establishment of a church in the Horse Prairie area.

Harriet "Hattie" (nee Geiger) was a cousin of Martha and the wife of Isaac. She was an exemplary woman who founded a Baptist Church in the Kissimmee area (more details later under Isaac Barber).

Moses, Sr., was a dichotomy; he could be religious and moral while he was blatantly breaking a few of the Old Testament's ten commandments. He was a —good Baptist in that he gathered himself together with the brethren at every opportunity. In fact, he insisted his entire family, permanent and temporary boarders, and slaves be in church service whenever possible. He was a vain man who blackened his large mustache with fireplace smut and dressed in his finest when it was meeting time. All the family and most of the residents of Barber's Station were loaded into wagons for the trip to whatever Baptist Church in the vicinity was meeting that Sunday or weekend (low church services lasted a weekend in backwoods Florida and Georgia in those days). Only a core was left behind to watch over the place and superintend the slaves who were needed for the day-to-day activities on the plantation.

Some known meeting houses of worship within several hours of Moses's home were Emmeus in the Georgia Bend, Pigeon Creek in Nassau County, and Providence in the present Union County. Mount Zion on the North Prong is believed to have been meeting in the mid nineteenth century, although the church wasn't constituted until later in the century.

From every branch of the family came this unwavering statement about their ancestor: —Moses Barber was never known to have taken a drink of liquor in his life.‖
Most old time Barbers said they had heard the family was originally Anglican before becoming Baptists and Methodist Episcopal. Some would laugh and say that they knew of a few who had backslid into the Episcopal Church (pronounced jokingly as —Piss-on-the-palin').

104

A reputation has been ascribed to Moses as a stealer of Indian cattle. The probability of truth is great since it was the habit of most Crackers to rustle cows, branded and unbranded, that were ranging among the wiregrass flats and marshes of the area. Before his move to Florida, Moses was said to have joined other Georgia Crackers, including his probable kinsman Grandison Barber, in slipping across the border into Florida and taking whatever cows were found. Some stories held that the Indians' raids were in retaliation for Moses stealing their cows. That could be a fact, but the Indians were going to attack white settlers whether or not any cattle had been purloined; other events and actions as well as cattle stealing made the conflict inevitable.

Some old time Barbers defended Moses on this count and believed the smear had come from the Mizell family with whom the Barbers had been at odds from the families' days in southern Georgia. The older Barbers maintained that some Mizells held an unquenchable envy of the Barbers and had a habit of stealing their cattle when both families lived in old Camden County, Georgia. I suspect, regarding envy, the shoe might have been on the other foot. But whatever is true, it is almost certain the infamous 1870 feud had its beginnings a half century before in Georgia when envy and ugly accusation reared their damning and destructive heads (see the Barber-Mizell Feud story later).

Be advised that even in the beginning of the 21st century, there are still some Barbers who blame the Mizells for every plague and sin ever visited on mankind. It is prudent to insert here that this is not a condemnation of the Mizell family. They tend to be folks of good repute, and the Barbers of both north and central Florida became related in the classic end of so many family feuds. William P. Barber wed the former Miss Mary Ida Bass, a Mizell descendent, in Osceola County. My own G-grandfather George Garrett's first wife was Louvilla, a daughter of Uncle Billy Mizell of Charlton County, Georgia (see Uncle Billy's story and an account of the Mizells in my PRESS columns).

Another negative trait ascribed to Moses by his amateur biographers (that includes myself) was that of philandering. Later research has suggested the probability that most – not all - of his reputation as a ladies' man was due to confusing him with his son Moses Edward, Jr. —Little Mosesand Little Moses's son Moses W. (the label —Much Marryin' Moses was tacked onto Moses the elder and his grandson Moses W.). His common-law arrangement with the young Rebecca Clements might have added fuel to the story of his womanizing. It should be noted that common-law marriage was not at all uncommon at the time (it might come as a surprise to learn that sin is not a discovery of the present generation). It seems some of his children by Mary Leah and his in-laws were very resentful of Rebecca, and they might have been responsible for helping to darken more his already denigrated name.

Moses Barber's extracurricular activities

There was truth in the rumors regarding his bent to concupiscence. After Mary Leah died he kept his women for convenience, as noted earlier, at his cattle stop stations along the peninsula. So did his sons. Whether we like it or not (this does not signify approval), the Barber men were men and they were men with needs, and the times were lusty. No story has ever been heard that he was guilty of infidelity when he was married to Mary Leah.

There was a case in Orange County charging a Moses E. Barber with bigamy. We cannot be certain from the information given whether it was Sr. or Jr., but we can guess, from knowledge passed down, that both were capable. Moses Ben Barber was given a hefty fine for adultery in Orange County just prior to the feud, and that could have been tacked onto Moses Sr.'s, reputation in the misty memories of his descendents.

He also met and wooed ladies on his trips to the land, cattle, and government offices in Saint Augustine, Newnansville, Tallahassee, Charleston, and Savannah. In the ten or more years since Mary Leah's death Moses did his part in peopling Florida, Georgia, and South Carolina with his affairs (as I was roaming the states of Florida and Georgia searching for Moses material I frequently met up with people who claimed Moses Barber as an ancestor but not via a legitimate branch).

The letter that follows under the next heading might shed light on the old family story that Moses had become intimate with a Miss or Mrs. Margaret Cook of New Smyrna and Saint Augustine…or it might add to the confusion. The older folks said Moses was a frequent guest at an inn on Saint George Street in Saint Augustine that was operated by the lady in question. The family story had it that two children, a girl and a boy, were from that liaison, and that the daughter became important in the Democrat party in Florida soon after the advent of women's suffrage, and the son was a brilliant man though alcoholic (another unfortunate Barber trait). Were these two tales from the same situation but with different details, or was there still another Ms. Cook in Moses's life? Did this have connections with the bigamy case in Orange County? My mind is boggled. Read on about the other Miss Cook.

Susan Letitia (nee Cook) Barber

An interesting instance of Moses's right hand keeping secrets from his left is in a letter that I will include below. Many of us in the family had heard of the situation related in the letter, and I was happy to read that still another oral tradition was more than just a tale. Although the details differ, there are enough similarities in the letter and story to take both seriously. It was written by Moses Edward Barber's own daughter – Mrs. S. B. (nee Meddie Barber) Wilson - to a distant relative – Mrs. Ola (nee Barber) Pittman of Valdosta, Georgia. Mrs. Wilson's letter was written on the 14th of May in 1924. Please note she speaks of her brother William James Barber and her half brother Moses Edward, Jr. and of a half brother whose name she cannot recall (doubtless Isaac since Little Moses and Isaac were the only two who were in central Florida any length of time). Her address was 516 N. Clara Ave., DeLand, Florida. This piece of history came to me from Col. Joe Finley, a Barber in-law. I had carried on a correspondence with Mrs. Pittman many years ago in which she had told of the letter, but we lost contact before she was able to send me a copy (copied as written).

Dear Cousin Olie, I suppose you will let me call you cousin. I was in Barberville (Fla.) last week and Mrs. Barber was telling me of your attempt to trace our ancestors. I"m very much interested and would like to know anything you can tell me. I can tell you so little, for mother never talked a great deal about my father Moses Edward Barber who died when I was still too young to remember him. I think my mother"s reticence was because she wished us, my one brother and myself, to be loyal to our stepfather. She always, when speaking of him [Moses] at all spoke of how very good he was to her, his love, devotion, etc., etc. He was a very wealthy man, nearly a millionaire in horses and cattle. He was known as the cattle king of Ga. And Fla. For that very reason he had many jealous enemies during the Reconstruction days who did everything in their power to ruin him by stealing, killing, and in every way destroying his property. He grew so tired of persecution that he went out to Texas and bought a farm and ranch and was on the point of sending for Mother, Brother, and I when the enemies got in their final bit of work and had him poisoned, so my mother always thought. She never even tried to claim the Texas property. Her life was made so miserable by Father"s enemies that she finally sacrificed everything she had left (after these same enemies got through stealing and marauding) and moved from Kissimmee to Emporia where we lived for many years. My mother"s name was Susan Letitia Cook. These Cooks settled in S. C. when they came to this country, and they are a large connection and have a large re-union every year.

My only whole brother"s name was William James Barber. He was an architect of some ability and note at the time of his death, a very sudden death too, in St. Louis. Mo., about ten or eleven years ago. My mother married soon after my father"s death in order to have a protector, more for Brother and myself than for any other reason I verily believe. My stepfather"s name was William Preston De Russ, but he never used the De before the Russ. He was French descent and came from a very fine family. He died about six months ago. Mother died some 15 or more years ago, still a comparatively young woman. Trouble no doubt hastened her death. I"ve often heard my grandmother Cook say that my father was a very handsome man and one of the best she ever knew. My mother was his second wife. He had two sons at the time he and Mother married, the name of one was Moses Edward (for my father) and just at this time I can"t remember the other boy"s name. Mother was very much younger than my father. She was considered the most beautiful woman in all this *part of the county. We have Barber relatives, many of them in this state, Chicago, Ill. And no telling where else. I would be so glad to hear from you and to get any information you can give me for the sake of my two daughters, the only children we have living. If there is expense please let me know and share it. Would be so glad to have you visit me. I usually spend the summer \with the girls in Hendersonville N. C. and Laurens, S. C.*

Hoping to hear from you soon, I am very sincerely your [signed by hand] Cousin Meddie"

Either G-g-g-grandpa Moses held back the truth from Miss Cook, or Miss Cook held back the truth from her daughter Mrs. Wilson. Whichever, it reads as a sad commentary on our ancestor. He left Miss Cook in dire circumstances.
I haven't found a record of Moses and Ms. Cook's marriage.
For those who insist on labeling Little Moses as Moses B. F., please note his own half-sister used his correct name of Moses Edward (as did his wife, sisters-in-law, nephews, and grandchildren). I will not swear that Little Moses did not alter his name to Moses B. F.; he was capable, and such was not rare in generations past.

Descendant Register, Generation No. 5

---

27. **James Israel Barber** (Henry Obadiah Barber[4], Isaac Barber[3], Moses Barber[2], William Barber[1]) was b. 28 MAR 1852 in Bryan, Georgia, United States, and died 22 OCT 1926 in Ware, Georgia, United States. He m. **Mary Ann Blackburn** 27 AUG 1873, dau. of Martin Ebenezer Lieurgis Blackburn and Mary Ann Cason. She was born 24 FEB 1854 in Ware County, Georgia, United States, and died 15 MAY 1935 in Waycross, Ware, Georgia.

Children of James Israel Barber and Mary Ann Blackburn are:
+ 47   i.   Amabel Barber was born 27 NOV 1879 in Ware County, Georgia, United States, and died 15 SEP 1970.
  48   ii.   Nancy Elizabeth Barber was born 9 AUG 1875, and died 18 DEC 1939.
+ 49   iii.   Edward Albert Barber was born 20 JUL 1877, and died 9 JUL 1957.
  50   iv.   Mary Etta Barber was born ABT 1882.
  51   v.   Martha Lavinia Barber was born ABT 1884.
+ 52   vi.   Zelpha Lee Barber was born 4 APR 1887 in Georgia, United States, and died 17 FEB 1921.
  53   vii.   Margaret Mae Barber was born ABT 1889.
+ 54   viii.   Estella Hortense Barber was born 16 SEP 1891.
  55   ix.   James Ira Barber was born ABT 1896.

28. **Julie Ann Barber** (Henry Obadiah Barber[4], Isaac Barber[3], Moses Barber[2], William Barber[1])

was born 12 DEC 1849 in Bryan County, Georgia, United States, and died 14 JUL 1923 in Brantley County, Georgia, United States.

Children of Julie Ann Barber are:

  56   i.   Flemming Darvey Altman was born 25 FEB 1872, and died 15 DEC 1894. He married Martha M. Dowling 8 FEB 1894. She was born 19 MAY 1875, and died 16 MAR 1931.
  57   ii.   Arrelia Altman was born 15 JAN 1871, and died 15 SEP 1883.
+ 58   iii. Amanda Altman was born 10 JUN 1869, and died 25 JUN 1955.
+ 59   iv.   Charles Hyson Altman was born 12 JUN 1873, and died 4 MAR 1930.
+ 60   v.   Charlotte Rosetter Altman was born 30 JUL 1875, and died 2 NOV 1965.
  61   vi.   Henry Altman was born ABT 1878.
  62   vii. James Altman was born ABT 1880.
+ 63   viii. Alfred Clarence Altman was born 24 JAN 1878 in Charlton County, Georgia, United States, and died 28 DEC 1924 in Brantley County, Georgia, United States.
  64   ix.   Elmore Tinsely Altman was born 2 FEB 1880, and died 29 MAY 1881.
  65   x.   Lulu Corrine Altman was born 17 OCT 1883, and died 12 JUN 1960. She married Harmon Thomas Jeffords 21 JAN 1900. He was born 23 JAN 1877, and died 16 OCT 1964.
  66   xi.   Valie Viola Altman was born 20 OCT 1886 in Georgia, United States, and died 23 JAN 1907. She married Pleasant Udolphie Griffin 11 FEB 1903. He was born 31 MAR 1884, and died 15 MAY 1958.
  67   xii. Myrtie Satilla Altman was born 1 OCT 1881, and died 19 JAN 1959. She married Burnis Agafa Griffin 7 FEB 1900 in Pierce County, Georgia, United States. He was born 14 AUG 1877, and died 3 OCT 1939.
+ 68   xiii. Julia Gertrude Altman was born 18 NOV 1888 in Brantley County, Georgia, United States, and died 23 MAY 1944 in Brantley, Georgia, United States.

29. **Laura Emily Barber** (Henry Obadiah Barber[4], Isaac Barber[3], Moses Barber[2], William Barber[1]) was born 20 JAN 1855, and died 15 AUG 1942. She married **James Daniel Sweat**. He was born 16 MAR 1851, and died 22 DEC 1916.

Children of Laura Emily Barber and James Daniel Sweat are:
  69   i.   Edward Sweat.
  70   ii.   Nancy Sweat.
  71   iii. William Sweat.
  72   iv.   Julia Sweat.
  73   v.   Henry Sweat.
  74   vi.   Joseph Sweat.

75 vii. Lawton Sweat.

76 viii. Eve Sweat.

77 ix. James Charley Sweat was born 26 JAN 1875, and died 12 APR 1840. He married Melissa Rose Etta Robinson. She was born 22 AUG 1882, and died 24 FEB 1958.

78 x. Mary Sweat was born ABT 1893, and died ABT SEP 1988. She married Robert Davenport.

79 xi. David Oscar Sweat was born ABT 1896, and died ABT 1942. He married Nola Latham. She was born 25 FEB 1900, and died 24 NOV 1974.

80 xii. Eugene Edgar Sweat was born 24 APR 1898, and died 12 FEB 1971. He married Hilda Hagins ABT MAY 1917.

31. **Nancy Angeline "Angie" Barber** (Henry Obadiah Barber[4], Isaac Barber[3], Moses Barber[2], William Barber[1]) was born 25 JAN 1861, and died 27 MAR 1924.

Child of Nancy Angeline "Angie" Barber is:

81 i. Israel Melton was born 16 NOV 1892, and died 11 FEB 1977.

32. **Edmond Obadiah Barber** (Henry Obadiah Barber[4], Isaac Barber[3], Moses Barber[2], William Barber[1]) was born ABT 1866 in Pierce County, Georgia, United States, and died 26 DEC 1931.

Children of Edmond Obadiah Barber are:

82 i. Amy Ellen Barber was born 3 DEC 1886, and died 16 MAR 1945.

83 ii. Henry James Barber was born 8 AUG 1888, and died 24 DEC 1930.

84 iii. William Riley Barber was born 7 JUN 1890, and died 23 NOV 1949.

85 iv. Richard Barber was born 13 MAR 1892, and died 19 JAN 1968.

86 v. Lonnie Barber was born 12 APR 1896.

87 vi. Josie Rena Barber was born 15 OCT 1900, and died 31 OCT 1969.

88 vii. Walter J. Barber was born 25 APR 1902, and died 30 MAR 1974.

89 viii. Robert Lester Barber was born 23 MAR 1907, and died 4 OCT 1969.

Children of Edmond Obadiah Barber are:

90 i. Jesse Mae Barber.

91 ii. Emmett Barber was born 7 JUL 1912, and died 21 JUN 1973.

Children of Edmond Obadiah Barber are:

92 i. Doris Barber.

93 ii. Hampton Barber was born 1 DEC 1919, and died 10 JUL 1920.

94 iii. Edward Obediah Barber III was born 14 MAY 1921, and died 22 MAR 1979.

95 iv. Ellis Aldine Barber was born 14 MAY 1921, and died 18 APR 1990.

33. **William Albert Barber** (Henry Obadiah Barber[4], Isaac Barber[3], Moses Barber[2], William Barber[1]) was born 23 NOV 1857, and died 14 JAN 1898.

Children of William Albert Barber are:

96	i.	Everett Obediah Barber was born 17 NOV 1887.
97	ii.	Julia Barber was born ABT AUG 1894 in Georgia, United States.
98	iii.	Moses Barber was born ABT AUG 1881.
99	iv.	Jesse James Barber was born ABT JAN 1891 in Georgia, United States.
100	v.	William Riley Barber was born 30 SEP 1882 in Georgia, United States, and died 21 NOV 1951 in Ware County, Georgia, United States.
101	vi.	Claud Johnson Barber was born 14 JAN 1894 in Georgia, United States.
102	vii.	Mary Emma Barber was born ABT JUL 1889 in Georgia, United States.
103	viii.	Albert C. Barber was born ABT AUG 1886 in Georgia, United States, and died 19 SEP 1940 in Ware County, Georgia, United States.
104	ix.	Hard "Hardy" Starling Barber was born 13 NOV 1896 in Georgia, United States, and died 31 DEC 1984 in Ware County, Georgia, United States.

Descendant Register, Generation No. 6

47. **Amabel Barber** (James Israel Barber[5], Henry Obadiah Barber[4], Isaac Barber[3], Moses Barber[2], William Barber[1]) was born 27 NOV 1879 in Ware County, Georgia, United States, and died 15 SEP 1970. She married **Benjamin Westberry Holt** 18 MAR 1894. He was born 12 DEC 1869, and died 12 APR 1935.

Children of Amabel Barber and Benjamin Westberry Holt are:

+ 105	i.	Bulah Lavina Holt was born 17 DEC 1896 in Ware County, Ware, Georgia, United States, and died 27 NOV 1988 in Searcy, White, Arkansas, United States.
+ 106	ii.	James Barber (J.B.) Holt was born ABT 1910 in Ware County, Georgia, United States, and died ABT 1991.
+ 107	iii.	Martin Holt was born 25 MAR 1895 in Ware County, Georgia, United States, and died 19 SEP 1970.
+ 108	iv.	Joseph Holt was born ABT 1907, and died ABT 1986.
109	v.	Alphonso Holt died ABT 1935.
110	vi.	Nancy Holt was born 16 FEB 1906, and died 4 OCT 1990 in Mobile, Alabama, United States. She married Bill Moll. He was born 22 NOV 1898, and died ABT SEP 1973 in Mobile, Alabama, United States.
+ 111	vii.	Mary Holt was born 3 APR 1913, and died 7 JUL 2004.
112	viii.	Thomas Holt was born ABT 1904, and died ABT 1972. He married Lilly LNU.
113	ix.	Aaron Holt was born ABT 1899, and died 12 AUG 1918 in France.

111

114   x.   Hoke Holt was born 7 MAR 1911, and died 13 FEB 1990 in Jacksonville, Florida, United States. He married Maude LNU. She was born 2 OCT 1919, and died 11 NOV 2002 in Jacksonville, Florida, United States.

115   xi.   Vida Holt was born 4 MAY 1900, and died 14 JUL 1995 in Waycross, Georgia, United States. She married Hall Watson.

+ 116   xii.   Palma Holt was born ABT 1915, and died ABT 2008.

49. Edward Albert Barber (James Israel Barber[5], Henry Obadiah Barber[4], Isaac Barber[3], Moses Barber[2], William Barber[1]) was born 20 JUL 1877, and died 9 JUL 1957. He married **Sallie Ogletree** ABT 1900. She was born 6 JUL 1875, and died ABT 1952. He married **Mamie Corbett** ABT 1952. She was born ABT 1881.

Children of Edward Albert Barber and Sallie Ogletree are:

117   i.   Lillie Mae Barber was born ABT 1901.

118   ii.   Charles Barber was born ABT 1905.

+ 119   iii.   Virginia "Lucille" Barber was born 12 JUN 1904 in Athens, Georgia, United States, and died 15 JUN 1987 in Rockingham, North Carolina, United States.

120   iv.   James C. Barber was born ABT 1916.

52. Zelpha Lee Barber (James Israel Barber[5], Henry Obadiah Barber[4], Isaac Barber[3], Moses Barber[2], William Barber[1]) was born 4 APR 1887 in Georgia, United States, and died 17 FEB 1921. She married **Leon Thomas Henderson** 25 AUG 1907. He was born 1 MAR 1882 in Manor, Georgia, United States, and died 20 NOV 1940.

Children of Zelpha Lee Barber and Leon Thomas Henderson are:

121   i.   Gilbert Kenneth Henderson was born 6 DEC 1909, and died 9 OCT 1970 in Georgia, United States. He married Willie S. Howard 18 SEP 1935. She was born 12 APR 1914.

122   ii.   Samuel Alton Henderson was born 29 AUG 1911 in Georgia, United States, and died 28 DEC 1972.

54. Estella Hortense Barber (James Israel Barber[5], Henry Obadiah Barber[4], Isaac Barber[3], Moses Barber[2], William Barber[1]) was born 16 SEP 1891. She married **Richard Crum James.**

Child of Estella Hortense Barber and Richard Crum James is:

+ 123   i.   Randall Walker James was born 16 JUL 1914 in Argyle, Georgia, United States, and died 15 DEC 1961 in Jacksonville, Florida, United States.

58. Amanda Altman (Julie Ann Barber[5], Henry Obadiah Barber[4], Isaac Barber[3], Moses Barber[2],

William Barber[1]) was born 10 JUN 1869, and died 25 JUN 1955. She married **Matthew Shuman**. He was born 2 JUL 1866, and died 16 NOV 1937.

Children of Amanda Altman and Matthew Shuman are:
 124 i. Irene Shuman was born ABT 1910.
 125 ii. Rufus Shuman was born ABT 1902.
 126 iii. Julia Shuman was born ABT 1905.

59. **Charles Hyson Altman** (Julie Ann Barber[5], Henry Obadiah Barber[4], Isaac Barber[3], Moses Barber[2], William Barber[1]) was born 12 JUN 1873, and died 4 MAR 1930. He married **Amarintha Sorento Dowling** 8 FEB 1894. She was born 11 NOV 1877, and died 16 FEB 1965.

Children of Charles Hyson Altman and Amarintha Sorento Dowling are:
 127 i. Ida B. Altman was born ABT NOV 1894.
 128 ii. Mary Altman was born ABT 1901.
 129 iii. Wilbur Noah Altman was born 22 AUG 1898, and died 6 MAR 1977. He married Rosa Lee. She was born 30 DEC 1902.
 130 iv. Ira Altman was born ABT SEP 1896.
 131 v. Goldie Calista Altman was born ABT 1910.
 132 vi. Darling Orbie Altman was born 19 APR 1902 in Georgia, United States, and died 29 JAN 1981.
 133 vii. Reje J. Altman was born ABT 1915 in Georgia, United States.
 134 viii. Clara L. Altman was born ABT 1919.
 135 ix. Charlie H. Altman was born ABT 1904 in Georgia, United States.
 136 x. Oscar L. Altman was born ABT 1917 in Georgia, United States.
 137 xi. Sadie Lee Altman was born ABT 1908. She married Lewis Jefferson Griffin.
 138 xii. Albert G. Altman was born ABT 1913 in Georgia, United States.

60. **Charlotte Rosetter Altman** (Julie Ann Barber[5], Henry Obadiah Barber[4], Isaac Barber[3], Moses Barber[2], William Barber[1]) was born 30 JUL 1875, and died 2 NOV 1965. She married **Manning Darling Griffin** 28 MAR 1900. He was born 14 NOV 1869, and died 28 DEC 1927.

Child of Charlotte Rosetter Altman and Manning Darling Griffin is:
 + 139 i. Rhoda Griffin was born 13 SEP 1909 in Pierce, Georgia, United States, and died 12 OCT 1971 in Hickox, Georgia, United States.

63. **Alfred Clarence Altman** (Julie Ann Barber[5], Henry Obadiah Barber[4], Isaac Barber[3], Moses

Barber[2], William Barber[1]) was born 24 JAN 1878 in Charlton County, Georgia, United States, and died 28 DEC 1924 in Brantley County, Georgia, United States. He married **Minnie Corine Lee** 8 MAR 1899 in Pierce County, Georgia, United States. She was born 23 APR 1878 in Wayne County, Georgia, United States, and died 3 MAY 1910 in Wayne County, Georgia, United States.

Children of Alfred Clarence Altman and Minnie Corine Lee are:
140   i.   Vandilla Altman was born ABT 1909 in Georgia, United States.
141   ii. Corine Altman was born ABT 1905 in Georgia, United States.
142   iii. Nolan Altman was born 14 MAY 1901, and died 28 AUG 1978.
143   iv. Clara Altman was born ABT 1908.
144   v.   Raymond Altman was born ABT 1906.
145   vi. Cyrus Jefferson Altman was born 17 FEB 1900, and died 3 FEB 1988.

68. **Julia Gertrude Altman** (Julie Ann Barber[5], Henry Obadiah Barber[4], Isaac Barber[3], Moses Barber[2], William Barber[1]) was born 18 NOV 1888 in Brantley County, Georgia, United States, and died 23 MAY 1944 in Brantley, Georgia, United States. She married **Charles Britton Crews** 24 MAY 1904 in Pierce County, Georgia, United States. He was born 1 FEB 1885 in Pierce County, Georgia, United States, and died 12 DEC 1953 in Ware County, Georgia, United States.

Child of Julia Gertrude Altman and Charles Britton Crews is:
146   i. Mabel Crews was born 31 JAN 1908 in Brantley County, Georgia, United States, and died 26 JAN 2000 in Charlton County, Georgia, United States.

1. **John SIKES**[1] was born about 1750 in   , Edgecombe Co., North Carolina.[1] He resided   , Bladen Co., North Carolina.[1]
He was married.[1] John SIKES had the following children:

+2 i. Edward SIKES.
3 ii. **Jacob SIKES**[1] was born about 1770.[1] He resided a place along Black Creek about 1792 in   , Effingham Co., Georgia.[1]
4 iii. **Joseph SIKES**[1] was born about 1776.[1] He resided a place along Black Creek about 1792 in   , Effingham Co., Georgia.[1]

1. Joseph E. Spann
Library Manager - Historical and Genealogical Library
Bartow, Polk County, Florida.
2. Carolyn Jarrard. E-mail message from information in Data Base of Carolyn Jarrard.
3. Ibid. 1880 Census of Bryan County, Georgia.
4. Doris E. Williams
P.O.Box 151
Waverly, Florida 33877-0151.
5. Ann Britton

CompuServe #71140,307.

6. Carolyn Jarrard. E-mail message from information in Data Base of Carolyn Jarrard. 1850 census of Bryan County, Georgia.

7. Ibid. 1850 census of Bryan County, Georgia.

8. S. A. (Butch) and Linda SIKES. The Database of S. A. (Butch) and Linda SIKES. P.O.Box 221

Lorman, Mississippi 39096

(601) 437-3705.

9. Dennis McGuire. Family Group Record of Samuel SIKES. 2900 Liberty Lane

Meadow Vista, California 95722 Phone 916-878-2361.

10. Carolyn Jarrard. E-mail message from information in Data Base of Carolyn Jarrard. 1850 census of Bryan County, Georgia.

11. Ibid. 1850 census of Bryan County, Georgia.

12. Ibid. 1850 census of Bryan County, Georgia.

13. Ibid. 1850 census of Bryan County, Georgia.

14. Ibid. 1850 census of Bryan County, Georgia.

15. Ibid. 1850 census of Bryan County, Georgia.

16. Ibid. 1850 census of Bryan County, Georgia.

17. Ibid. 1850 census of Bryan County, Georgia.

18. Ibid. 1850 census of Bryan County, Georgia.

19. Ibid. 1850 census of Bryan County, Georgia.

20. Ibid. 1850 census of Bryan County, Georgia.

21. Ibid. 1850 census of Bryan County, Georgia.

22. S. A. (Butch) and Linda SIKES. The Database of S. A. (Butch) and Linda SIKES. P.O.Box 221

Lorman, Mississippi 39096

(601) 437-3705. Death Certificate of John J. (Joshua) Sikes, born 15 March 1851, died 19 Dec 1944.

23. Carolyn Jarrard. E-mail message from information in Data Base of Carolyn Jarrard. 1850 census of Bryan County, Georgia.

24. Ibid. 1850 census of Bryan County, Georgia.

25. Ibid. 1850 census of Bryan County, Georgia.

26. Ibid. 1880 census of Bryan County, Georgia.

27. Ibid. 1880 census of Bryan County, Georgia.

28. Ibid. 1880 census of Bryan County, Georgia.

29. Ibid. 1880 census of Bryan County, Georgia.

30. Ibid. 1880 census of Bryan County, Georgia.

31. Ibid. 1880 census of Bryan County, Georgia.

32. Ibid. 1880 census of Bryan County, Georgia.

33. Ibid. 1880 census of Bryan County, Georgia.

34. Ibid. 1880 census of Bryan County, Georgia.

35. Ibid. 1880 census of Bryan County, Georgia.

36. Obituary - The Macon Telegraph. 29 Nov 1929 edition.

37. Carolyn Jarrard. E-mail message from information in Data Base of Carolyn Jarrard. 1850 census of Bryan County, Georgia, lists an Isaac J. Sikes, 13 years of age. That would place his date of birth in 1837, the same as other records indicate being the date of birth of Samuel Isaac

Sikes. On this basis, I have assumed them to be the same person as of 8 October 1997, pending additional information.

38. U.D.C. application of Annie Sikes Whitt, 2 Sep 1930.

39. Obituary - The Macon Telegraph. 29 Nov 1929 edition.

40. Carolyn Jarrard. E-mail message from information in Data Base of Carolyn Jarrard. 1850 census of Bryan County, Georgia.

41. Georgia State Archives. Muster Roll, Cavalry Battalion, Phillip's Legion, Company E, Georgia Volunteers.

42. Anne H. Rogers. Washington Memorial Library Research Letter Dated 5 Aug 1997.
Genealogical & Historical Room
Washington Memorial Library
1180 Washington Avenue
Macon, Georgia 31201. First Paragraph of letter; reference to Georgia Death Certificate Index.

43. Personal Knowledge of David Whitt DORSEY, Sr. Phone call to Bonaventure Cemetery, Savannah, Georgia.

44. Obituary - The Macon Telegraph. 29 Nov 1929 edition.

45. Ibid. 29 Nov 1929 edition.

46. Ibid. 29 Nov 1929 edition.

47. Ibid. 29 Nov 1929 edition.

48. Anne H. Rogers. Washington Memorial Library Research Letter Dated 5 Aug 1997.
Genealogical & Historical Room , Washington Memorial Library, 1180 Washington Avenue Macon, Georgia 31201. First paragraph; reference to Georgia Death Index.

49. Relationship not confirmed. Based on a gold on black printed Memorial card in the effects of Nell Ross Whitt Dorsey. Birthdate calculated as: abt 14 Sep, 1873.

Text:

In Loving Rememberance of) on image of card held in beak of a dove.

Samuel Isaac Sikes)
Died June 14, 1895) on image of Holy Bible.
Aged 21 Yrs. 9 Mos.)
A precious one from us has gone,)
A voice we loved is stilled;)
A place is vacant in our home,)
Which never can be filled.) on image of a scroll.
God in His wisdon has recalled)
The boon His love has given,)
And though the body slumbers here)
The soul is safe in heaven.).

50. Obituary - The Macon Telegraph. 30 Dec 1962 edition.

51. Gravestone. Grave Marker in Riverside Cemetery, Macon, Georgia.

52. Obituary - The Macon Telegraph. 30 Dec 1962 edition.

53. Gravestone. Riverside Cemetery, Macon, Bibb co., Georgia.

54. Obituary - The Macon Telegraph. 30 Dec 1962 edition.

55. Ibid. Sunday, 30 December, 1962 edition.

56. Carolyn Jarrard. E-mail message from information in Data Base of Carolyn Jarrard. 1850 census of Bryan County, Georgia.

57. Ibid. 1850 census of Bryan County, Georgia.

58. Ibid. 1880 census of Bryan County, Georgia.

59. Census - Florida State 1895
City of Calahan, Nassau County, Florida. City of Callahan, Nassau County, Florida.

60. Carolyn Jarrard. E-mail message from information in Data Base of Carolyn Jarrard. 1880 census of Bryan County, Georgia.

61. Census - Florida State 1895
City of Calahan, Nassau County, Florida. City of Callahan, Nassau County, Florida.

62. Gravestone in Greenwood Cemetery, Highland Ave. at Lincoln Road, Montgomery,Montgomery,Alabama,.

63. Death Certificate. David Sears Whitt Death Certificate #510101.

64. Obituary from Montgomery Advertiser, October 15, 1936.

65. Gravestone in Greenwood Cemetery, Highland Ave, at Lincoln Road, Montgomery,Montgomery,Alabama.

66. Death Certificate. David Sears Whitt Death Certificate #510101.

67. The Church of Jesus Christ of Latter-day Saints. LDS Ancestral File.
http://www.familysearch.org
50 East North Temple Street
Salt Lake City, Utah 84150. Batch #: M712893, Sheet #: , Source Call #: 0409850 V. I
International Genealogical Index.

68. Death Certificate. David Sears Whitt Death Certificate #510101.

69. Ibid. David Sears Whitt Death Certificate #510101.

70. Obituary - The Macon Telegraph. Page 13a, 8 May 1961 edition.

71. Ibid. Page 13a, 8 May 1961 edition.

72. Ibid. Page 13a, 8 May 1961 edition.

73. Ibid.

74. Personal Knowledge of David Whitt DORSEY, Sr.

75. The Church of Jesus Christ of Latter-day Saints. LDS Ancestral File.
http://www.familysearch.org
50 East North Temple Street
Salt Lake City, Utah 84150. 9004410 - 1553663.

76. Carolyn Jarrard. E-mail message from information in Data Base of Carolyn Jarrard. Jan 1870.

77. S. A. (Butch) and Linda SIKES. The Database of S. A. (Butch) and Linda SIKES. P.O.Box 221 Lorman, Mississippi 39096
(601) 437-3705. 1880.

78. Census - Florida State 1895
City of Calahan, Nassau County, Florida. City of Callahan, Nassau County, Florida, 1879.

79. S. A. (Butch) and Linda SIKES. The Database of S. A. (Butch) and Linda SIKES. P.O.Box 221
Lorman, Mississippi 39096
(601) 437-3705.

80. Carolyn Jarrard. E-mail message from information in Data Base of Carolyn Jarrard. Shows as Leon N. Sikes.

81. S. A. (Butch) and Linda SIKES. The Database of S. A. (Butch) and Linda SIKES. P.O.Box 221

Lorman, Mississippi 39096

(601) 437-3705. Shows as Otis Sikes.

82. Census - Florida State 1895

City of Calahan, Nassau County, Florida. City of Callahan, Nassau County, Florida, shows as L. O. Sikes.

83. George Winston Sikes. The database of George Winston Sikes. Crystal River, Florida.

84. Census - Florida State 1895

City of Calahan, Nassau County, Florida. City of Callahan, Nassau County, Florida.

85. Henry M. UFFORD Family Group Record.

86. Tombstone Rosemere Cemetery, Opelika, Lee, Alabama.

87. Nell Ross WHITT's scrapbook. Newspaper Clipping of Wedding Event.

88. Opelika-Auburn News Local Newspaper for Opelika, Lee, Alabama. Obituary Thursday, 20 Feb 1947.

89. Obituary - Opelika-Auburn News.

90. Death Certificate. Alabama No. 004085, State File Number 101.

91. Ibid. Alabama No. 004085, State File Number 101.

92. Ibid. Alabama No. 004085, State File Number 101.

93. Kevan Michael Dorsey Family Group Record.

94.

95. Grace Rackley DORSEY interview.

2. Edward SIKES [2] was born about 1774 in   , Bladen Co., North Carolina.[3][4][1] Carolyn Jarrard advises that the 1880 Census of Bryan County, Georgia, shows Samuel Sikes' father, Edward, as being born in South Carolina. He resided a place along Black Creek about 1792 in   , Effingham Co., Georgia.[1] Edward Sikes came to Effingham County, Ga. with his brothers Jacob Sikes (b. 1770) and Joseph Sikes (b. 1776) in about 1792. All three brothers settled along Black Creek in Effingham County. In 1793 Screven and Bryan Counties were cut out of Effingham County. The lands of Joseph Sikes wound up in the new County of Screven. The lands of Jacob and Edward Sikes were placed in the new County of Bryan. Then in 1796 Bulloch County was formed out of Screven County and the lands of Joseph Sikes were part of that area. However, during this entire time the three brothers only lived a few miles apart, along Black Creek.

From Mr. Joseph E. Spann, Library Manager/Historical and Genealogical Library, Bartow, Polk County, Florida.

He died in 1828 in   , Bryan Co., Georgia.[2] He had an estate probated on 13 Sep 1828 in   , Bryan Co., Georgia. [4][5] 1799; Edward SYKES was one of six jurors for the trial of Estate of Houston v. Estate of HARN

1799; Edward SIKES, 200 AC in land lottery in Bryan Co., Georgia.

1817; Edward SIKES, 250 AC in land lottery in Bryan Co., Georgia.

1822; Edward SIKES, 100 AC in land lottery in Bryan Co., Georgia.

Edward SIKES and James ALEXANDER were property owners next to William DUKE in 1822 in Bryan Co, Georgia.

1828 Sept 13--Catherine SIKES is appointed guardian to Catherine, Samuel, Rebecca, and Isaac SIKES, the orphans of Edward SIKES, Trustees: Jacob SIKES, Alex. BIRD.

Source: Ann Britton 71140,307 CompuServe email 18 Jun 1997 to David Whitt Dorsey from "Court Records of Bryan Co., GA, 1793-1826" abstracted by Caroline P. Wilson.
He was married to Catherine MCGEE (daughter of Shadrack MCGEE) about 1795 in   ,
Bryan Co., Georgia.[2][4][1] **Catherine MCGEE**[2][1] was born in   ,   Co., Georgia.[2]
1880 Census of Bryan County, Georgia, shows Samuel Sikes' mother, Catherine, as being born in
Georgia. 1828 Sept 13--Catherine SIKES is appointed guardian to Catherine, Samuel, Rebecca, and Isaac SIKES, the orphans of Edward SIKES, Trustees: Jacob SIKES, Alex. BIRD. Source: Ann Britton 71140,307 CompuServe email 18 Jun 1997 to David Whitt Dorsey from "Court Records of Bryan Co., GA, 1793-1826" abstracted by Caroline P. Wilson.
Edward SIKES and Catherine MCGEE had the following children:

+5 i. Frances SIKES.
6 ii. **Rebecca SIKES** was born about 1806.[4]
+7 iii. Samuel SIKES.
8 iv. **Catherine SIKES** was born before 1828.
9 v. **Isaac SIKES** was born before 1828.
5. Frances SIKES [2] was born about 1803.[2]
She was married to Isaac BARBER.[2] **Isaac BARBER**[2] was born in 1808 in   , Bryan Co., Georgia.[2] He died in 1856 in   , Bryan Co., Georgia.[2] According to the minutes of 7 July, 1844/17 April 1898, Issac Barber helped constitute Old Fellowship Baptist Church in Bulloch County, Georgia. Frances SIKES and Isaac BARBER had the following children:

+10 i. Susan BARBER.
+11 ii. Obadiah BARBER.
12 iii. **Isaac BARBER Jr.**[2] was born in 1825 in   , Bryan Co., Georgia.[2]
+13 iv. Israel M. BARBER.
14 v. **Martha BARBER**[2] was born in 1833 in   , Bryan Co., Georgia.[2]
+15 vi. Mary Ann BARBER.
+16 vii. Caroline BARBER.
+17 viii. Angeline Lydia BARBER.

JEREMIAH SMITH BADEN

Jeremiah Smith Baden was the son of Thomas George Baden and Sarah Sabina. He was born in 1840, Prince Georges County, Maryland. He died 30 Mar 1903, Suwannee County, FL. In Jul 1865 he married Angeline Lydia Barber, b. 1843, Bryan Co., Georgia. Angeline died 1923 in Live Oak/Suwannee County, FL.

In the St. Paul's Church records:

20 May 1839: Baptized in the Church Chapel **Jeremiah Smith Baden**, son of Thomas George & Sarah Sabina Baden, born 8 December 4 1838 [B1, 40-41].

Brothers and Sisters of Jeremiah Smith Baden:
5 April 1832.   Baptized in the home of Mrs. Naylor, John Baden, son of Thomas George & Sarah Sabina Baden, born 7 August 1831 – also a coloured child named Pheby. On this same evening I married George A. Baden to Martha Naylor, and received a $5 note for the same [B1, 2].
7 July 1833.   Baptized in the home of Capt. James Baden, Susanna Isabella Rebecca Baden, daughter of Thomas George & Sarah Sabina Baden, born 16 December 1832 [B1, 18-19].
Married unknown: Children, Billy, Emma, John, Ellen, Sadie, an unnamed child.
23 June 1834. Baptized in the Church Chapel, Martha Ann Baden, daughter of Thomas George & Sarah Sabina Baden, born 6 February 1834 [BL, 22-23].
20 March 1836. Baptized in the Church Chapel, James Thomas Baden, son of Thomas George & Sarah Sabina Baden, born 12 December 1835 [B1, 32-33].
James Thomas Baden married Anna Maria Yates, 1 Jul 1836, Washington, D.C. She was born 6 Jan 1842, Alexandria, VA and died 25 Nov 1941, Washington, D.C. Both are buried in the Arlington Claim File XC2676.419.
1.   Flora Baden married Langley
2.   Harry E. Baden b. 1873, still living 18 Apr 1898 (sworn affadivit by father)

A letter dated 21 November 1913, Washington, D.C. and signed by Anna Maria Yates Baden, the widow of James Thomas Baden to Idella Jeanette Baden Frier is abstracted below:
—. . . of course you know that the Baden family belonged to the old families of Maryland slave holders, and at one time they were considered —somebodies' in the County. Since the Civil War they have had to hustle. My husband James T. [Thomas] Baden was an Officer of the Regular Army when the War broke out and he remained in the Union Army. He was promptly dis-inherited by his Grandfather, Capt. John Baden, who characerically remarked _that you stayed in the Union Army, now let the damn Yankees take care of you! . . .‖

The Uncle John mentioned above married his cousin Nellie Townsend. He met a sad fate, being murdered on his way to Washington, by whom it was never discovered . . .‖ An entry in the Church Registrar of St. Paul's — . . . John Baden found dead on the road supposedly to have been murdered the 17th day of November 1873 . . . buried 11 January 1874, . . .‖ [B2, 159]
Further on in the letter she speaks of — . . . your Aunt Belle . . . .‖ No doubt a corruption of the name of Susanna Isabella Rebecca Baden, sister of James Thomas and Jeremiah Smith Baden.
Later on she speaks of —Mattie‖ which again is the accepted nickname for Martha, born prior to James Thomas Baden.

James Thomas Baden: —Enlisted 23 Oct. 1857 as a Private in the General Mounted Services in Baltimore, Maryland. He served as a private, Corpral, Sergeant and a First Sergeant in Troop —F‖, 5th Cavalry until 30 October 1862. Granted a commission of 2nd Lieut. 31 October 1862 in the Cavalry. He rejoined his Regiment at St. James, MD [about 5 miles from Sharps-burg, MD where he participated in that bloody battle as the 1st Sgt. of Troop —F‖, 5gh Cav. 17 Sept. 1862. The Yankees called this Antietam.]

Promoted to 1st Lt. 2 Nov. 1863.

Resigned 12 Sep 1864 due to an injury received in the —Seven Days Battle‖ when his horse fell from under him, during a Cavalry Charge by his Regt. Discharged 12 Sep 1864 at City Point, VA. 5' 8 tall, fair complexion, brown hair, grey eyes, date of birth 12 Sept 1835.

In his sworn affidavit to his pension application he states: name, J. Thos. Baden; residences, resided in Prince George's County from birth until May 1853 when I moved to Washington, D.C. He is buried in the present-day National Arlington Cemetery.
In a book compiled by Maurice Walter Frier, March 1978, Honolulu, Hawaii a grandson on the maternal side —My oldest sister Hilory (Mrs. J. A. Bishop, Riverview, FL) was born in his log cabin in Suwannee County, FL. She said she remembered him well but knew little of any detail about him. In a later interview with Bessie she said he was from Maryland, he never spoke of his parents, no one ever heard him express a desire to visit his former home, those of his —far south‖ family knew nothing of his family in the —far north. Bessie and Hilory had been told he had taught school in Georgia before the War of the Rebellion, that he had met our Grandmother, Miss Angeline Lydia Barber, during the War and that he promised he would return and marry her when the war was over. He did just that for the license for the wedding was issued 14 Feb 1865. He was still fighting for the Yankee cause.

Jeremiah Smith Baden enlisted in Chatham County, Georgia, served as 4th Corporal, Company L, Georgia 25th Infantry Regiment on 9 Aug 1861. Mustered out on 16 Nov 1861, Camp Wilson, Savannah, Georgia. (Roster of Confederate Soldiers of Georgia, 1861-1865).

He served in Company —E‖, 47th Georgia Regiment of Infantry. He saw military service as a Sergeant at Chickamauga, Chattanooga, Atlanta Campaign, and throughout the Caroline Campaign. In the last campaign, his unit was under the command of General Joseph E. Johnson who surrendered 26 April 1865, 17 days after General Lee (Confederate Army Records).

It is recorded in his Confederate Army Records, the papers on file in the courthouse in Suwannee County, FL for the settlement of his estate, and it is the same on Grandmother Baden's Confederate Pension Application Records [3158].

No explanation has been found as to why Jeremiah Smith Baden was left out in the will of his great grandfather John Baden, Jr., while his two brothers reaped so much.
Jeremiah went south either on 8 December 1859, the day he became 21 or soon after. He has not been located on any census for 1860 either in Maryland, Washington, D.C. or Georgia nor on the 1870 census.
1.   Thomas Luther Baden b. 1868, Georgia, d.   , married Mary E. and was a woodsman.
2.   Susan Frances (Anna) Baden, b. 5 Sep 1871, Florida, d. 14 Jan 1960, married William Author Roberts, b. 31 Dec 1863, Florida, d. 30 Apr 1925.
3.   Idella Jeanette (Nettie) Baden, b. 12 Jun 1875, Florida, d. 15 May 1964, married 15 May 1896 Warren Walter —Mack‖ Frier, b. 23 Jan 1873, Florida,d. 5 Aug 1959.
4.   Isaac Barber Baden, b. Sept 1877, Florida, married Ola Sapp.
5.   James Edward Baden, b. Feb 1880, married Annie
6.   Will H. Baden, b. Oct 1881, Florida, married Willow Sapp

7.   Lily Belle Baden, b. 6 Oct 1883, Florida, d. 2 Feb 1919, married James Edard Vann, b. 22 Jan 1880, d. 23 Dec 1945.

8.   Mary Harriet Baden b. 22 Oct 1885, McAlpin/Suwannee Co., FL, d. 18 Nov 1962, Clearwater/Pinellas Co., FL. On 25 Dec 1911 she married Marion Hampton Hicks, b. 21 Nov 1889 New Bern/Suwannee Co., FL. He died May 1970 at Clearwater/Pinellas Co., FL.
a.   George Olin Hicks, b. 25 Nov 1912, Live Oak, FL.
b.   Vivian Olive Hicks, b. 27 Apr 1914, Live Oak, FL; d. She died 26 Oct 2008, Dunedin/ Pinellas County, FL. On 1 Jun 1942, she married Joseph Lindsey Land in Clearwater, FL.
        Robert Brice Land is the son of Vivian Olive Hicks and Joseph Lindsey Land. He was born 12 Jun 1943, Clearwater/Pinellas County, Florida. He is a veteran of the Korean War.
c.   Elizabeth Inez Hicks, b. 10 Sep 1915, Live Oak, FL, married John Wilks, Jr. resided in Largo, FL.
d.   Hilda Videl Hicks, b. 30 Aug 1917, Live Oak, FL, married James Eubanks.
e.   James Lloyd Hicks, b. 10 Apr 1926, Largo, FL, married 10 Apr 1947, Janet Ruth Hancock.
Jeremiah and Angeline are buried in the Mt. Pisgah Church cemetery in Suwannee County, FL. His headstone announces he was born 8 December 1840, died 30 March 1903. This all tallies with his Army records and census records.

The application for Grandmother Baden's Confederate Pension Application had to be a sworn statement or it could not be accepted in Tallahassee, FL. It was a sworn statement and accepted.

Marriages

Angeline Barber and Jerry Baden Feb 16, 1865
William Roberts and Susana Baden Feb 14, 1886
Thomas Luther Baden and W.E. Cofalfard nov, 1890
Mack W. Frier and Janet Baden May 16, 1894
Isaac B Baden and Ola Sap Jan. 8 1902
James Edward Vann and Isabel Baden 26, 1904
William Horas Baden and Willa Sapp 28, 1906
James Edward Baden and Annie Lee Sept, 1910.
Marion Hampton Hicks and Harriet Baden Dec 24, 1911

A. Edgar Baden   Deaths — July, 13, 1874.
W. Oma Baden   Aug. 10. 1874
JerryMicah S. Baden   March 30. 1903
Pearl Roberts   nov 1902
Jewel Angaline Baden   nov Feb 21, 1408
Bell Vann   Feb. 2. 1919
William Angaline Baden   nov, 17, 1923
William Horace Baden   March 29. 1946
Isaac Barber Baden May or June   1962

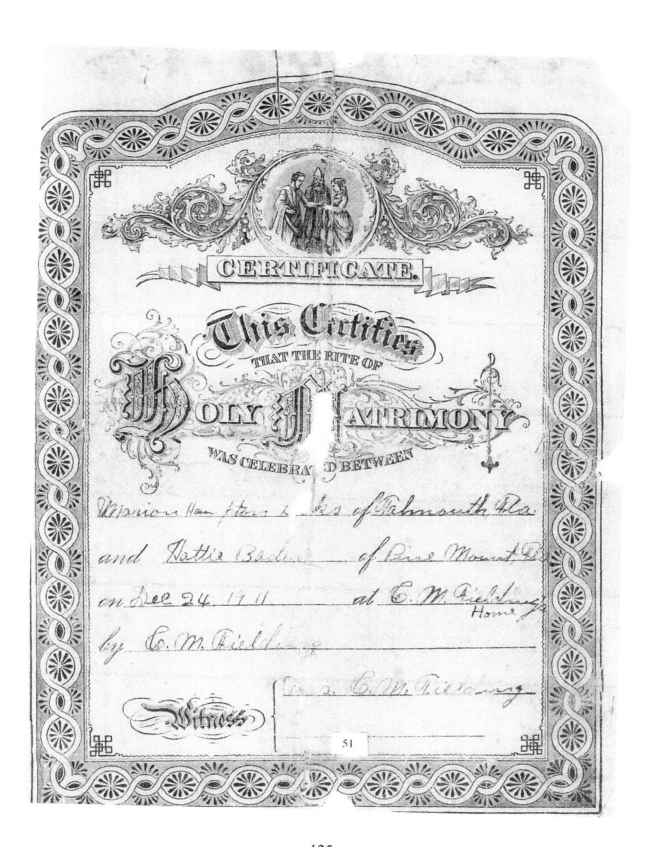

CERTIFICATE.

This Certifies

THAT THE RITE OF

HOLY PATRIMONY

WAS CELEBRATED BETWEEN

Marion Hampton _____ of Falmouth, Fla.

and _Hattie Baden_____ of Pine Mount, Fla.

on _Dec 24 1911_____ at _C. M. Fielding's_
Home

by _C. M. Fielding_

Mrs C. M. Fielding

Witness

51

125

1	2	3	4	5	6	7	8	9	10 11 12	13
6	61	Isaac Barber	63	m		Cordi, Wasp Est acc	1000	Ga		
		Frances "	47	f				"		
		Susan "	27	f				"		
		Israel "	25	m		Farmer		"		
		Martha "	17	f				"		
		Mary Ann "	15	f				"	1	
		Caroline	13	f				"	1	
		Georgina	7	f				"	1	
61	62	Riddick Crubbs	30	m		Farmer	300	Ga		
		Susan "	34	f				"		
		Green "	6	m				"		
		Shepard "	6	m				"		
		Moses G "	3	f				"		
		Cornelia "	2	f				"		
		James G Moss	1	m				"		
63	63	Elkanah Barber	25	m		"	300	Ga		
		Nancy "	21	f				"		
		Julian "	16	f				"		
		Cornelia Barber	11	f				"		
64	64	Thomas Conway	43	m		"	500	Ga		
		Sarah "	40	f				"		
		James "	15	f				"	1	
		John "	13	m				"		
		Thomp "	12	m				"	1	
		William "	10	m				"	1	
		Elizabeth "	5	f				"	1	
		Sarah "	6	f				"		
		Mary "	1	f				"		
65	65	James Thompson	28	m		"	300	Ga		
		Rebecca "	27	f				"		
		Wm C "	7	m				"	1	
		Cornelia "	5	f				"		
66	66	John Negro	60	m		"	600	N S		
		Elizabeth "	50	f				Ga		
		Catherine Thompson	27	f				"	1	
		John Thompson	30	m		"		"		(?)
17	67	Solomon Thompson	40	m		"	300	Ga		(?)
		Susan Ann "	35	f				"		10
		Joshua "	12	m				"		
		Elizabeth "	11	f				"		
		Julian "	7	f				"		
		Rebecca "	7	f				"		

52

① Georgia }
Bryan county } by W. H. Hayman Ordinary of Bryan co.
Greeting, to any Minister of the Gospel or Judge
I. I

Justice of the Inferior court or justice of the peace for said
County you are hereby authorized to Join in marriage Mr.
Jeremiah S Baden and Miss Angeline Barber of said county
according to the Laws and constitution of this State for which
this Shall be your sufficient License given under my hand and
private seal of office this July the 14th 1865
(L.S.) W. H. Hayman O.B.C.

I hereby certify that Jeremiah S Baden & Miss Angeline Barber
were duly Joined in matremony this day by me this July the 16th 1865
James Sherman J.P.

Recorded July the 20th 1865 By W.H. Hayman Ordinary B.C.

_____

Georgia Bryan County By W. H. Hayman ordinary of said county
To any minister of the Gospel Judge Justice of the Inferior court or Justice
of the peace for said county you are hereby authorized to Join in marriage
Mr. A. Jr Sapp and Miss Ann Brown of said county according to the con-
Stitution and Laws of Said State for which this Shall be your sufficient
License Given under my hand and private seal there being no Seal of office
this fourteenth day of April A.D. 1865
(L.S.) W. H. Hayman O.B.C.

the above Joined was duly Married by W.B. McHan upon
the 16th day of April 1865
Recorded this April the 17th 1865

53   W. H. Hayman Ordinary B.C.

CONFEDERATE PENSION RECORD ABSTRACT

VETERAN'S NAME (LAST, FIRST, MIDDLE):				FILE NO.
BADEN, JEREMIAH S.				3158

STATE	UNIT DESIGNATION(S):			FLA. RESIDENT SINCE:
GEORGIA	Co. E, 47TH GEORGIA			NOT GIVEN

ENLISTMENT DATE:	PLACE OF ENLISTMENT:	APPLICATION FILED:	CITY AND/OR COUNTY OF RESIDENCE:
MARCH 1862	NOT GIVEN		NONE FILED
DISCHARGE DATE:	PLACE OF DISCHARGE:	APPLICATION FILED	CITY AND/OR COUNTY OF RESIDENCE:
CLOSE OF WAR	NOT GIVEN		
DATE OF BIRTH:	PLACE OF BIRTH:	APPLICATION FILED:	CITY AND/OR COUNTY OF RESIDENCE:
NOT GIVEN	NOT GIVEN		
DATE OF DEATH:	PLACE OF DEATH:	APPLICATION FILED	CITY AND/OR COUNTY OF RESIDENCE:
3-30-1903	SUWANNEE COUNTY, FLORIDA		

WIDOW'S NAME (FIRST, MIDDLE, LAST):		APPLICATION FILED:	CITY AND/OR COUNTY OF RESIDENCE:
ANGELINA LYDIA BADEN		8-4-1903	COOPER (SUWANNEE Co.)
DATE OF MARRIAGE:	PLACE OF MARRIAGE:	APPLICATION FILED:	CITY AND/OR COUNTY OF RESIDENCE:
2-14-1865	EDEN (BRYAN) GEORGIA	7-28-1909	PINE MOUNT (SUWANNEE Co.)

FLA. RESIDENT SINCE:	DATE OF DEATH:	AGE/YEAR (AS GIVEN ON APPLICATION):	APPLICATION FILED:	CITY AND/OR COUNTY OF RESIDENCE:
2-20-1867	BEFORE 1934	60 IN 1903		

	PAGES:	STATE OF FLORIDA
	8	DEPARTMENT OF STATE Division of Archives, History and Records Management Form DS-AR 1 (10-74)

This abstract card is NOT an original source document. The original documents are preserved in the Archives of the State of Florida.

The Archives of the State of Florida cannot certify the accuracy of any statement made on a pension application. Certification is made only as to the accuracy of the abstracted data which appears on this form.

ARC 3-1 (21)
Ref. 104

NOTE:
The license was issued 14 Feb 1865
The marriage ceremony was performed 16 July 1865
M. Fries

54

The United States of America,

TO ALL TO WHOM THESE PRESENTS SHALL COME, GREETING:

Homestead Certificate No. 4884
Application 3302

Whereas there has been deposited in the GENERAL LAND OFFICE of the United States a CERTIFICATE of the Register of the Land Office at Gainesville, Florida whereby it appears that, pursuant to the Act of Congress approved 20th May, 1862, "To secure Homesteads to actual settlers on the public domain," and the acts supplemental thereto, the claim of Jeremiah S. Paten has been established and duly consummated in conformity to law for the north half of the north-east quarter, the north-east quarter of the north-west quarter and the south-west quarter of the north-east quarter of section thirty-six, in township four south of range fourteen east of Tallahassee Meridian in Florida, containing one hundred and sixty acres and eighteen hundredths of an acre

according to the Official Plat of the Survey of the said Land returned to the GENERAL LAND OFFICE by the SURVEYOR GENERAL.

Now know ye, That there is therefore granted by the UNITED STATES unto the said Jeremiah S. Paten the tract of Land above described TO HAVE AND TO HOLD the said tract of Land, with the appurtenances thereof, unto the said Jeremiah S. Paten and to his heirs and assigns forever.

In testimony whereof I, Grover Cleveland President of the United States of America, have caused these letters to be made Patent, and the Seal of the General Land Office to be hereunto affixed.

[L.S.]

Given under my hand, at the City of Washington, the twentieth day of June in the year of Our Lord one thousand eight hundred and eighty five, and of the Independence of the United States the one hundred and ninth.

By the President: Grover Cleveland

By M. McKean Sec'y.

S. H. Clark, Recorder of the General Land Office

55

Jeremiah Smith Baden

&

Wife, Angeline Lydia (Barber)

Now know ye, That there is therefore granted by the UNITED STATES unto the said Jeremiah S. Baden the tract of Land above described. TO HAVE AND TO HOLD the said tract of Land, with the appurtenances thereof, unto the said Jeremiah S. Baden and to his heirs and assigns forever.

In testimony whereof I, Grover Cleveland President of the United States of America, have caused these letters to be made Patent, and the Seal of the General Land Office to be hereunto affixed.

Given under my hand, at the City of Washington, the twentieth day of June, in the year of Our Lord one thousand eight hundred and eighty five, and of the Independence of the United States the one hundred and Ninth.

By the President: Grover Cleveland

By M. McKean, Sec'y.

S. W. Clark, Recorder of the General Land Office.

[L.S.]

131

132

136

Sand. Wright Lindsay *John Square (illegible)*

Limer Margaret K	R B	Shoco
Lynch May Ellen	Sidney	Judkins
Latta Mary E	J P	Norlina
Lynch Geo W	Ed	Fishing Creek
Lynch Ben J	Sidney	Judkins
Lynch Ashley	June	"
Little *Murphy Cuxgll*	W G	River
~~Lynch Hester~~ *Lola Cromell*	Fred *Baird*	"

B. V. S. FORM 33
10,000-4-57

North Carolina State Board of Health

BUREAU OF VITAL STATISTICS

No 145022

STANDARD CERTIFICATE OF BIRTH

1. PLACE OF BIRTH—

County .... Warren .... Registration District No. .... 93-2673 .... Certificate No. 6

Township .... River ....

City .... Vaughan .... No. .... St. .... Ward
(If birth occurred in a hospital or institution, give its name instead of street and number)

2. FULL NAME OF CHILD .... Joseph Lindsey Land ....
If child is not yet named, make supplemental report, as directed

| 3. Sex Male | If plural births / 4. Twin, triplet, or other .... 5. Number in order of birth .... | 6. Premature .... Full term .... | 7. Are parents married Yes | 8. Date of birth June 25, 18 (Month, day, year) |

9. Full name FATHER	18. Full maiden name MOTHER
John Thomas Land	Lois Rebecca Brice
10. Residence (usual place of abode) (If non-resident, give place and State) Vaughan	19. Residence (usual place of abode) (If non-resident, give place and State) Vaughan
11. Color or race White	12. Age at last birthday — (years)	70. Color or race White	21. Age at last birthday — (years)
13. Birthplace (city or place) S. C. — (State or country)	22. Birthplace (City or place) S. C. (State or country)
14. Trade, profession or particular kind of work done, as spinner, sawyer, bookkeeper, etc. Truck Foreman	23. Trade, profession or particular kind of work done, as housekeeper, typist, nurse, clerk, etc. Housewife
15. Industry or business in which work was done, as silk mill, sawmill, bank, etc.	24. Industry or business in which work was done, as own home, lawyer's office, silk mill, etc.
16. Date (month and year) last engaged in this work 19	17. Total time (years) spent in this work	25. Date (month and year) last engaged in this work 19	26. Total time (years) spent in this work

27. Number of children of this mother (at time of this birth and including this child) (a) Born alive and now living .... 4 .... (b) Born alive but now dead .... (c) Stillborn ....

CERTIFICATE OF ATTENDING PHYSICIAN OR MIDWIFE

I hereby certify that I attended the birth of this child, who was born alive at .... 5:A ...... m. on the date above stated.

WHEN THERE WAS NO ATTENDING PHYSICIAN OR MIDWIFE, THEN THE FATHER, HOUSEHOLDER, ETC., SHOULD MAKE THIS RETURN.

(Signed) .... L. J. Picot .... M. D

or .... Midwife

Given name added from a supplemental report ....

(Date of) ....

Address ...... Littleton, North Carolina ......

Filed .... 19 .... J.H. Harris .... REGISTRAR

REGISTRAR

THIS IS TO CERTIFY that the above is a true copy of the birth certificate

of .... Joseph Lindsey Land ....

filed in this office.

J.W.R. Norton

State Registrar.

FILE ...... 725 ...... PAGE ...... 387 ......

Date Issued: .... 11-24-1958 ....

65

APPLICATION FOR MARRIAGE LICENSE   C. J. NO. 13503

Name   J. L. Lund ....   Address   Aberdeen, N.C.

Age   23   Color   white   Birthplace   Vaughan, N.C.

Married before?   no   Divorced?   ---   Where?   ------   Occupation S.A.L.R.R.

and

Name   Vivian Hicks ....   Address   Clearwater, Fla.

Age   28   Color   white   Birthplace   Live Oak, Fla.

Married before?   no   Divorced?   ---   Where?   ------   Occupation bookkeeper

It is expected that   John C. Brown

Address   Clearwater, Fla.

will perform the ceremony.

STATE OF FLORIDA	STATE OF FLORIDA
COUNTY OF _____	COUNTY OF Pinellas
Before me, the undersigned authority, personally appeared	Before me, the undersigned authority, personally appeared the persons above named, who, being first duly sworn, depose and say that the information given by each of them as above set forth is true and correct, and that neither of them is married at this time and that they are not related within the prohibited degree.
_____ and	
_____	J. L. Lund
who being first duly sworn, depose and say that ___ he ___ the parent ___ of the said	Vivian Hicks
_____	
who is ___ years of age, and that ___ he ___ do ___ hereby consent to the marriage of the said	Subscribed and sworn to before me this, the 1 day of June 19 42
_____	John C. Brown
to _____	Notary Public
_____	(TITLE)
Subscribed and sworn to before me this, the ___ day of ___ 19 ___	
_____	
(TITLE)	
FORM V. S. NO. 44	

Marriage License

C. J. No. 13503   CENTRAL BUREAU OF VITAL STATISTICS

State of Florida, Pinellas County

To any Minister of the Gospel, or any Officer Legally Authorized to Solemnize the Rite of Matrimony:

Whereas, Application having been made to the County Judge of Pinellas County, of the State of Florida, for a license for marriage, and it appearing to the satisfaction of said County Judge that no legal impediment exist to the marriage now sought to be solemnized:

These are, therefore, To authorize you to unite in the

Holy Estate of Matrimony

J. L. Land   and   Vivian Hicks

and that you make return of the same, duly certified under your hand, to the County Judge aforesaid.

Witness my name as County Judge, and the seal of said Court, at the Courthouse in Clearwater, this 1st day of June, A. D. 19 42   (SEAL)   Jack F. White, County Judge.

CERTIFICATE OF MARRIAGE

I Certify that the within-named J. L. Land

and Vivian Hicks were by me, the undersigned, duly united in the Holy Estate of Matrimony, by the authority of the within License.

Done this 1st day of June A. D. 19 42 at Clearwater, Florida.

Witness Mrs. Johnny Williams   (SEAL)   John C. Brown - Notary Public
MINISTER OR LEGALLY AUTHORIZED OFFICER

Witness Johnny Williams   Clearwater, Fla.
ADDRESS

Returned this 1 day of June A. D. 19 42, and recorded in Marriage Book 23, page 2.

Jack F. White, County Judge.
J.B.

VT

RTIFI

FLORIDA CERTIFICATE OF DEATH

Olive   LANE

Live Oak, Florida   Pinellas

Dunedin

Bookkeeper   Retail Department Store

Marion Hicks   Mary Harriet Baden

Florida   Pinellas   Dunedin

Sylvan Abbey Memorial Park   Florida   Clearwater

F043031

Sylvan Abbey Funeral Home   Florida

Clearwater   7853 Sunset Pt. Rd.   33765

0846

Florida   Clearwater   1969 Sunset Point Road   Suite 15   33765

41488457

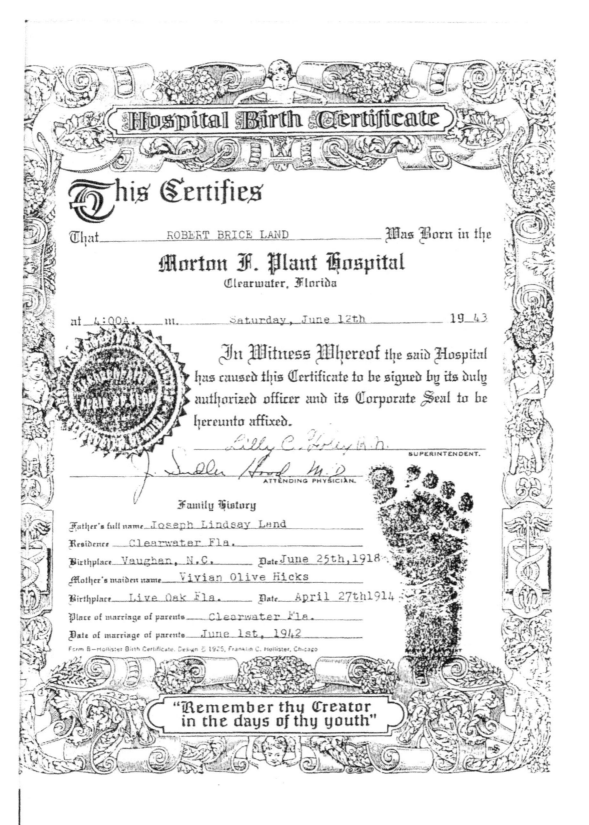

Hospital Birth Certificate

This Certifies

That ROBERT BRICE LAND Was Born in the

Morton F. Plant Hospital
Clearwater, Florida

at 4:00A. m. Saturday, June 12th 19 43

In Witness Whereof the said Hospital has caused this Certificate to be signed by its duly authorized officer and its Corporate Seal to be hereunto affixed.

Lilly C. Foley R.N.
SUPERINTENDENT.

J. Snelle Hood M.D.
ATTENDING PHYSICIAN.

Family History

Father's full name Joseph Lindsay Land
Residence Clearwater Fla.
Birthplace Vaughan, N.C. Date June 25th, 1918
Mother's maiden name Vivian Olive Hicks
Birthplace Live Oak Fla. Date April 27th 1914
Place of marriage of parents Clearwater Fla.
Date of marriage of parents June 1st, 1942

Form B—Hollister Birth Certificate. Design © 1929, Franklin C. Hollister, Chicago

"Remember thy Creator in the days of thy youth"

142

Florida
State Board of Health

BUREAU OF VITAL STATISTICS
JACKSONVILLE

This is to Certify that a **Birth Certificate** *has been filed for*

Robert Brice Land   Sex Male

Child of: Born on June 12, 1943

Mr. & Mrs. Joseph Lindsay Land
914 E. Turner St.
Clearwater, Fla.

This Record is filed in

Book No. 1571

Page No. 20645

Henry Hanson
State Health Officer

Edward M. K'Eagle
Director Bureau of Vital Statistics

143

FOURTH GENERATION

10. Susan BARBER [2] was born on 26 May 1823 in   , Bryan Co., Georgia.[2] She died on 30 Jun 1906 in   , Bryan Co., Georgia.[2]

She was married to Richard Barlow JONES on 22 Jul 1851 in   , Bryan Co., Georgia. [2] Mary Walbert and Sarah J. English were witnesses to this wedding. Mary was Susan's sister. **Richard Barlow JONES**[2] was born on 10 Mar 1828 in _   , Washington Co., Georgia.[2] He died on 26 Nov 1903 in   , Bryan Co., Georgia.[2] Susan BARBER and Richard Barlow JONES had the following children:

11. Obadiah BARBER [2] was born on 25 Jul 1825 in   , Bryan Co., Georgia.[2] He died on 28 Dec 1909 in   , Ware Co., Georgia.[2] Martha Collins, age 11, was in this household in the 1850 census of Bryan County, Georgia.

Before 1852 Obadiah built a log cabin on the edge of the Okefenokee swamp about eight miles from Waycross, Ware County, Georgia. This cabin is still standing as of March, 1999.

He was married to Nancy STEPHENS (daughter of Isham STEPHENS) on 1 Feb 1849 in   , Tattnall Co., Georgia.[2] **Nancy STEPHENS**[2] was born on 19 Feb 1829 in   , Tattnall Co., Georgia.[2] She died on 6 Nov 1874 in   , Ware Co., Georgia.[2] Obadiah BARBER and Nancy STEPHENS had the following children:

+33 i. Julia Ann BARBER.
+34 ii. James Israel (Isaac) BARBER.
+35 iii. Laura E. BARBER.
+36 iv. Wiliam A. BARBER.
+37 v. Elizabeth BARBER.
+38 vi. Mary Marjory BARBER.
+39 vii. Nancy Angeline BARBER.
+40 viii. Lydia Lavina BARBER.
+41 ix. Edward Obadiah BARBER.
42 x. **Charlotte BARBER**[2] was born in 1868. [2] She died died young.[2]
+43 xi. Ella BARBER.

He was married to Matilda TATUM (daughter of George TATUM and Sarah   ) in 1876.[2] **Matilda TATUM**[2] was born on 9 Sep 1848.[2] She died on 11 Aug 1898. [2] Obadiah BARBER and Matilda TATUM had the following children:

+44 i. Perry BARBER.
+45 ii. Rosa BARBER.
+46 iii. Charles BARBER.
47 iv. **Cleveland BARBER (Private).**
+48 v. Virginia BARBER.
49 vi. **John BARBER**[2] was born in 1886. [2] He died in 1899.[2] John Barber was accidently shot and killed at age 13.
+50 vii. Samuel J. BARBER.
+51 viii. Lucinda BARBER.
52 ix. **Lee BARBER (Private).**

He was married to Martha Ann KIGHT.[2]

13. Israel M. BARBER [2] was born in 1827 in   _, Bryan Co., Georgia.[2]
He was married to Edey M.   .[2] One source says his wife's name was Nancy. **Edey M.**
[2] was born about 1827.[2] Israel M. BARBER and Edey M.   had the following children:

53 i. **Ann F. BARBER**[2] was born in 1852 in   , Bryan Co., Georgia.[2]
54 ii. **Sarah BARBER**[2] was born in 1854. [2]
55 iii. **James B. BARBER**[2] was born in 1857. [2]

Search

NORTH CAROLINA BARBERS

(1) WILLIAM of NC, and MOSES EDWARD of GA and FL
(2) WILLIAM and JOHN of Anson Co
(3) HENRY and WILLIAM BRYWOOD BARBER of Martin Co

RICHARD and MICAH BARBER, Onslow Co NC -The descendancy for this family is found under the file of Andrew Barber in North Carolina Barbers (A)

(1) WILLIAM BARBER OF NORTH CAROLINA and MOSES EDWARD BARBER of GEORGIA and FLORIDA

References:
Thomas H Lindsay: Tlind44@aol.com
Nancy Catlett:
Thomas Parker: twparker@sprynet.com
Jacki Barber:
Kathy Carroll at WorldConnect:
Carl Wendell Mobley, 7031 Gondola Dr, Orlando FL 32809; at LDS FamilySearch
Gene Barber: gbarb@nefcom.net
Charles H Jones: dfayejones1@juno.com
Diane Barber McColl
Kaycie Beckman: kaycie@alltel.net
Cindy Swords
Earl R Bates
David W Dorsey, Sr. at WorldConnect ddorsey@mindspring.com
Kimberly Barber Gaylord: ddsealman@msn.com
Larry R Youmans: lyoumans@waxcable.com
Jack Thompson:
Barbara Goodson: BEG@tntech.edu
Kay Rockett: KayRockett@webtv.net
Dick Wilson: WRW83@aol
Margaret Taylor: GENFORUM
William G Cassady at WorldConnect – cassady at gulftel.com

(2) WILLIAM and JOHN BARBER OF ANSON COUNTY, NORTH CAROLINA

William and John are probably brothers, and have been shown by DNA to be not sons of George Barber and Elizabeth (Moore) of VA and NC.

References:
Betty Barber:
Elise Johnson: R1, Box 179B, Lobelville TN 37097
Terry Sutton:

Dan Sullivan at WorldConnect, Dan_Sullivan@prodigy.net
Elaine K Kubinski at WorldConnect - <elainekubinski@cs.com>
David McKerchen at WorldConnect - <davemphx@mindspring.com>
Lacey Sparks at WorldConnect - <ccsparks@flash.net>
Nancy Hart Servin – nharts@silcon.com
Daniel K Edwards: 1237 Ocotillo Dr, El Centro CA 92243
Lynn Dawson: dawson@gbso.net
Glenn Spradley: Rootsweb Worldconnect

FIRST GENERATION

1. WILLIAM[1] BARBER, 172?; m ?; res Anson Co NC.   [Ref: IGI:NC]
    KEZIA[2], 1750; m William Henry **Cone**; d Camden or Bullock Co GA.
    CASSANDRA[2], ; m Matthew **Carter**.

2. JOHN[1] BARBER, 1738; m Mary Ann **Allen**; res Anson Co NC.   [Ref: IGI:NC; Lt:Betty Barber;(John was likely a brother of William); Website: Dan Sullivan, including work of Eleanor Barbour; FTM: —Luersen Family‖, by Betty Joan Jones]
  3   ABRAHAM[2], 1755; m Rhodah ?**Braswell**.
      NICEY[2], 1755; ?m John **Davis**
      LIDDY[2] (ELYDA), 1756; m ?John ?**Davis**
  4   WILLIAM[2], 1757; m Mary ---; d NC.
      ARBY[2], 1758; m ---; had ch.
      ZIBARY[2] (ZIBY), 1759; m ---; had ch.
      JAMES[2], 1760; was in Anson Co.
  5   JOHN[2], 1761; m Mary Amarenthia **Smith**.
      NANCY[2], 1762; m John **Davis**; had ch.
      ALLEN[2], 1763; m ---; had ch.
            CHARLOTTE[3]
            NANCY ANN[3]
            JOHN[3]
            DANIEL[3]
            MARTHA E[3]
            ANDREW[3], 1820
            JOHN[3], 1830
      GATSEY/GATSBY[2], 1765; m ---; had ch.
      MARY B[2], 1767; ?m John **Curlee**; d Rutherford City TN. ?? See NC2, family of Richard Barber, son Thomas D's
      family.
      SIDNEY[2], 1769

SECOND GENERATION

3. ABRAHAM^2 BARBER, 1755; m Rhodah ?**Braswell**; res Anson Co NC. [Ref: IGI:NC; Lt:Elise Johnson; Virkus:Compend,Vol.7; Gendex; Lt: Terry Sutton]

ELIZABETH^3, 1777; m Richard **Sasser**.

      MARY POLLY^3, 1779; m Uriah **Tyson**; r Montgomery Co TN.

6   ABRAHAM^3, c 1782; m Sarah **Edwards**.

9   JAMES^3, 1790; m Sarah **Richardson**.

7   NOAH^3, 1793; m Mary Susannah **Moore**

      ANNA^3 (?same as DANE M), 1793; m Thomas **Hemby**.

9a   ?ZIBA DANIEL^3,   ; m Permelia ---

8   JOHN RICHARDSON^3, 1806; m Mary **Goldston**. (maybe son of a John^3, Abraham^2, John^1)

4. WILLIAM^2 BARBER, 1757; m Mary ---; d NC; r Anson Co NC.   [FTM: Agnes Marie DePriest]

      ABRAHAM^3, 1780

10   ZIBARY^3, 1784; m Sarah **Dobbs**.

      JOHN E^3, 1790; m Sarah ---

      ENOCH^3, 1791

      JAMES^3, 1793; m Ann ---; r Hickman and Perry Cos, TN.

            BENJAMIN^4, c 1826

            ANN^4, c 1832

            MARTHA^4, c 1833

            MARY^4, c 1834

            LUVINA^4, c 1837

            ELLENDER/ELLA^4, c 1838

            ALLEN^4, c 1841

11   ALLEN^3, 1795; m Martha **Kilpatrick**.

12   ELIDA^3, c 1806; m Jane B **Dowdy**.

5. JOHN^2 BARBER, 1761; m Mary ?Amarenthia **Smith**; res Anson Co NC.   [Ref: IGI:NC; Lt:Elise Johnson]

12a THOMAS^6, 1807; probably m Martha **Edwards**.

THIRD GENERATION

6. ABRAHAM^3 BARBER, c 1782; m Sarah **Edwards**; res NC, TN, and Hale or Choctaw Co AL. [Ref: Lt:Elise Johnson; FTM: —Luersen Family▌, by Betty Joan Jones]

      FANNIE^4, 1800; m Richard **Campbell**

13   ENOCH^4, 1804; m Susan **Hinson**

14   JOHN E^4, 1809; m/1 Sarah ?**Hinson**; m/2 Sarah **Land**.

      JENNIE^4,   ; m Cyrus **Campbell**

      NANCY^4, 1811; m Tubal **Campbell**

      MICHEL^4, 1815; m Richard Henderson **Campbell**; r Perry Co TN.

15 CALVIN[4], 1817; m Nancy **Dowdy**.
16 JAMES[4], 1821; m Jane **Hilburn**
17 ZIBA J[4], 1823; m Mary Elizabeth **Hilburn**
   SUSAN A[4], 1824; m Simon **Campbell**.
18 ALLEN H[4], 1826; m Margaret **Harper**
   ABRAHAM[4], c 1826; m Dolly **Baucom**.
           JAMES H[5], b MO c 1854
           JOHN[5], b MO c 1856
           MARY M[5], b TN c 1857; m James Delefate **Henson**; r TX, and Beckman Co OK.
           ABRAM L[5], b TX c 1862
           DOLLY[5], b TN c 1867
           THOMAS[5], b TN c 1871
           WILLIAM[5], b TX c 1874

7. NOAH[3] BARBER, 1793; m Mary Susannah **Moore**; res NC, Hale or Choctaw Co AL, and Jasper Co MS.   [Ref: IGI:NC; Virkus:Compend,Vol.7; Dan Sullivan at WorldConnect, Dan-_Sullivan@prodigy.net]
           WASHINGTON[4], 1812/3
           JOHN THOMAS[4]
           HENRY[4]
18a ABRAHAM[4], b NC 1819; m Martha **Henry**.
   HELENA[4]
   JEMIMA[4]
   LURINEY V[4], 1825/6; m William L **Brock**.
 19 JAMES FRANCIS[4], 1827; m Sarah **Puckett**
   ALEX M[4], 1829
   ALMIRA LOU COLSON[4], b NC 1832; m Seth Granberry **Travis**; r Jasper Co MS.
   RHODA[4], b bef. 1832; m Alfred **Edwards**.
   NICEY JANE[4], b NC
   CALOM H[4], b AL 1834
   ENOCH N[4] b AL 1836
   CALVIN M[4], b AL 1839
   WILLIAM A[4], 1835
   JULIA A[4], 1838
   EMELINE[4], 1840

8. JOHN RICHARDSON[3] BARBER, b NC 1806; m Mary **Goldston**; res Anson Co NC.
[Ref: Gendex; Laura Buckmaster, Worldconnect: laurabuckmaster at sbcglobal.net]
           LYDIA ANN[4], 1834; m Willis Hertley **Mills**; r Anson Co.
           ROBERT[4], 1836-63
           SARAH[4], 1838; m James R **Briley**; r Anson Co.
           JAMES[4], 1840-72
           GEORGE[4], 1842-64
           SIDNEY R[4], c 1845; m Nancy Anne **Garris**; r Caliborne Parish LA and Stamps AR.
               ANN VADER[5], 1867
               ROBERT E[5], 1870

JOHN BENJAMIN[5], 1872; m Sarah **Hurst**.
WALTER J[5], 1875
WILLIAM E[5], 1877; m A L **Wedgworth**.
JAMES S[5], 1880
JULIUS GARRIS[5], 1883; m Sarah Elizabeth **Bruce**; r Stamps, Lafayette Co AR.
    SIDNEY GEORGE[6]
    JOHN HURST[6]
    THELMA[6], 1912; m Earle Haynes **Fischer**.
HUGH P[5], 1886
SPURGEON S[5], 1889
20   WALTER J[4], 1848; m Eliza Cornelia **Lanier**
MARY A[4], 1853; m James F **Ross**

9. JAMES[3] BARBER, 1790; m Sarah **Richardson**; res Anson Co NC; late in Stewart Co GA. [Lt: Terry Sutton]
21   ABRAHAM CALVIN[4], b NC 1812; m Bethany **Davenport**.
LLOYD[4], 1816
CULLEN[4]
JAMES C[4], 1822; m Catherine ---.
NANCY[4] (Nicey), 1825; m 1850 --- **Austin**; to LA.
ELLENA[4], 1827; d Millican TX; m Solomon Bartholomew **Scrimshire**; r Montgomery Co AL.
NOAH W[4], 1830; m Celia ---.
POLLY[4], b NC ; m Cana **Everett**. (or Averett); to LA.

9A. ?ZIBA DANIEL[3] BARBER, ; m Permelia ---. [FTM Website; Ziba C Barber]
MARY LUCINDA[4], 1843; m William **Curtis**.
KIZZIAH[4], 1849
JAMES JEFFERSON[4], MO 1850; m Ealy Jane **Pittman**.
    JOHN[5]
    WILLIAM[5]
    CHARLES[5]
    MOLLIE[5]
    MATTIE[5]
    ADA BELLE[5]
    MAUDE[5]
    JIM[5]
    ZIBA[5]
21a ANDREW JACKSON[4], c 1853; m/1 Sinthy Ann **Grady**; m/2 Rebecca Jane **Sellers**.
SOPHRONIA[4], b Independence Co AR 1859; m Drewery Bird **James**.
AMELIA[4], 1860

10. ZIBARY[3] BARBER, 1784; m Sarah **Dobbs**; r Perry Co TN.   [FTM:—Luersen Family, by Betty Joan Jones; Website of David Kircher at Rootsweb World Connect; Glenn Spradley at Rootsweb Worldconnect]
    AMANDA[4], 1832; m Eli **Brison**; r TN.

21b JOHN M[4], 1833; m Sarah C **McDonald**.

SARAH L E[4], 1835; m William **Baucom**; r TN and Perry Co AR; d in AR.

MARTHA PATRICIA[4], 1837; m/1 Isham **Quarles**; m/2 Anthony Henry **Baucom**; r Perry Co; d in AR.

ISABELL JANE[4], 1841; m Dennis **Baucom**; r TN and Newton Co AR.

JAMES C[4], 1843; m Mary ---; r Newton Co AR.

ZIBARY ANDREW[5], 1870; m Martha S **Davis**; r Newton Co AR.

WILLIAM A[6], c 1906

MARY E[6], c 1913

EULA BEATRICE[6], c 1918

MILDRED G[6], c 1920

CUTELLA F[6], c 1927

SARAH L[5], 1881; r AR.

WALCY M[6] BARBER, 1899; m James **Kirwin**; r Johnson Co AR.

NANCY CAROLINE[4], 1846; m Frederick J **Clayborn**; r Perry Co; d Johnson Co AR.

ALSEY B[4], 1848; m Noble **Stone**; r Johnson Co AR.

11. ALLEN[3] BARBER, 1795; m Martha **Kilpatrick**. r. Perry Co TN. [FTM: —Luersen Family‖, by Betty Joan Jones]

22 ANDREW D J[4], 1820; m Tabitha Deliah **Smith**.

MARY[4], 1822; d Perry Co AR; m/1 Jordon **Dowdy**; m/2 Alvin or Allen **Warren**; m/3 Elijah **Warren**.

GATHASA[4] (GATSEY), 1824; m Elijah **Warren**, Sr; d Perry Co TN.

23 JOHN[4], 1826; m Rhoda S A **Beckham**.

CHARLOTTE[4], 1830

NANCY ANN[4], 1833; m Rufin Sanders **Stephens**; r Perry Co.

JOSEPH[4] *1839; d yg.

24 DANIEL[4], 1844; m/1 Mary Ann **Kilpatrick**; m/2 Martha ---; m/3 Sarah **Kilpatrick**; m/4 1897 Nora Neumigah
Duncan.

MARTHA E[4], 1846

12. ELIDA[3] BARBER,   ; m Jane B **Dowdy**; r Perry Co TN. [FTM: —Luersen Family‖, by Betty Joan Jones]

FRANCES B[4], 1825; m Roberson **Warren**.

NANCY B[4], 1830; m Elkanah Anderson **Land**.

25 WILLIAM THOMAS[4], 1835; m Ellender Phinetta **McCallister**.

12A. THOMAS[3] BARBER, b VA 1805; m Martha **Edwards**; res Perry Co TN. [Lt: Daniel K Edwards; Ancestry.com: OneWorldTree]

ALLEN[4], 1826

25a ZIBA DAVID[4], 1828; m Arilla Caroline (**Gardner**) Wyatt.

NANCY[4], 1830

ALSEY[4], 1832

FRANCIS[4], 1834

151

DAVID L⁴, 1839; m Francis M ---; r AR.
    MARTHA I⁵, 1864; m L C **Phillips**.
    THOMAS G⁵, 1867
    MARY F⁵, 1870; m --- **Magness**.
    JOHN M⁵, 1870; m Dora ---.
        EDITH LORAS⁶, 1903; d 1903.
        ARTHUR C⁶, 1904; d 1912.
        MYRTLE VELMA⁶, 1914; d 1918.
        PAUL L⁶, 1921; m Alverta **Murphee**.
    WILLIAM D⁵, 1875
    SARAH F⁵, 1880
    TENNIE⁵, 1880; m John **Hurt**.
    JAMES E⁵, 1883; d 1901.
MARTHA P⁴, 1842
AMOS A⁴, 1845; m S A ---.
    G L⁵, 1873
    MARY S⁵, 1875
    L E⁵, 1879
JOHN J⁴, 1849

FOURTH GENERATION

13. ENOCH⁴ BARBER, 1804; m Hickman Co TN Susan **Hinson**; r TN.   [FTM: —Luersen Family‖, by Betty Joan Jones; Cathy Cagle – ccagle9482@aol.com]
    SARAH⁵, 1832
    JAMES A⁵, 1834; m Nancy ---; r Hickman Co TN.
        A G⁶, 1856
        JAMES H⁶, 1857
        SPARK W⁶, 1858; m Mary E--; d Hickman Co.
        William A⁶, 1860
26 WILLIAM W⁵, 1836; m Rachael ---.
    HENRIETTA (RITTA)⁵, 1836; m Balam **Barham**.
    MARY⁵, 1840
    NANCY JANE⁵, 1841; m Stephen B **Johnson**.
    ?MANDY⁵, 1842
    LOUISA C⁵, 1848; m Linden, Perry Co TN Andrew Jackson **Kilpatrick**.

14. JOHN E⁴ BARBER, 1809; m/1 Sarah ?**Hinson**; m/2 Sarah **Land**; res NC ?Johnston Co and Linden, Perry Co TN. [Ref: IGI:NC; FTM: —Luersen Family‖, by Betty Joan Jones]
    First wife:
    ENOCH W⁵, 1829; ?m Susannah Caroline **McAllister**; r Perry Co TN.
        ANDREW J⁶, b Perry Co 1876; m Nancy Jane **Stephens**.
            EVA⁷, ; m Rushton **Hinson**.
            EVERT⁷, 1904
            WILLIAM CLAUDE⁷, 1905; m Isabelle **Warren**.
            DOCHIA MAGILINE⁷, 1909; m Sam **James**.

ISAAC[7], 1914
MELVIN[7], 1918
MARY MELINDA[5], 1831; m David Andrew **Lancaster**.
JORDAN[5], 1833; m Elsie **Dobbs**.
ABRAM E[5], 1836; m Margaret **Edwards**.
IBBY E[5], 1837
JOHN H[5], 1839; m Mary **Cochran**.
SARAH ELIZABETH[5], 1841; m Reuben Murphy **Copeland**; r Caldwell Co TX.
LARKIN Z[5], 1847; m Sarah **Edwards**.
?JAMES R[5], c 1847
27　?CHARLEY[5], 1849; m Zillie **Hamilton**
RETTA C[5], 1853
AMANDA F[5], 1855 ?same as Amanda, below?
Second wife:
RACHEL L ELIZA[5], 1865; m Levi W **Baucom**; r Perry Co TN.
AMANDA FREDONIA[5], 1866; m Milton Brown **Copeland**; r Lavaca and Caldwell Co
TX.

15. CALVIN[4] BARBER, 1817; m Nancy **Dowdy**.; r TN. [FTM: —Luersen Family‖, by Betty
Joan Jones]
ELIZABETH JANE[5], 1841; m Hiram **Campbell**.
RICHARD A[5], 1843
WILLIAM[5], 1846
28　ABRAHAM E[5], 1849; m Nancy Adeline **Warren**.
28a　JEREMIAH TAYLOR[5], 1858; m Caldonia Alice **Warren**.
JOSEPH H[5], 1859; m Parley **Tucker**.

16. JAMES[4] BARBER, 1821; m Jane **Hilburn**; Jane was murdered along with 2 of her sons, in
Atacosta Co TX, 1899; r TN. [FTM: —Luersen Family‖, by Betty Joan Jones]
RILEY BRITTEN[5], 1841; m Ginney/Jenny **Allen**.
WILL R, 1869
BARBARA ALLEN[6], 1873; m Jesse Cass Gipson, Jr.
RUTH[6]
CARVER[6]
FLORENCE[6]
WILEY A[5], 1843; murdered in Pleasanton, Atacosa Co TX, 1899.
BETTY[5], 1845; m William Frederick **Jenkins**; she died in DeWitt Co TX. William F was the
murdered, with his son John.
SARAH[5], 1846
ZIBA LEVI[5], 1849; murdered.
LEVI[5], 1862

17. ZIBA J[4] BARBER, 1823; m Mary Elizabeth **Hilburn**; r Perry Co TN. [FTM: —Luersen
Family‖, by Betty Joan Jones]
MARY[5], 1841
LUCINDA[5], 1843

KEZIAH^5, 1844
WILLIAM A^5, 1849
SIMEON JAMES^5, 1854; m Annice Madora **Berry**.   [Ancestry.com: OneWorldTree]
    JOHN WILLIAM^6, 1874; m Minnie May **Harris**; r Dale TX.
        SIMEON HENRY^7, 1899; d 1899.
        CHARLES IVAN^7, 1902; m Ruth Armettie **Clifton.**
            HERSHEL^8
            RAEDALE^8
            CLIFTON OVAN^8, 1922
            MARGIE^8, 1926
        RUDELLA^7, 1905; d 1907.
        EMITT ALVIN^7, 1908; m Vella Ada **Pritchard**.
        AMIE RUTH^7, 1911
        WILLIAM ALBERT^7, 1913; m Mavis Oleta **Bridgewater**.
        MARY ALICE^7, 1916; m Clarence Albert **Pritchard**.

18. ALLEN H^4 BARBER, 1826; m Margaret **Harper**; r TN.
    WESLEY D^5, 1844
    WILLIAM^5, c 1850; m Louisa **Ammons**; r Perry Co TN.
        JOHN ANDREW, 1867; m ---; r Perry Co.
            DOUGLAS AUSTIN, 1891; m Bessie Lee **Breece**.
            OMAR ZENAS, 1893; m Nannie **Witherspoon**.
            DONNIE ESTHER, 1896; m Fred **Bates**.
            GRADY THOMAS, 1900; m ---.
            JOHN NOLESS, 1903; m Mary **Lowe**.
        JASPER B, 1872; m Sarah **Cagle**.
        WESLEY W, 1875; m/1 Anna **Chessor**; m/2 Ollie **Daniel**.
        JIM HURT, 1880; m Eliza **Chessor**.
    SARAH^5, c 1851; m James R **Ammons**.

18A. ABRAHAM^4 BARBER, b NC 1819; m in AL Martha **Henry**.
    CALOM H^5
29   JEREMIAH C^5, b 1846; m Martha Emily **Sisson**.
    LELITHA^5, 1848
    FRANCES^5, 1855
    SARAH^5, 1860

19. JAMES FRANCIS^4 BARBER, 1827; m Sarah **Puckett**; res Butler AL.
[Ref:Virkus:Compend.Vol.7]
30   CALVIN CAINE^5, 1863; m Lena **Newcomb**

20. WALTER J^4 BARBER, 1848; m Eliza Cornelia **Lanier**; res Anson Co NC. [Ref: Gendex]
    WILLIAM LANIER^5, 1879; m Selean **Martin**.
        WALTER LANIER
    HORACE^5
    ROBERT JULIAN^5, 1887

VIRGINIA[5], 1881; m Lotte W **Humphrey**.
      KATE JONES[5], 1892-1906

21. ABRAHAM CALVIN[4] BARBER, b NC 1812; m Bethany **Davenport**; res. Stewart Co GA; Summerfield, Claiborne Parish LA. [Lt: Terry Sutton; Nancy Hart Servin – nharts at silcon.com; Elaine Kubinski, Rootsweb Worldconnect]
      JOHN CALVIN[5], 1835; m Rebecca **Stewart/Bennet**. He d. 1862, in Civil War; r LA.
            ALBERT[6], died young
            CATHERINE[6]
      SARAH ELIZABETH[5], 1836; d Pearsall, Frio Co TX; m/1 James F **Skinner**; m/2 James Farmer **Hightower**; r Claiborne Parish
30a JAMES MERRILL[5], 1838; m Mary Elizabeth **Morgan**.
      NANCY CAROLINE[5], 1839; m James Marion **Bridges**; r Claiborne Parish.
30b ELIJAH WARREN[5], 1840; m Carrie J **Smith**.
      MARY ETTA[5], 1842; m William Riley **Kennedy** II; r Claiborne Parish.
      LUCINDA CATHERINE[5], 1844; bur. Salesville TX; m William Parsons **Bethell**.
      MELITA[5], 1847; bur Hopkins Co TX; m Sidney Columbus **Harper**; r Hopkins Co TX.
      PHILLIP P[5], 1848; m Alice Merrill **Harper**; r LA; r Hopkins Co TX.
            ALLEN MELVIN[6], 1872; m Levera Maude **Lile**.
                  F MILDRED[7], 1898-98.
                  ALICE A[7], 1900-00
                  ALINE[7], 1900-00
                  VIOLET E[7], 1903
                  OMIE LOU[7], 1904
                  MARY[7], 1908
            ?WILSON[6], 1872
            WILLIAM CALVIN[6], 1874
            FLORENCE[6], 1876; m --- **Chawning**.
            ANNIE VIOLA[6], 1878; m F J Ovid **Moore**; r TX.
            ORA M[6], 1880; m Robert H **Mason**; r Hunt Co TX.
            JOSEPHINE[6]
            PHILIP ERNEST[6], 1884; m Mabel **Rout**; r Alexandria, Rapides Co LA.
                  PHILIP ERNEST[7], 1907; m Jessie C ---.
                  ROSA LEE[7], 1913
                  JAMES[7], 1916
            WALTON I[6], 1887; m/1 1910 Alice **Prewitt**; m/2 1925 Minnie M **Sprinkle**; r Hunt Co TX.
                First wife:
                WALLACE[7], 1911
             OMI[6]
30c THOMAS JEFFERSON[5], 1849; m Sarah Anne **Kennedy**.
      WILLIAM WORTH[5], 1851; m Mary **Dean**; r Claiborne Parish LA.
            LELA GERTRUDE[6], 1874; m Merideth Fledwood **Home/House**.
            LULA CATHERINE[6], 1876; m George Lee **Scott**.
            WILLIE[6], ; m --- **Crowder**.
OPHELIA B[5], 1853; m Leonidas **Thurman**; r Claiborne Parish.

GEORGE WALTON[5], 1854; d 1883; unmarried.

HENRY ARTHUR[5], 1857; d 1858.

KATURA B[5], 1858; bur Stephens Co TX; m George Alexander **Dean**.

BOY[5], twin; 1859

BOY[5], twin; 1859.

BOY[5], 1860

GIRL[5]. 1863

21A. ANDREW JACKSON[4] BARBER, c 1853; m/1 Sinthy Ann **Grady**; m/2 Rebecca Jane **Sellers**; r Melbourne AR.

[FTM Website: Ziba C Barber; Ancestry.com: OneWorldTree]

First wife:

31　GEORGE LEWIS[5], 1872; m Sarah Adeline **Strother**.

MARY SUSAN[5], 1874

LUCINDA JANE[5], 1880; m David Perry **Strother**.

PARALEE CINTHIA[5], 1881; m William Hardy **Coker**.

Second wife:

32　YANCY JEFFERSON[5], 1885; m/1 Rebecca Jane **Sellers**; m/2 Ada Aldona **Lamons**.

21B. JOHN M[4] BARBER, 1833; m Sarah C **McDonald**; r Pleasant Hill, Newton Co AR.

[Glenn Spradley at Rootsweb Worldconnect]

ALCEY T[5], 1855

WILLIAM R[5], 1857

NANCY E J[5], 1859; m Joseph **Edwards**; r Newton Co AR.

MARTHA A T[5], 1860; m John H **Thomas**; r Newton Co.

MANDA J[5], 1862

MARY MALINDA[5], 1864; m William Morrison **Spradley**; r Johnson Co AR.

LOUISE ELIZABETH[5], 1868; m Thomas Joseph **Tripp**; r Newton Co AR.

32a　JAMES ANDERSON FRANKLIN[5], 1874; m Victoria Mahala **Boatman**.

22. ANDREW D J[4] BARBER, 1820; m Tabitha Deliah **Smith**; r Perry Co TN and Newton Co AR. [FTM: —Luersen Family‖, by Betty Joan Jones]

NANCY J[5], 1841; m Thomas Benton **Nuckolls**.

JOHN[5], 1843

AMANDA[5], 1844; m/1 --- **Nuckolls**; m/2 William Washington **Nuckolls**; r Newton Co AR.

MARY[5], 1847

LOUISA[5], 1849; d Newton Co AR; m James Franklin **Brison**; r TN, AR.

JAMES[5], 1852; m Mary ---.

MARTHA[5], 1854; d Little Rock AR; m Jesse **Cowan**.

GATSEY[5], 1859; m John Thomas **Brisson**.

23. JOHN[4] BARBER, 1826; m Rhoda S A **Beckham**; r Perry Co TN.　[FTM: Anc. of David Earl McKercher]

34　ALLEN WILLIAM or WILLIAM ALLEN[5], 1847; m Amanda Frances (**Nuckolls**) **Wilcox**.

JORDAN[5], 1849; m Margarette **Crowell.**
    ISAAC[6], 1875
    CORA[6], 1878
    CALLIE[6], 1883; m Jonathan Harvey **Hinson**; r Perry Co TN.
    CARRY M[6], 1878
    JAMES A[6], 1892
35 DAVID WILSON[5], 1849; m Elizabeth **Nuckolls.**
ELIJAH THOMAS[5], 1853; m Mary Bell Arizona **Cowan**; r AR.
    WILLIAM HENRY[6], 1888
    JOHN TAYLOR[6], 1890; m Maggie May **Warren**; r Ft Douglas AR.
        MINNIE J
        J T
        WILLIAM HENRY
        MARY ELLEN
        ROSETTA
        ANNA BELL, ; m Earl **Freeman.**
        WANDA JEAN, ; m --- **Crumrine.**
        BILL
        FLORA BERTHA, 1922; m Gorman **Wilson.**
    JASPER A[6], 1892
    GEORGE ELVIN[6], 1896
    JAMIE E[6], 1900
JOSHUA F[5], 1856
ANDREW FRANCIS[5], 1860; m/1 Elizabeth J ---; m/2 Fay O Lee **Wilson**; r AR.
    First wife:
    PRISCILLA M[6], 1885
    CHARITY E[6], 1890
    ANDREW J[6], 1892; m ---.
        LENA[7], c 1913
        HUGH[7], c 1914
    CHARLES S[6], 1895
    C I—IKEI[6], 1896; m Stella M ---.
    Second wife:
    IDA M[6], 1898; m/1 Bill **Roland**; m/2 Hugh **Wyrick.**
    FRED R[6], 1905; d Crawford Co AR.
    JAMES TROY[6], 1907; m Grace H ---.
    ROBERT ROY[6], 1907 (twin); m Stella A ---.
    CONSOILAR F[6], 1909; m John Henry **Ritchie.**
NELLY A[5], 1863
JOSEPH DANIEL[5], 1867; d MO; m Clara Ann **Moore.**

24. DANIEL[4] BARBER, 1844; m/1 Mary Ann **Kilpatrick**; m/2 Martha ---; m/3 Sarah **Kilpatrick**; m/4 1897 Nora Neumigah **Duncan**; r Lewis Co TN. [FTM: —Luersen Family, by Betty Joan Jones; Website of David Kircher at Rootsweb World Connect]
    Children of First wife:
    ROBERT ALLEN[5], 1868; m Donna **Brown.**

GENERAL SIMPSON[5], 1871; m Mary A —Polly‖ **Hickerson**; r TN.
    ANDREW JAMES[6], 1891
    NARCISSA[6], 1893; m George Washington **Dobbs**; r Trenton TN.
    JOHN DANIEL[6], 1898
    HERSHALL[6], 1902
    GILBERT[6], 1906
    BEULAH[6], 1908
36 WILLIAM FRANKLIN[5], 1875; m Georgianna Alice **Qualls**.
Third wife:
DAVID[6], ; d 1990.
Fourth wife:
MARY[5], ; m --- **Harder**.

25. WILLIAM THOMAS[4] BARBER, 1835; m Ellender Phinetta **McCallister**; r Perry Co TN.
[FTM: —Luersen Family‖, by Betty Joan Jones]
    JACOB[5]
36a JAMES[5], 1853; m Mary Ann **Fuller**.
36b JOHN LEWIS[5], 1855; m Harriet **Edwards**.
    SARAH JANE[5], 1856; m George Thomas **Rogers**; r Napier, Lewis Co TN.
    ROBERT[5], 1858; m Martha **Warren**.
    MARTHA[5], 1860; m William Allen **Trull**; r Perry Co.
    JOSEPH[5], 1865; m Mariah Ann **Fuller**.
    MARY[5], 1868; m Pete **Beasley**; r Perry Co.
    FANNIE[5], 1870; m Rufford **Gibbons**.
37 ANDERSON LEVINE[5], 1873; m Sarah Elizabeth **Morgan**.

?25A. ZIBA DAVID[4] BARBER, 1828; m Arilla Caroline (**Gardner**) **Wyatt** (her 1st husb. was --- **Wyatt**); res Decatur Co TN and Newark, Independence Co AR. [Ancestry.com: OneWorldTree]
    AMOS REYNOLD[5], 1857; m/1 Eliza J **Locke**; m/2 Amanda **Clark**.
        Second wife:
        WOODROW[6]
        MABEL[6]
        TROY[6], 1888
        WILLIAM AMOS[6], 1891; m Rose Etta **Marshall**.
            EMMA GENE[7]
            AMOS COE[7]
            BENNY DALE[7]
            BLANCHE[7]
            NINA JANE[7]
            MARY ETTA[7]
            MARSHALL REED[7], ; m Sarah Ann ---.
            MAUDE[7]
            ELOISE[7]
            EULA MAE[7]
        LILLY[6], 1894

JAMES T^6, 1905
37a   JAMES JACKSON^5, 1859; m Julia Hannah **Linebaugh**.
37b   WILLIAM DAVID^5, 1862; m/1 Vica Jane **Huffman**; m/2 Lettie **Waits**.
       ROBERT RILEY^5, 1865; m Kathy **Limbough**.
           ROBERT LEE^6
           FRANK D^6, 1899; m Myrtle **Clark**.
               FRANK^7
               NAOMI^7
               RAYBORN LEROY^7
       ALBERT A^5, 1869

FIFTH GENERATION

26. WILLIAM W^5 BARBER, 1836; m Rachael ---; r TN. [FTM: —Luersen Family, by Betty Joan Jones]
       ELIJAH^6, 1855
       ALVIN^6, 1857
       RUFUS^6, 1859; m Alice ---; r TX.
           LIGE^7, c 1884
           FANNY^7, c 1890
           ORA^7, c 1892
           PAUL^7, c 1894
           FLORENCE^7, c 1897
       LOTTE^6, c 1861
       NANCY J^6, c 1863
       MAMIE^6, c 1864
       WILLIAM RILEY^6, c 1867
       MARY^6, c 1870
       MARTHA^6, c 1874

27. ?CHARLEY^5 BARBER, 1849; m Zillie **Hamilton**; res Johnston Co NC. [Ref: IGI:NC]
       WILLIAM B^6, 1875; m Maggie **Jones**
       SARAH^6, 1880

28. ABRAHAM E^5 BARBER, 1849; m Nancy Adeline **Warren**; r TN. [FTM: —Luersen Family, by Betty Joan Jones]
       IZORA^6, 1878; m/1 Joseph T **Lewis**; m/2 Joe **Beasley**.
       WILLIAM KINCHEN^6, 1884; m Edna **Hinson**.
       MARY NANCY^6, 1886; m J C **Devore**.
       CALVIN D^6, 1888; m Jessie **Lewis**.
       MARTHA JANE^6, 1890; m Eli Thomas **Qualls**; r Perry Co TN.

28A. JEREMIAH TAYLOR^5 BARBER, 1858; m/1 Caldonia Alice **Warren**; r Hohenwald, Lewis Co TN; d Ethridge, Lawrence Co TN. [Patricia Wright: wright.p.e@att.net]
       First wife:
       LULA M^6, 1882; m Taylor **Chandler**.

159

BRADEN[6], 1885; m Ruth Ann **Pitts**; 4 children.
JESSE CASEY[6], 1887; m Jennie **Pitts**.
BULAH LEONA[6], 1889; m Wesley **Tharp**.
HADEN PEARLESS LEVI[6], 1892; m Annie **Gray**.
    DAUGHTER[7], ; m --- **Payne**.
CASRLEE[6], 1893
EARLESS[6], 1896; m Delia Susan **Holland**; 4 children.
FLOYD WILLIAM[6], 1899; m Bertha Elizabeth/Melissa **Cromwell**; r Weirton, Hancock
Co WV.
    DAUGHTER[7], ; m/1 **Richardson**; m/2 **Bartholomew**.
    FLOYD ANCIL[7], ; m --- **Neverly**; 4 children.
        SON[8], ; m ---
        SON[8], ; m --- **Quigley**.
        DAUGHTER[8], ; m --- **Hinds**.
        SON[8], ; m --- **Olmstead**.
    MARY ELLEN[7], 1928; m/1 Horace Hubert **Skinner**; m/2 Albert Rufus **Webb**.
    DAUGHTER[7], ; m --- **Saunders**.
LLOYD[6], 1902; m/1 ---; m/2 Thetis ---. He bur. In Odenville, St Clair Co AL.
DAUGHTER[6], ; m --- **Fields**.

29. JEREMIAH C[5] BARBER, b GA 1846; m Martha Emily **Sisson**.
  38 WILLIAM E[6], 1868; m Cynthia Jane **Everett**.

30. CALVIN CAINE[5] BARBER, 1863; m Lena **Newcomb**; res Butler AL, and MS.
[Ref:Virkus:Compend.Vol.7; David McKerchen at WorldConnect -
<davemphx@mindspring.com>]
    LENA ORA[6], 1886; m/1 Clayton **Myers**; m/2 Allen **Fountain**
    WILLIAM LEE[6], 1887; m Callie **Daniels**
    MAMIE EVELYN[6],1890
    IDA VARY[6], 1892; m John **Thrower**.
    FRANK PUCKETT[6], 1894; m Laurette **Shaw**.
    CALVIN CAINE[6], 1899; m Lida **Lovett**.

30A. JAMES MERRILL[5] BARBER, 1838; m Mary Elizabeth **Morgan**; r Claiborne Parish LA.
[Elaine K Kubinski; Nancy Hart Servin – nharts@silcon.com]
    W MERRELL[6], 1872; m Alice **Raley/Railey**.
        VIVIAN[7]
        ERWIN[7]
        RUPERT[7]
        VAUGHN WILLIAM[7], 1901
        HOWARD[7], 1907
        FRED[7], 1913
    CARRIE O[6], 1873; m J Ernest **Glover**.
    METIER[6]
    MARTIS DAVENPORT[6], 1877; m Nancy Ellen ---.
        HERBERT M[7], 1905

RACHEL[7], 1913; m --- **Taylor**.
MILDRED[6], 1882; m Oscar I **Tanner**.
J RANDALL[6], 1879-1889.
EMILY EDNA[6], 1884-1889.
PEARL[6], ; m --- **Tanner**.
?EMMA[6]
?SALLIE[6]
?CALVIN[6]

30B. ELIJAH WARREN[5] BARBER, 1840; m Carrie J **Smith**; r Claiborne Parish LA. [Nancy Hart Servin – nharts at silcon.com; Ancestry.com: OneWorldTree]
FANNIE O[6], 1866; m W **Taylor**.
MATTIE C[6], 1867; m Will **Brown**.
VIRGINIA V[6], 1869; m Tom **Waller**.
BETTIE[6], 1871, twin; m --- **Teekle**.
HENRIETTA[6], 1871, twin; d 1871.
KATHRON[6], 1874
CORINTHIA LUCINDA[6], 1876; d 1883.
OPHELIA[6], 1878; m Cicero **Davidson**.
LAURA[6], 1880; m --- **Wages**.
ELISHA CASPER[6], 1883, twin; m Ruth **Ferguson**; r Claiborne Parish LA.
　　　ALVERNE[7], 1909
　　　J WARREN[7], 1912
　　　VERNON[7], 1914-1915.
　　　J DURELL[7], 1916
　　　EDWIN WILLARD[7], 1919; m Ruby **Brown**.
　　　　　JOHN[8], ; m Sandy **Jacobs**.
　　　　　WAYNE[8], ; m Carol **Finklea**.
　　　　　PENNY[8], ; m Johnny **Culpepper**.
　　　　　BETTY[8], ; m Ralph **McKarkie**.
　　　　　PATSY[8], ; m Roger **Barton**.
　　　　　FRANCES[8], ; m Gene **Sweat**.
　　　　　REGGIE LOU[8], ; m Dalton **Box**.
　　　MALCOLM O[7], 1924
　　　ERNIE R[7], 1929
ELIJAH JASPER[6], 1883, twin; m Willie K **Smith**; r Claiborne Parish LA.
　　　ESTELLE[7], 1905
　　　AGNES[7], 1908
　　　INEZ[7], 1911
　　　WALTER W[7], 1914-1936.

30C. THOMAS JEFFERSON[5], BARBER, 1849; m Sarah Anne **Kennedy**; r Summerfield, Claiborne Co LA. [Ronald Grames: gramesronaldl at qwest.net]
FRANCES MARTHA ETTA[6], 1872; m John Thomas **McBride**.
STEPHEN T[6], 1874; m/1 Mary **Odem**; m/2 Golda **Hargrove**.
　　Children by first wife:

THEO[7], 1900
MAUD[7], 1903
LULA[7], 1908
Second wife:
MATTIE L, 1914
CARMELO, 1916
LAURENDA[6], 1875; m James A **Peevy**; r LA.
LOUISA[6], 1878; m Hampton Franklin **Bush**.
MARY B[6], 1879; m/1 Ike S **Crouch**; m/2 R F **Grider**.
SARAH ELIZABETH[6], 1881; m Thomas Edmon **Teekell**.
WILLIAM ABRAHAM[6], 1883; d Winfield, Winn Co LA; m Ollie Maybell **Cox**.
ELVIN BRODIE[7], c 1906; d Many, Sabine Co LA 1993; m Vendora Celia
Grames.
MERTIE[7], ; m --- **Bartley**.
BERTIE[7], ; m --- **Green**.
CATHERINE[7], ; m --- **Apel**.
THOMAS[7]
BERNETTE[7], ; m --- **Duke**.
JAMES THOMAS[6], 1885; d infancy.
JOSEPH J[6], 1886; d infancy.
M OLIVER[6], 1887-1907.
ADA AMANDA[6], 1889; m/1 James Leo Vickery **Black**; m/2 Torrence T **Chubb**; r LA
and OK.
BRODIE EDGAR[6], 1892; m/1 Lula **Chandler**; m/2 Clyde Spence **Coiv**; d Winnfield LA.

31. GEORGE LEWIS[5] BARBER, 1873; m Sarah Adeline **Strother**. [FTM Website: Ziba C
Barber]
39   DAVID LEWIS[6], 1894; m/1 Lelitie **Stone**; m/2 Bamma **Parkerson**; m/3 Lottie Lorene
Jones; m/4 Cora David
Thomas.
BESSIE CLEMENTINE[6], 1895; m William Harve **Jones**.
CLARA ELIZABETH[6], 1898; m/1 Jim **Dillard**; m/2 John **Neal**; m/3 Steve **Tooley**.
HESTER IZORA[6], 1901; m Clifton **Armstrong**.
40   ZIBA JEFFERSON[6], 1904; m Bertha Christine **Belcher**.
41   CHESTER JACKSON[6], 1908; m Ruby **Wisdom**.

32. YANCY JEFFERSON[5] BARBER, 1885; m/1 Rebecca Jane **Sellers**; m/2 1907 Ada
Lamon; r Independence Co AR.
[FTM Website: Ziba C Barber; Ancestry.com: OneWorldTree]
Second wife:
ODENE[6], ; m Harry **Clanton**.
ZELLA MELISSA[6], 1909; m Homer Richmond **Goodman**.
ARLENE[6], 1913; m/1 T J **Clark**; m/2 Borden **Finney**; m/3 Hugh **Finney**.
DELBERT HENRY[6], 1916; m Gladys S Mary **Gorman**.
GENITA MAYE[7], ; m --- **Spain**.
MICHAEL ANTHONY[7], 1946

ROBERT LEE[7], 1947

RAYMOND HENRY[7], 1953; m Sindra Ann **Manchester**.

LOUIS EUGENE[6], 1921; m Pansy **Finster**.

LARRY GENE[7], ; m Diane **Johnson**.

ANGELA DIANE[7], ; m John **Richardson**.

ELVIN EMMIT[6], ; m Ethel Leora **Creech**; d Independence Co AR.

WILLIAM DARREL, ; m Marjorie Jane **Salter**.

SHERRY GAIL, ; m Michael Everett **Todd**.

VIOLA MAY, ; m John Everett **Via**.

LANNIE ROSS, ; m Cynthia Bennett **Britton**.

LOIS JANE, ; m Arthur Leroy **Weakley**.

GERALD WAYNE, ; m --- **Haegele**.

BERNICE LEE, ; m Anna **Zaremba**.

REGINALD DALE,   ; m Janie **Inman**.

DONNA FAYE, ; m John Wesley **Ramsey**.

CHARLES LYNN, ; m Carol Ann **Brown**.

TERREL MARLIN, 1944; d 1944.

BOYCE EDWARD, 1946

BETTY CAROL, 1954; m Danny **Knatcal**.

DOYLE JULIUS[6], 1927; m Easter Marie **Clark**.

BRUCE LEE[7]

32A. JAMES ANDERSON FRANKLIN[5] BARBER, b Pleasant Hill, Newton Co AR 1874; m Victoria Mahala **Boatman**. [Glenn Spradley at Rootsweb Worldconnect]

ROXIE GERTRUDE[6], 1900; m/1 Tom **Dyer**; m/2 James E **Clark**; r OK.

WILLIAM LESTER[6], 1902; d Bakersfield, Kern Co CA; m/1 Delilah **Foster**; m/2 Bertha Leola **Ishmael**.

First wife:

CINDY[7]

WESLEY LESTER[7], 1925

Second wife:

WILLIAM LESTER[7], b Trinity Co TX 1926

DOROTHY[7], b Trinity Co TX 1929

DAUGHTER[7], ; m Kenneth **Clark**.

NAOMI TENNESSEE[6], 1903; m Marvin Lee **Jernigan**; r Checotah, McIntosh Co OK.

JOHN WILLIS, 1905[6]; m/1 Lela Cordelia **Borum**; m/2 Mozelle **Shastid**; r Checotah.

First wife:

NEVA[7], 1927; m Alvie **Bookout**.

NEDA RAE[7], 1928; , John Henry **FARRAR**.

SON[7], ; m/1 Alma Lou **Stone**; m/2 --- **Kerbow**.

Second wife:

JOHN WILLIS[7], 1945; m --- **Akins**.

MINNIE ARKIE[6], 1906; m/1 Fred **Crawford**; m/2 Jesse Floyd **Thompson**; they d Tulare Co CA.

ANNIE MAE[6], 1907; m John Harry **Ford**; they d KS.

VIRGIL FRANKLIN[6], 1908; d Riverside Co CA; m/1 Bessie **Hill**; m/2 Ethel **Lawham**.

JAMES MONROE[6], 1910; m Faye **Martin**; r Bakersfield CA.
    BETTY LOU[7], 1933; m James Vershall **Hall**.
RUSSELL HOMER[6], 1912; d Contra Costa Co CA; m Loy **Martin**.
MALINDA BERTHINIA[6], 1913; d Visalia CA; m/1 Luther Richard **Jennings**; m/2 Fate
Dudley **Head**.
    PERSHING —DICK[6], 1917; d Contra Costa Co; m/1 Verda Francis **Cutler**; m/2 Bettie -
---.
    ORLANDO CECIL[6], 1919; m/1 --- **McComas**; m/2 Hazel **Karr**.
    DENNIS ROSS[7]; d Modesto CA.
RUBY VICTORIA[6], 1921; m/1 C W **Swift**; m/2 Eugene E **Jones**.
VICTOR IVIS[6], 1923; d Topeka, Shawnee Co KS; m --- **Payton**.
ORA LEE[6], 1926-1932.

34. ALLEN WILLIAM or WILLIAM ALLEN[5] BARBER, 1847; m Amanda Frances
(**Nuckolls**) **Wilcox**; TN, AR. [FTM: Anc. of David Earl McKercher]
    MIRANDA F (AMANDA)[6], c 1869
    ZIBARY[6], ; m Sarah **Dobbs**.
    JOHN H[6], 1869-69
    SUSAN E[6], 1870-187?
    K H L[6], 1870-187?
    SARAH J[6], 1872-99
42   JOSHUA KINSEY[6], 1876; m Ida Mae **Samuels**.
    LUCY ANN[6], 1879
    MARY M[6], 1881
43   WILSON E[6], b AR 1887; m/1 Margaret Elizabeth **Gray**; m/2 1923 Ola **Kindricks**.
    THEOPHILUS B J[6], 1890-90
    LEVI THOMAS[6], 1891-1905

35. DAVID WILSON[5] BARBER, 1849; m Elizabeth **Nuckolls**; he d Madison Co AR. [FTM:
—Luersen Family, by Betty Joan Jones]
44 JOHN RILEY[6], 1871; m Nancy Leona **Baucom**.
    RHODA A[6], 1873; m William **Wilson**.
    WILLIAM T[6], 1875; m Tennie B ---.
    DAVID W[6], 1880
    ELIJAH THOMAS[6], 1886; m Flora Jane **Newton**; r AR.
        ?FLOY[7]
        IDA[7], c 1911
        OLIVER[7], c 1913
        OLLIE[7], c 1919

36. WILLIAM FRANKLIN[5] BARBER, 1875; m Georgianna Alice **Qualls**; r TN. [FTM:
—Luersen Family, by Betty Joan Jones]
    LILLIE[6], ; m George **Treadway**.
    DANIEL[6], 1896
    GEORGE D[6], 1899

36A. JAMES[5] BARBER, 1853; m Mary Ann **Fuller**. [Rhonda Cravins, Worldconnect: RC373 at yahoo.com]

    JAMES[6]
    SARAH[6]
    ROBERT[6]
    MARTHA[6]
    JOSEPH[6]
    MARY[6]
    FANNIE[6]
    ANDERSON[6]
    WILLIAM[6], c 1890
    THOMAS[6]

36B. JOHN LEWIS[5] BARBER, 1855; m Harriet **Edwards**. [Rhonda Cravins, Worldconnect: RC373 at yahoo.com]

    IDA MARIER BIRTHLEE[6], ; m Richard Tyler **Qualls**; r Perry Co TN.
    SARAH MARY CELINE HEITIRE[6], ; m William Arthur **Qualls**.
    ERA ELISE[6], ; m Bud Black **McAllister**.
    JOHN CHESLEY EDWARD[6], 1891; m Ola **Mathis**.
    JESSIE JOE[6], 1896; m Virginia **Staggs**.
    SALLY LENORA DAISY[6], ; m Cecil **Chandler**.
    NANCY ELIZABETH JANE[6]
    MARTHIE FERNETTIE AMERICA[6]
    WILLIAM ROBERT[6], 1888; m Lena Eva **Barber**; r Perry Co TN.

37. ANDERSON LEVINE[5] BARBER, 1873; m Sarah Elizabeth **Morgan**. [FTM: ⸺Luersen Family⸹, by Betty Joan Jones]

    CLAGETT[6], 1900; m Gertie **Qualls**.
    EVE[6], 1902; m William **Barber**.
    FLOYD[6], 1905; m Lillian **Rogers**.
45   JAMES[6], 1911; m Geneva **Qualls**.
    EARLINE[6], 1913; m Kent **Warren**.

37A. JAMES JACKSON[8] BARBER, 1859; m Julia Hannah **Linebaugh**; d Jonesboro, Craighead Co AR; res Newark, Independence Co AR. [Lt: Lynn Dawson]

    JOHN R[9]
    CHARLIE OSCAR[9], 1891; m Willie Lee **McCoy**; res Newark, Independence Co AR.
        WREATHA ELLAREE[10], 1916; m Sherrod **Magness**.
        OPAL PAULINE[10], 1918; m Fred B **Smith**.
        CHARLES EUGENE[10], 1919; m Winnie Lou **Sneed**.
        FORREST GLYNN[10], 1921; m Geraldine **Gardner**.
            GLINDA SUE[11], ; m Jimmy Neal **Austin**.
            LYDA ANN[11], ; m James Larry **Harris**.
            FREDDIE MACK[11], ; m Linda Sue **Liles**.
        HOMER VON[10], 1924; m Annie Mae **Jenkins**.
            SHARON LYNN[11], ; m John **Wyatt**.

DONALD GENE[11], ; m Brenda **Glover**.
DEBORAH GALE[11], ; m John Morris **Ross**.
BRENDA KAY[11], ; m David **Schaufler**.
FANNY LOUISE[10], 1925; m Ben A **Joyce**.
ERMA[10], 1928; m Robert V **Barnes**.
JIMMY DEAN[10], 1931; m Carroll **Walker**.
    KARI[11]
    DANA[11]
LYNN[10], 1933; m Barbara **Broadwater**.
DONALD RALPH[10], 1936; m Jane **Wilson**.
    RICHARD[11]
    MELINIE[11], ; m James **Atwell**.
    MELINDA[11], ; m Rusty **Wyatt**.
MAGDALENE[9], 1894
ROSA ETHEL[9], 1896; m --- **Michaels**.
FRANK D[9], 1899
TINA MAY[9], 1902; m Hubert Edgar **Brightwell**.
JEFFERSON DAVIS[9], 1904; m Hattie **Prater**.
    KENDALL ROY[10]
    WALLACE[10]
    GINA LEE[10], ; m Joe **Riccio**.
    RETHEL MYRON[10], ; m Elise Jane **Holt**.
        JUSTIN WAYNE[11], ; m Summer **Delaney**.
        JENNIFER JANE[11], ; m Byron Geoffrey **Cook**.
        JEFFERY LEE[11], ; m Debra Lou **Scheele**.
ALETHA[9], 1911; m James R **Marshall**.

37B. WILLIAM DAVID[8] BARBER, 1862; m/1 Vica Jane **Huffman**; m/2 Lettie **Waits**; res Ozark Co MO; Newark, Independence Co AR.
    First wife:
JAMES ARTHUR[9], 1886; m Eliza Fidella **Luna**; r Newark, Independence Co AR; d Jonesboro, Craighead Co AR.
RAEL SAMPSON[10], 1909; m ---.
    EVERETT TALMADGE[10], 1910; m ---.
    COYE ESTER[10], 1913; m James Tracy **Clark**; r Newark.
    JAMES DEE[10], 1915; m ---.
    ANNIE OCTAVIA[10], 1917; m ---.
    VIRGIE LOUVICY[10], 1920; m ---.
    ROBERT LUNA[10], 1923; m ---.
LUTHER[9], 1888; m Katie ---.
EARL[9], 1889; m Dora **Ramsey**.
ENOS[10]
    ARNOLD[10]
    MAYBELLE[10]
    WILLENE[10]
ARLEY ROCK[9], 1891

CHARLES J^9, 1893
Second wife:
JOYCE^9
ELBER^9 (—DOCK!)
CECIL^9, c 1894
HUGH^9, ; m Elma ---.
FLOYD^9, c 1895
JETTIE^9
DARRELL^9, c 1896
CLIFFORD^9, c 1898
LAWRENCE^9, c 1899
CARL^9, c 1900

SIXTH GENERATION

38. WILLIAM E^6 BARBER, 1868; m Cynthia Jane Everett.
  VINCE^7
  ARTHUR^7
  IRA^7
  ETHEL^7
  ANNIE MAE^7
  JERRY C^7, 1888; m Minnie **Lee**.
  WILLIAM E^7, 1894
  NATHAN CLARK^7, b Chunky MS 1896; m Ida Belle **McGee**.
    ERLEEN^8

39. **DAVID LEWIS^6 BARBER**, 1894; m/1 Lelitie **Stone**; m/2 Bamma **Parkerson**; m/3 Lottie Lorene **Jones**; m/4 Cora David **Thomas**. [FTM Website: Ziba C Barber]
  Third wife:
  GERALD DEAN^7, 1925-1935
  GRACE ADELINE^7, 1926; m Murrel Eugene **McDaniel**.
  WINFORD BURLEY^7, 1931; m/1 Billei **Keys**.
  BONNIE LEE^7, 1933; m Elmer Earl **Belcher**.
  CHESTER LEE^7, 1933; m Madeline **Simpson**.
  HILDA L^7, 1938; m/1 Dewayne **Thomason**; m/2 James **Glen**; m/3 ----; m/4 Bill **Webb**.

40. **ZIBA JEFFERSON^6 BARBER**, 1904; m Bertha Christine **Belcher**. [FTM Website: Ziba C Barber]
  SARAH DORIS EVELYN^7, 1924; m Jack Whitt **Harrison**.
  THOMAS JEFFERSON^7, 1925; m Christine **Richmond**.
  DOLLY BEATRICE^7, 1930; m/1 James **Bolding**; m/2 Roy **Carter**; m/3 Eugene **Hale**.
  JOHNNIE BERTHA^7, 1934-1938
  BILLY JOE, 1938^7; m/1 Mary ---; m/2 Mary **Hagar**.
  ZIBA JAMES^7, 1947; m Shelley Inez **Fuller**.

41. CHESTER JACKSON[6] BARBER, 1908; m Ruby **Wisdom**. [FTM Website: Ziba C Barber]

      BILLY GENE[7], 1932; m Martha Lovetta **Week**.
      NORMA RUTH[7], 1934; m Iran Leonard **Bare**.
      CAROLYN SUE[7], 1940; m Ronald Glynn**Cooley**.

42. JOSHUA KINSEY[6] BARBER, 1876; m Ida Mae **Samuels**; r AR.   [Website of David Kircher at Rootsweb World Connect]

      HENRY[7], c 1901
      SAMUEL C[7], c 1906; m Olga **Tolsch**.
      WILLIAM F[7], c 1909; m Dorothy **Music**.
      JAMES WILSON[7], 1912; m Betty **Rook**.
      AMANDA HESTER[7], c 1915; m Max C **Downing**.
      ELMER[7], c 1916
      ANNA AMELIA[7],   ; m/1 Valney **Boyd**; m/2 Laurence **Bema**; m/3 Edward **Hall**.

43. WILSON E[6] BARBER, b AR 1887; m/1 Margaret Elizabeth **Gray**; m/2 1923 Ola **Kindricks**; r Franklin Co AR.
[FTM: Anc. of David Earl McKercher]

      First wife:
      JAMES WASHINGTON[7], 1918
      THOMAS JEFFERSON[7], 1920-43
      MARY ELLEN PEARL[7], 1922; m/1 Tilman Russell **Wolfinbarger**; m/2 Walter Earl **McKaercher**; m/3 John **Parker**.
      Second wife:
      IVA MARTHA[7], 1925
      EFFIE INEZ[7], 1928; m Jeff J.----
      LOUIS EDWARD[7], 1931
      LUCY ANN[7], 1933
      LINNIE[7], 1935
      JAMES EARL[7], 1937
      OPAL JUNE[7], 1939; m William A **Miller**.
      DOLLY ROY[7], 1941; m Robert L **H(K)esterson**
      THOMAS LEVI[7], 1945

44. JOHN RILEY[6] BARBER, 1871; m Nancy Leona **Baucom**; r Clarksville, Johnson Co AR.
[FTM: ―Luersen Family‖, by Betty Joan Jones; Website of David Kircher at Rootsweb World Connect; Lacey Sparks, Worldconnect: ccsparks at flash.net]

      WILLIAM RILEY[7], 1890; d Bannock Co ID.
      HENRY ANTHONY[7], 1892-1910.
      DAVID WILSON[7], 1894; m Jessie May **Perry**.
          VIRGINIA HELEN[8],   ; m Joseph Daniel **Baker**.
      MILDRED VALENTINE[7], 1896-1910.
      CHARLES THOMAS[7], 1899; m Martha Wilson **Osborn**.
      JAMES JOHN MONROE[7], 1901-1925
      MARTHA ELIZABETH JANE[7], 1905; m Clayton C **Cowan**; r Sequoyah Co OK.

45. JAMES[6] BARBER, 1911; m Geneva **Qualls**. [FTM: —Luersen Family, by Betty Joan Jones]

    HAROLD DEAN[7]

    BROWNIE SUE[7]; m Roger I **Barber**.

        ROGER DANIEL[8] BARBER; m/1 Lisa **Carter**; m/2 Lisa **Shelton**.

        TIMOTHY WACO[8] BARBER; m Mia **Shelton**.

    JERRY[7]

GEORGIA BARBERS

(1) CHARLES of NC and Appling Co GA
 (2) JESSE, 171? of GA and White Co IL
(3) JESSE, 1788, Oglethorp and Walton Co
(4) JAMES and GRAY BARBER OF CLARKE CO GA and ST CLAIR CO AL
 (5) JOHN, 177? and PLEASANT of Carroll Co
(6) JOHN of NC, to Screven and Bullock Co GA
(7) SETH of VA and GA
(8) WILLIAM and CHOICE of NC and GA
(9) WILLIAM of Screven Co GA

(1) CHARLES BARBER of NORTH CAROLINA and GEORGIA

FIRST GENERATION

1. **CHARLES[1] BARBER**, b Robeson Co NC c 1750; m Frances ---.
     ISRAEL[2], 1770
     WILLIAM[2], 1775; d Bryan Co GA.
     MOSES[2], 1777; d Bryan Co 1928.
     CORNELIUS[2], 1780; d Wayne Co GA.
2   JOHN[2], 1795; m Nancy **Dampier**.

SECOND GENERATION

2. **JOHN[2] BARBER**, 1795; m Nancy **Dampier**; r Appling Co GA.
 3   JEPTHA[3], 1820; m Martha **Medders**.
     FRANCES[3], 1831; m William Henry **Lewis**; r Jesup, Wayne Co GA.
 4   CORNELIUS[3], 1832; m Harriett **Altman**.
     SARAH[3], 1835; m --- **Ishon**.
     ADALINE[3]

THIRD GENERATION

3. **JEPTHA[3] BARBER**, 1820; m Martha **Medders**; r Appling Co.
 5   JOHN BENJAMIN[4], 1853; m Mary Ellen **Smith**.
     MARY[4], 1856; d young.
 6   CORNELIUS M[4], 1862; m Elizabeth **Taylor**.

4. **CORNELIUS[3] BARBER**, 1832; m Harriett **Altman**; r Appling Co GA.
     CHARLES[4], 1857
     FRANKLIN[4], 1860
     MARY[4], 1861

GEORGIA A[4], 1864
    ELIZABETH[4], 1866
    JOHN M[4], 1869
FANNIE[4], 1872
    JEPTHA[4], 1872
    JESSIE GORDON[4], 1872; m Mollie Victoria **Carter**; r Baxley, Appling Co GA
        GEORGE CORNELIUS[5], 1892
        ETHEL MAY[5], 1896
        EULA LEE[5], 1898; m Lothridge Newton **Norton**.
        JAMES I[5]
        ERNEST WILLIE[5], 1902
        VERNON HYMERIC[5], 1905; m Lois **Johnson**.
        VIRGIL ESTUS[5], 1907; m Velma Leona **Peacock**.
        BEULAH ELIZABETH[5], 1909
        JOHN HENRY[5], 1911
        JESSIE GORDON[5], 1914; m Ellen T ---.
        ALIFF[5], 1916
    JAMES E[4], 1875; m Keziah **Carter**; r Alma, Bacon Co GA.
        WILLIAM HARVEY[5], 1898; m Edna Earl **Douglas**.
    FREDERICK[4], 1876
    DANIEL MARTIN[4], 1878
    JEFFERSON[4], 1879
    FLORA[4], 1882

FOURTH GENERATION

5. JOHN BENJAMIN[4] BARBER, 1853; m Mary Ellen **Smith**; r Appling Co GA and Bunnell FL.
    JEPTHA DENNIS[5], 1878; m Minnie **Sweat**; r Bunnell FL.
        GARRIE HOBART[6], 1899; m Bernice **Bates**.
        GRACE[6], 1905-1905.
        ELLIE[6], 1907
        JOHN EULICE[6], 1909; m Lina Mae **Smith**.
        AUDREY[6], 1917
    MARTHA NANCY[5], 1880; m Robert **Moody**.
    CORNELIUS BENJAMIN[5], 1882; d Waycross GA; m/1 Julia Ann **Taylor**; m/2 Martha ---; m/3 Leila ---.

        First wife:
        LENOX CARL[6], 1904; m Mamie Alberta **Hickox**.
            LENOX CARL[7], 1928
        CHARLES[6], ; d 1959
        MARVIN ALTON[6], ; m/1 Leary **Snowden**; m/2 Bobbi **Woolard**.
        WOODROW[6], 1920; m/1 Christine **Strickland**; m/2 --- **Boatwright**.
        MARY ALICE[6], ; m James L **Walker**.
        NANCY[6], ; d young.

ESTELLE[6], ; m/1 --- **Sweat**; m/2 --- **Jenkins**.
AGNES[6]
EDWIN[6], ; d young.
NELLIE LOUISE[6], ; m --- **Ford**.
LEVY[6], ; d young.
CHARLES JACKSON[5], 1884; m/1 Kedie Mae **Sweat**; m/2 Mildred **Johnson**.
　　First wife:
　　JOHN BROWARD[6], 1906; m Jessie Mae **Olsteen**.
　　ODESSA[6], 1910
　　LLOYD[6], 1912
　　EDITH[6], 1912
　　WARD[6]
JOHN MARION[5], 1886; m Bessie Althea **Lee**.
WILLIAM LEMUEL[5], 1888; m Mamie **Kemp**.
　　GEORGE EUGENE[6], 1911; m Dorothy Marie **Cauley**.
GUILFORD MALCOLM[5], 1890; d Bunnell FL 1973.
MARY ELIZABETH[5], 1892; m Edward E **Howard**; d Jesup GA 1969.
ELIZA JANE[5], 1894; m/1 Ira Quinton **May**; m/2 B L **Lovett**.
IRA LEE[5], 1896; m Grace Helen **Brown**; d Mayo FL.
　　RUBY LOUISE[6]
FLORA L[5], 1898; m Arthur **Brown**.
JOSEPH SPENCER[5], 1902; m Myrtle **Willberry**.
DAVID WARREN[5], 1902; m Gladys **Deese**.

6. CORNELIUS M[4] BARBER, 1862; m/1 Elizabeth **Taylor**; m/2 Margaret **Head**; r Applinig Co GA. [Ancestry.com: OneWorldTree]
　　First wife:
　　SARAH ELIZABETH[5], 1884; d Appling Co; m Levi **Deen**.
　　JOHN B[5], 1886; m Elmira ---.
　　　　SIDNEY D[6], 1910
　　　　LINDY M[6], 1912
　　　　MARTHA E[6], 1914
　　WILLIAM EMORY[5], 1888; m Emma **Thorton**.
　　　　MEARLINE ELIZABETH, 1925; m --- **Hutte**.
　　　　LAURA ESTELLE, ; m/1 --- **Cook**; m/2 --- **Dorsey**.
　　CORNELIUS A[5], 1890
　　EDDIE OLIN[5], 1893; m Ava **Jenkins**.
　　　　MANNING W[6], 1919
　　MARY E[5], 1895
　　LUCINDA[5], 1898; m Thomas **Kimbrell**.
　　LEON[5], 1900
　　JOSEPH L[5], c 1903 ; m Elsie Mae ---.
　　　　MERLE L, c 1918
　　WILLIAM EMORY[5], 1904; d 1932; m Emma **Thornton**.
　　　　MEARLINE ELIZABETH[6], 1925; m Ivey Sammie **Hutto**.
　　　　LAURA ESTELLE, 1927[6]; m/1 --- **Cook**; m/2 Glen **Dorsey**.

172

JEFFRIE[5], 1905
JEPTHA[5], 1907; m Eddie Mae **Thorton**; r Surrency, Appling Co.
EMILY[5], 1911

DR. LUKE BARBER

Dr. Luke Barber, b. 1615, Wickham Hall, Yorkshire, England, A surgeon, and member of the Cromwell Court; came to MD 1655 married Elizabeth Younge (Younger?) b. 1615/1621, England and died 1725/1726. Dr. Luke Barber was awarded 1000 acres on the Wicomico River in St Mary's MD by Lord Baltimore; res Charles Co, MD. (Governor of MD 1657-58). [Ref: Ewing: "Barber, Briscoe, Story, Yates, Hanson, and other Maryland Families" by Elizabeth Colton Ewing."]

"Barber / Barbier, Luke, St. Mary's Co., 31st July, 1664; 4th Jan., 1674. To wife Eliza:, "Michan Hall" during life. To wife eld. son Luke and his eld. son and in succession to sons Edward, Thomas and their male hrs., "Michan Hall" afsd. In event of sd. sons dying without male issue, sd. property to pass to next of kin, Barber Vel Barber. To son Edward afsd., 500 A. "Lukeland"; subject to entail. To son Thomas afsd., "Michan Hills,"; subject to entail. To eld. dau. Eliza: and young. dau. Mary, personalty. Exs.: Capt. Richard Bankes, Randall Hinson. Test: Walter Hall. 1. 534.

A surgeon, member of the Cromwell Court. Came to Maryland in 1655. Was awarded 1000 acres on the Wiconico river in St Mary's MD by Lord Baltimore.
=====
Dr. Luke Barbier 1.191 A SM #40713 Mar 9 1674
Payments to: John Blomfield who married relict (unnamed).
Administrator/Executor: Joachim Guibertt."

Spouse: Sybil, d.?. 2. Edward BARBER who married bef. 1664 Cibbil (_____. He died in 1694. Maryland Calendar of Wills: Volume 2: "Barber, Edward, St. Mary's Co., 2nd Mch., 1693; 21st May, 1694. To wife Cibbil, plantation and 200 A. during life; to revert to son Edward. To dau. Mary, of certain tract (unnamed), To unborn child, residue of sd. tract and 200 A. (unnamed) nr. Bird's Ck. To brother Thomas, rights in 300 A., part of Michan Hills, and 200 A. nr. Bird's Ck., formerly belonging to Jno. Barecroft. To cous. Thomas Nicholls, and to Adam Clarke and hrs., rights of 200 A. (unnamed). To child. afsd., residue of land equally. To godsons, Jas. Morris and Jno. Bratson, and Mary and Martha Williamson, daus. of Sam'l Williamson, personalty. In event of death of child. afsd. without issue, the child. of sister Eliza: Guibert to be co-heirs with brother Thomas afsd., and in event of death of sd. Thomas afsd. without issue, sister Mary Nichols and Ann Clarke to be co-heirs. Wife Cibbil, extx. and residuary legatee. Overseers: Thos. Clarke, Thos. Barber. Test: Sam'l Williamson, Stephen Caward, Wm. Dutch. 2. 287."

Luke BARBER
ABT 1680 - 1743
ID Number: I63856

RESIDENCE: St. Mary's Co. MD
BIRTH: ABT 1680

DEATH: 1743, St. Mary's Co. Maryland [S2930]

Father: Edward BARBER Sr.

Family 1 : Rebecca WHITE
MARRIAGE: 1704, St. Mary's Co. Maryland
+Barnett White BARBER
Notes

"Cornelius White 37C.141 A CH £150.1.3 £227.1.9 Jan 19 1716
Received from: Richard Lewellin on account of Mrs. Mason, Thomas Hebb, Will.
Farthing, Will. Jones, George Vennables, Mrs. Jane Jones, Peter Watts, Thomas
Jameson.
Payments to: Col. Henry Lowe, Mr. Richard Lewellin, Mr. Cheseldyne, Mr.
Dullany, Mr. Rogers, Mr. Macnemara for fees against administratrix of W,
Davis, Robert Hall, Charles Carroll, Esq.
Executors: John Parry, Luke Barber, Andrew Norton."

MARYLAND BARBERS, LUKE and GEORGE

(1) THE FAMILY OF LUKE BARBER OF MARYLAND

References:
Ewing = "Barber, Briscoe, Story, Yates, Hanson, and other Maryland Families" by Elizabeth
Colton Ewing (an LDS microfilm)
Sara Clark: 524 Central Ave, Lapel IN 46051
Laura Birmingham: Bama470@aol.com
Lois Trunick:
Susan Clark:
Anna S Agee, 1670 Walleye Dr, Crofton, MD 21114; at LDS FamilySearch.

FIRST GENERATION

1. DR. LUKE[1] BARBER, b Yorkshire, England c 1615; A surgeon, and member of the Cromwell Court; came to MD 1655; m Elizabeth **Younge**; she m/2 John **Bloomfield**.   Luke was awarded 1000 acres on the Wiconico river in St Mary's MD by Lord Baltimore; now in Charles Co, MD. He was Governor of MD 1657-58.   [Ref: Ewing: "Barber, Briscoe, Story, Yates, Hanson, and other Maryland Families" by Elizabeth Colton Ewing (an LDS microfilm); Abbott-Adlum-Green Families; Lt: Lois Trunick; Lt: Sara Clark; Lt: Laura Birmingham]

    ELIZABETH[2], 164?; m Joachim **Guibert**

    LUKE[2], ; no male heirs

2   EDWARD[2], c 1650; m Cibbel

3   THOMAS[2], 1661; m Mary ---; she m/2 William **James** by 1719.

    MARY[2],   ; m William **Nichols**; res Calvert Co MD.

    ANNE[2],   ; m Thomas **Clarke**

SECOND GENERATION

2. EDWARD[2] BARBER, c 1650; m Cibbel ---.   [Ref: Ewing]

    MARY[3]

4   LUKE[3], ; m 1704 Rebecca **White**

5   EDWARD[3],   ; m Sarah **Myvert**

    JOHN[3], d yg

3. THOMAS[2] BARBER, m Mary ---.

    THOMAS[3]

    JOHN[3], possibly the one b 168? And m Sarah **Pingstone** (see RZ file: Rezin and John)

    MARGARET[3],   ; m Vinson **Taylor**

THIRD GENERATION

4. LUKE[3] BARBER, c 1679; m 1704 Rebecca **White**. He inherited the family home, —Micham Hall, on Chaptico Manor estate.   [Ref: Ewing; Lt: Susan Clark]

    LUKE[4], 1710-1733

    BARNETT[4], 1708-1724

6   EDWARD[4], 1719; m Elizabeth --

    BAPTIST[4], 1713; m Elizabeth **Sotheron**

7   CORNELIUS[4], 1715; m Rebecca **Yates**

    DOROTHY[4], 1717; m Thomas Truman **Greenfield**

    ELIZABETH[4], 1706-1720

    MARY[4], 1722-1724

5. EDWARD[3] BARBER,   ; m Sarah **Myvert**.   [Ref: Ewing; Virkus: Compendium, Vol 3]

8   THOMAS[4], m ?

9   LUKE[4],   ; m Ann **Edwards**

EDWARD[4]

10   JOHN MYVERT[4], ; m Lydia **Dent**.   [Abbott-Adlum-Green Families]
        ELIZABETH[4], ; ?m Meverell **Hulls**
        SARAH[4]
        REBECCA[4], ; m William **Moran**.

FOURTH GENERATION

6. EDWARD[4] BARBER, 1719; m Elizabeth ---; r St Mary's Co MD.   [Ref: Ewing]
        PRICE[5], (daughter),
11   BARNETT WHITE[5], 1748; m Elizabeth Story **Briscoe**
        LUKE[5], c 1752

7. CORNELIUS[4] BARBER, 1715; m Rebecca **Yates**; res St Mary CO MD.
           [Ref: Ewing; Abbott-Adlum-Green Families]
        MYHARD[5], 1752-1777
        CORNELIUS WHITE[5], 1754 - ?1785. (1790CS: 3-0-1)
        HORATIO[5], 1756; d yg
        MYVERT[5], 1756; d at age 9 mo.
12   LUKE WHITE[5], 1764; m Susannah **Rowles**.

8. THOMAS[4] BARBER, c 171?; m ?; res MD.
        ?CHARLES[5], 174?; m Elizabeth ---. [Ref: DAR Lineage; IGI:MD]
        CATHARINE[6], 178?; m James **Taylor**

9. LUKE[4] BARBER, ; m Ann **Edwards**; d 1793; res St Mary's Co MD.
[Ref: Ewing; IGI:MD; Virkus Compend.,Vol 3; 1790 CS; Lt: Susan Clark]
        LUKE[5]
14   ELIAS[5], 1752; m Elizabeth **Wainwright**
15   JONATHAN[5], 1764; m Elizabeth **Swann**
        JOSEPH[5]
        JANE[5]
        EDWARD[5], ; ? m Sarah ---.   [Ref: IGI:MD]
        EDWARD[6], 1797
        JOHN[5]
        ELIZABETH[5]
        ELINOR[5]
        MARGARET[5]

10. JOHN MYVERT[4] BARBER, ; m Lydia Swann **Dent**; res St Mary's CO MD. [Ref: 1790
CS; CSL: Billingsly Gen; Melissa T Alexander: mada@atcalexanderthompson.com]
17   THOMAS[5], 1775; m/1 Mary **Amery**; m/2 Susanna **Latimer**; m/3 Margaret **Wellmore**;
m/4
     Eleanor **McCubin**.
        MARY SARAH[5], ; m Thomas **Billingsly**
        CATHERINE[5], ; m Thomas **Billingsly**, after Mary died; no children.

MARGARET, ; m --- **Estep**.
HENRIETTA, ; m James **Primm**.
SARAH, ; m ---- **Edwards**.
ESTHER
HEZEKIAH

FIFTH GENERATION

11. BARNETT WHITE[5] BARBER, 1748; m Elizabeth Story **Briscoe**; res Luckland, St Mary's
CO, MD.   [Ref: Ewing; 1790 CS]
18   LUKE PHILIP[6], 1777; m Jane Bruce **Yates**; m/2 Violetta **Harris**.
JANE STORY[6], ; m 1813 Philip Thomas **Marshall**; no ch.
EDWARD WHITE[6], c 1779; d 1796
CHLOE HANSON[6], c 1781
ELIZABETH MARGARET[6], c 1785; d 1817
REBECCA WHITE[6], c 1787; m/1 Richard **Bond**; m/2 William **Briscoe**

12. LUKE WHITE[5] BARBER, Esq, 1764; m Susannah **Rowles**; res St Mary's CO, MD.
[Ref: Ewing; Lt: Brenda Rowles Parr; 1790 CS; Bible rec:Hutchins; IGI:MD]
19   CORNELIUS[6], 1803; m Margaret C **Adlum**.
CAROLINE REBECCA[6], ; m Joshua **Hutchins**.
JOHN L[6], ; ?m Maria **Owens**.   [Ref: IGI:MD]
ALFRED[7], 1842
        ROBERT[7], 1844
        JOSHUA[7], 1844
LUKE REASON[6], 1806-28
GUSTAVUS REASON[6], ; m/1 Eleanor **Williams**; m/2 1839 Isabella **Ridgely**.

14. ELIAS[5] BARBER, 1752; m Elizabeth **Wainwright**; res St Mary's CO MD, then moved in
1794 to what is now Barber, near Cleveland, Rowan Co NC. "Had 9 children".   [Ref:
IGI:NC; IGI:MD; 1790 CS; Ms:Wm. A Yates; Lt: Sara Clark]
        SARAH[6], 1780?; m John Dyson **Swan**; res Cape Girardeau Co MO.
21   WILLIAM[6], 1783; m 1816 Margaret **Hughey**
ELIZABETH[6], ; m John **Garner**
LUKE E[6], ; m/1 Catherine Nancy **Steele**; m/2 1818 Jane **Clementine**; m/3
        1835 Jane P R **Cansio**.   [Ref: IGI:MD]
Second wife:
        CLEMENTINE[7], c 1819; m 1839 Jonathan **Barber** #16.
23   ELIAS[6], 1793; m Elizabeth H **Ross**
ANN[6], ; m 1808 Levi **Higdon**
JOHN EDWARD[6], ; m 1814 Catherine **Young**
RICHARD W[6], ; m 1816 Polly K **Foster**
MARGARET[6], ; m Alex **Neely**

15. JONATHAN⁵ BARBER, 1764; m Elizabeth **Swann**; moved 1794 to Barber, near Cleveland, Rowan Co NC.
[Ref: IGI:NC; Ms:Wm A Yates; Virkus: Compend.,Vol.3]

      CATHERINE⁶, c 179?; m Richard **Swan**; res Perry Co MO.

      NANCY⁶, (Anne), 1798; m Wilson **Turner**

      MARGARET C⁶, ; m Isaac **Lyerly.**

24   THOMAS⁶, ; m Malinda **Weir**

      GEORGE⁶, 1805; m Lydia **Ross**; res Perry Co MO. [from Angela DiBlasi at WorldConnect]

      HANNAH⁷, ; m A M **McPherson.**

         EPHRAIM⁷

         NARCISSUS⁷

         MARGARET J⁷

         PIKNEY⁷

         JONATHAN⁷

      JANE⁶, ; unm.

      SAMUEL⁶, ; m Elvira **Martin**; res Perry Co MO.   [from Angela DiBlasi at WorldConnect]

      MARGARET E⁷, 1834

         MARY JANE⁷, 1836

         JOHN L⁷, 1838

         MARTHA ANN⁷, b MO 1839

         WILLIAM M⁷, b MO 1844

         ROBERT A⁷, b MO 1847

         JAMES L⁷

      JONATHAN⁶, 180?; m Clementine **Barber** (see 15C.)   [Ref: Ms:Wm. A Yates; Virkus:Compend.,Vol.3]

      HENRY HEZEKIAH⁷, ; d yg.

         ELIZABETH CATHERINE⁷, b 181?; m Joseph Franklin **Owens**; res Cleveland NC; had ch

         MARGARET ANN⁷, ; d unm.

         JANE⁷, ; m Locke **Thompson**

         INFANT⁷

         GEORGE⁷, ; d yg.

         WILLIAM PLEASANT⁷, ; m Martha **Walton**

         FRANCIS⁷, ; d yg.

         NANCY⁷, ; d yg.

      ELIZABETH⁶, ; d yg.

17. THOMAS⁵ BARBER, 1775; m/1 Mary **Amery**, who d 1796; m/2 1808 Susanna **Latimer**, d 1816; m/3 1819 Margaret **Wellmore**, d 1822; m/4 1824 Eleanor **McCubin**; res Baltimore MD, late.   [Ref: Barber Family Bible]

    First wife:

    MARY A⁶, 1796; m George **Slye**

    Second wife:

    LYDIA C⁶, 1809; m Chapman **Billingsley**

CAESAR A[6], 1811-1825

SIXTH GENERATION

18. DR. LUKE PHILIP[6] BARBER, 1777; m/1 Jane Bruce **Yates**; m/1 Violetta **Harris**; res
Prince George Co MD.   [Ref: Ewing]
     EDWARD BARNETT WHITE[7], 1804-1845; unm
     DR LUKE PHILIP JR[7], 1805-1875; unm.
25   CORNELIUS WHITE[7], 1819; m Elizabeth **Plummer**
     JONATHAN YATES[7], 1807; m Mary Wheeler **Kent**. ; r Silver Stone, Calvert Co MD.
[Anna S Agee]
     THOMAS KENT[8], 1842
         JOHN YATES[8], 1840; m Jane **Garner**.
         MARGARET K[8], 1850
         LYDIA[8], 1857
         Dr. PHILIP[8], 1833
         MARY J[8], 1845
         SALLY JANE[8], 1835; m William Boswell **Scrivener**.
     ELIZABETH[7], 1808; m Richard **Reeder**
     WALTER BRUCE[7], 1812-1881; unm
     SAMUEL HANSON BRISCOE[7], 1810-1849; unm
     MARY[7], 1813; m Joseph **Shemwell**
     YATES[7], 1822; m Eliza Crane **Morgan**
     REBECCA WHITE[7], 1817-1845; unm
     JANE BRUCE YATES[7], 1815; m William **Briscoe**

19. CORNELIUS[6] BARBER, 1803-1853; m Margaret C **Adlum**. She m/2 John **Bloomfield**.
Res. St Marys Co MD, and Georgetown, Washington DC. [Ref: Ewing; Abbott-Adlum-Green
Fam.]
     JOHN ADLUM[7], 1838; m/1 Fannie Ravenscroft **Brockenbrough** (d 1873); m/2
Margaret Green **Walls**. [Abbott-
Adlum-Green Fam]
     First wife:
         CORNELIUS[8],   ; m Sara **Cruxe**.
         MARGARET C ADLUM[8],   ; m William C **Looker**, Sr.
         EUGENIA FAUNTLEROY[8], 1874; m Cadwallader **Woodville**.
         FRANCES BROCKENBROUGH[8], 1866; m John William **Henry**.
     Second wife:
         MARY WALLS[8],   ; m Frederick Antes **Godcharles**.
     SUSAN ROWLES[7], 1842-49
     MARY VIRGINIA[7], 1843-49
     CAROLINE R YATES[7], ; d age 1 mo, 4 d.
     MARGARET[7] ADLUM, 1846; d young.
     LUKE WHITE[7], ; d 1 mo 6 d.

21. WILLIAM[6] BARBER, 1783; m Margaret **Hughey**; res Rowan Co NC.   [Ref: Lt: Sara Clark]
26   Rev. RICHARD WAINWRIGHT[7], 1823; m widow of John P **Peden**.

23. ELIAS[6] BARBER, 1793; m Elizabeth H **Ross**; res Perry Co MO.   [Ref: Ms:Wm. A Yates]
ROBERT WAINWRIGHT[7], 1825; m/1 Elizabeth **Garety**; ?m/2 Ada R ---; res. Cape Girardeau, Cape Gir. Co MO,
near Perry and Wayne Cos. [1880 CS: Cape Girardeau Co]
JOSEPH[8], 1860
THOMAS C[8], 1866
ROBERT[8], 1868
ADA BELLE[8], 1876
JOSEPH WILEY[7], 1828-49
JOHN EDWARDS[7], 1830; m Mary E **Slaughter**; res. Cowan, Wayne Co MO. [1880 CS: Wayne Co]
ROSA A[8], 1865
AUGUSTA[8], 1867
JAMES N[8], 1869
SARAH B[8], 1874
FLORA M[8], 1876
JOHN C[8], 1878
BARTON R[8], 1880
NANCY MATILDA[7], 1832; m --- **Garner**
LUKE[7], 1832
ELIZABETH CATHERINE[7], 1835; m Abel **Swan**
HANNAH ISABELLA[7], 1838-40
SARAH JANE[7], 1840; m --- **Oswald**
ELIAS NOBLE[7], 1842; m ?Irene **Noble**
RICHARD HARRIS[7], 1845, m Columbia **Cline**; res Cowan?, Wayne Co MO. [1880 CS: Wayne Co]
DURETTE[8], 1870
CORA C[8], 1872
ELNORA[8], 1874
CHARLES[8], 1876
CLARENCE[8], 1878
CARRIE[8], 1880
MARGARET ROSANAH[7], 1847; m Thomas **Swan**
AMANDA ADELIA[7], 1847; m --- **Milster**
LYDIA NARCISSA[7], 1850-64

24. THOMAS[6] BARBER, c 1800; m Malinda **Weir**. [from Angela DiBlasi at WorldConnect]
MARGARET[7], ; m Otho **Lyerly**.
WILLIAM[7], ; m Jane **Marlin**.
Rev. SAMUEL SWANN[7], ; m/1 Sarah **Patrick**; m/2 Adelaide **Mayhew**.
First wife:

FRANCIS COLLIN[8]
LAURA[8], ; m George **Brown**.
Rev. HENRY HOBART[8], ; m Sallie **Wolfenden**.
THOMAS PATRICK[8]
Second wife:
Rev. MILTON AUGUSTUS[8], ; m Henrietta ---.
CATHERINE E[7], ; m George **Keller**.
NANCY AMANDA[7], ; m Milton **Cowan**.
JANE MALINDA[7]
THOMAS DAVIS[7]
MARY ELIZA[7]

SEVENTH GENERATION

25. CORNELIUS WHITE[7] BARBER, 1819; m Elizabeth Plummer.   [Ref: Ewing]
ALBERT PLUMMER[8]
CORNELIUS BRUCE[8]
PHILIP YATES[8], ; m Lucy Briscoe **Young**   [Ref: Ewing]
PHILIP ALBERT[9], 1872
    ELIZABETH PLUMMER[9], 1873
    HELEN BRUCE[9], 1874
    ROBERT YOUNG[9], 1878
    LUCY BRISCOE[9], 1880
    JENNIE DEAN[9], 1881
    YATES MIDDLETON[9], 1885
    TOWNLEY WHITE[9], 1886; d yg
    EDWARD[9], 1889; d yg
    STANLEY WHITE[9], 1887

26. Rev. RICHARD WAINWRIGHT[7] BARBER, 1823; m widow of John P **Peden**; res
Wilkesboro, Wilkes Co NC.   [Ref: Lt: Sara Clark]
 27   WILLIAM WAINWRIGHT[8], 1855; m Mariana Martitia **Wilcox**
    MARY TAYLOR[8]

EIGHTH GENERATION

27. WILLIAM WAINWRIGHT[8] BARBER, 1855; m Mariana Martitia **Wilcox**; a lawyer, State
Senator; res Wilkesboro NC.   [Ref: Lt: Sara Clark]
MARGARET TAYLOR[9], ; m William Carroll **Moore** II.
WILLIAM WILCOX[9], ; m Zola **Gage**   [Ref: Lt: Sara Clark]
MARY GAGE[10]
    ELIZABETH WORTH[10]
ELIZABETH WORTH[9]
JOSEPH RICHARD[9],   ; m Nell **Somers**   [Ref: Lt: Sara Clark]

JOSEPH RICHARD[10]
SARAH ANN[1]

Dr. Lois Green Carr
Men's Career Files
MSA SC 5094

Barber, Luke   d. 1668   immi. free   Newtown

Date first rec. 1655 last rec. 1683   Arr. 1655
                      last rec. clue Newt/68
Wife: Elizabeth   who married John Blomfield

Occupation: Planter, Doctor

Office: Councillor July 10, 1656-1660
        Provincial Court 1656-1660

Religion: Roman Catholic   Literate   Dr. Gent
            prob petition for
Testate: yes but executor renounced executorship so   considered intestate.

Tev: 169.64   Labor: 0   Debts: 34.53   Bal: 159.19

Householder: yes

Children: Elizabeth who mar. Joachim Guibert; Luke, Edward, Thomas, Mary, and Ann Barber.

John Bloomfield left two children to the care of John Taunt. (see Taunts will)

        Barber had been in the army under the Lord Protector and also in his household
        as a domestic servant.

                                        MSA SC 5094 - 228

Dr. Lois Green Carr
Men's Career Files
MSA SC 5094

Blo[..]!hld· John	Bo m1	Died I 1692	Immigrant:free	Hundred: Chaptico
		(bond)		Newtowen ..
				St. Mary's City 1671
lat rec· 1667	lat rec1 1 1		Arrheclt here 'b7 1666/f	

t--rd:. ·....,,ve: 1 ·'8<1

Whnl UiNbeth ·· BloaCield by 1669· to'''erl7 ·· to Wke 1 r/ Bloathlcl bhr urrhd
,.rt>" John Twllt 11 111ter. Tnllt ldJire, Blo ield'· tate. ': \\.d .., ...;''\c..·>
f)f'   ;.,s.c ... -· '1'-·" ....

OcCUJiat.ioa l innholder. clerk, ettor11e7 ;r *-*-..

O!tic··· Minora Appra1Hr- 1671. 1672. 1677· 1682
            AttorMY o! the court ·1worn Dec. 8· 1668

Other: Chief Clerk o! the SecretarJ'· Office of the rro·- Ct. end Counoll – epptd ·
,.,,,,_ · . \:   H17 1669 – Ju}J' 1670J Mar, 1673/liJ reocoa. bJ Lt. G1n. Apr _ 1676
.(·''' ·_ Clerk o! the Couacil – "-1 1669 – .Jv}J' 1670; Aug. 167la
''''''l)a...·;. Clerk ot the Perocatin Office – pptd. MBJ 1668 – drtvea !roa office 'b7 tbe
            Proteatent AlBochtor· Jue. 1689
            Clerk o! St,)!erJ'I Co, – epptd. prtor to Apr. 1686 · forced out bJ t. .-.!
            Proteahnt Auocbtou SIJ!t 1689
            'f-ottfltA <00Jf ✓

| Relicionl Catholie1" | Literacy: literate / | Titles called Oent. in 161/J – frequent |
| | | 1)' re!. to ·· Gent.. t.bereetter |

Houeehold·r· yea   Testate: no

TEV1 8L.o6   Labor: 0   Debts Receiv: 42,76   Balence: (-19.23)

Children: son Patrick; dau. Maryeena; ? [...] d.1718 ; stepchildren – MSx SC 5094-434

Dr. Lois Green Carr
Women's Career Files
MSA SC 4040

```
                        P.  ! ( ··              ··   ···  ·· - 74
                                              First record: 16·8        ·ast: ···
          ·ame: Elizabeth ·arbier ·lomfield
                                                          ·usbands:        P. · ···
          Status: widow, wife                            First: Luke ·arbier
                                                         ID#: 21.2 ···· ···  · · 8
          Children:                                       ·eath: 1668
          ·ro· first husband: ·,·.: ·lizabeth (m. ·.·····t by ···)   ·econd: John ·lomfield
                             Luke ·r.                     ID#: 959 ·· ·## ·34
                             ·dward                       ·eath: 16·2
                             Thomas                       married by: 1669
                             ·ary
                             ·nn
          ·ro· ·econd husband: ·,·.: ·atrick
                             ·aryeena                        ·areers on next card...
                             Jamaele
                             ·ay ·e another.

          ·nheritance:
          ·rom first husband: Adnin. of estate and "·ichan ·all" for life
          ·rom ·econd husband: ·lizabeth was his first wife, and died before he did.
```

rchives of Maryland Onlin

search   this volume

Maryland State Archives | Index | Help | Search

Slave Statistics of St. Mary's County Maryland, 1864, Commissioner George B. Dent by Agnes Kane Callum
Volume 369, Page 48 View pdf image (33K)   Jump to page   *60*   << PREVIOUS NEXT

48.

OWNER Dr. Luke P. Barber by his Attorney Richard H.

Reeder,
DATE August ?, 1867

Name Of Slave	Sex	Age	Emancipated by State of Maryland	Remarks
Westly Smith	M	32		E-Jan. 5, 1864
James W. Yates	M	21		19th. USCT E-Jan. 5, 1864
Henry Brown	M	19	Nov. 1, 1864	19th. USCT
Filmor Brown	M	18	Nov. 1, 1864	
Webster Brown	M	15	Nov. 1, 1864	
Columbus Brown	M	15	Nov. 1, 1364	
Robert Dyson	M	12	" " "	
William Young	M	8	" " "	
Albert Young	M	6	" " "	
Samuel Butler	M	65	" " "	
Lydia Brown	F	45	" " "	
Gilbert Brown	M	15	" " "	
Josephine Brown	F	18	" " "	
Rosetta Young	F	30	" " "	
Ann Young	F	31	" " "	
Kizzy Ann Young	F	5	" " "	
Ann Tolbert	F	14	" " "	
Rebecca Brown	F	18	" " "	(102)
Jane Brown	F	2	" " "	
Martha Ann Brown	F	8	" " "	
				No. of Slaves #20

Dr. Luke Barber (Guardian to
Philip Y. Barber & Cornelius B. Barber)
by his Attorney Richard H. Reeder -Owners
August 7, 1867

John?	Gorden?	M	65	Nov. 1, 1864	
Thomas	Seward	M	40	Nov. 1	E-Jan. 5, 1864

Cornelius	Gorden?	M	21	, 1864	
Yates	Steward	M	18	" " "	
Morgan	Steward	M	16	" " "	
John	Steward	M	12	" " "	
Jenifer	Steward	M	10	" " "	
Bruce	Steward	M	8	" " "	
James	Yates	M	6	" " "	
Grant	Yates	M	5	" " "	
Matilda	Gorden?	F	50	" " "	
Estelle?	Young	F	25	" " "	
Eliza	Steward	F	40	" "	(103)
Mary R.	Steward	F	14	" " " "	
Lydia	Steward	F	6	" "	
Mary	Steward		28	" " " "	
Lucy A.	Yates	F	4	" " "	
Roseanna	Steward	F	3	" " "	
					No. Of Slaves #18

Dr. Lois Green Carr
Men's Career Files
MSA SC 5094

Guitert, Joshua F: 1645 D: 1713 Immig from Rheims, France - naturalized
1679
Late 1st Rec: 1669 Last Rec: 1721   Hundred: Chaptico 1671
last rec. alive   see 18th c. St, Clements by 1695
Arrived by:1667 file #10196
Wife: Elizabeth, eldest dau. of Luke Barbier by 1673
Occupation: Planter, Merchant 1682

Offices: Major: JP St. Marys 1674-1713   Minor: Commissioner for the town
Assembly 1708   of St. Marys 1708
Jury 1651
Appraiser 1675, '72, '84, '77
& '98

Householder: yes

Religion: Protestant Literacy: Literate Titles: gent

Testate: yes TLV: see 18th c. file Step daughter
Children: Joshua #11088 d. 1743 Thomas d.1729, Matthew #11227 d.1752
Elizabeth m. 1) John Blakiston 2) Thomas Turner 3). J.B
Carberry and Anne

REF.: John Blakiston #10330
Ann Blakiston Pippard
NSA SC 5094 - 1696

Dr. Lois Green Carr
Men's Career:..fi_les
MSA SC 5094

Image No: sc5094-0229-1 Enlarge and print image (8K)   << PREVIOUS NEXT>>

B&rher, wl<e Jr. Bol"Tl: Died: lli'Cidr.rant: ndred t   New town
                                            \Ot   r-·   ......,
Pate first rec: 1657   last rec: 169)/4 Date arrived Datefree :
                    Last recorded alive :1693/4

'1ii/nι:
l'alherr Luite Barber #24 '2 died 1668
             1 t..l.-4..   - ٦ \―   <..rn\ιP ιd.,_   ρ ᴄ᠍ᴸᴸ᠍ᴜ᠍ᴜᴏ=

Occupation
Otric&s
Religion   Literacy   Title

Testate
TIN
Children

189

Image: sc4040-0075-1   Enlarge and print image (2M)   << PREVIOUS NEXT >>

Name: Elizabeth Barbier   First record: 1664   Last: 167_
                                           Not married on date of record
Status: daughter   Generation: 1r

Daughter of:
Father: Luke Barber

Inheritance:
Father: 100 L sterling on her marriage day to be paid from England.

and a share in fathers estate.

Dr. Lois Green Carr
Men's Career Files
MSA SC 5094

Image No: sc5094-0221-01   Enlarge and print image (16K)   << PREVIOUS   NEXT >>

Barber, Edward   Born: bet. 1658   Died: 1694   Native   Hundred: Chaptico
(Barbier) #1043   & 1664*   (will &   "LURELAND"
                                      bond)
1st rec: 1664   last rec: 1700/1 last alive 1694   1st Generation
                   correc. cause; 1693/4
Father: Dr. Luke Barber #242 who d. 1674
Siblings: Luke, Thomas * 10Jan 1715; Eliz m J.Garbert; Mary m Nichols; Ann m Thos CLARE;
Wives: Sibilla(Cibill, Isabelle) his wife at time of his death; she married William Holmes
   .. by 1695(he is also called William Holins)
occupation : prob. planter

                         Literacy: literate   — m info 13** c.
                                                       per. Cncl m Assembly.
Householder: yes

Testate: yes.

TEV: 51.00   Labor: 0   Debts Receiv: 2.29   Balance: 31.91

Children: sons Luke & Edward; dau. Mary; unborn child

* called age 32 inv. which would be born 1662

                                                  MSA SC 5094-221

191

Dr. Lois Green Carr
Men's Career Files
MSA SC 5094

Barber, Edward   Died: 1764   Native   Hundred: St. Clement's or
#11787   Newtown
                     18th c file: #11787 inv. 1764   R.P. = West ham
1st rec: 1693/4   last rec: 1708(this file) ∧ 2nd Generation
Married. Sarah — 1st rec. ca. w.c ; 18th c file: #.11787
Father: Edward Barber #1063 who d. 1694; grandson of Luke 0242 d.1674
Mother: Isabella
Literacy: illiterate
Occupation
See 18th century file #11787 for further information.

Testate: Wills 32: 266

Inv: 84: 305-9; Acct. 53:89

OFFICES:
Title
Religion

no info 18th C.
Pro. Crul Armly

Children: John   Elizabeth, Sarah, Rebecca, Luke, Edward, Thomas, Mary
         Minort
         vinbor, eyer
    Kin Lacy & Sary Barber   MSA SC 5094-222

Dr. Lois Green Carr
Women's Career Files
MSA SC 4040

Name: Cibill (Sibilla) Barber Hollins   First record: 1694   Last: 1695   *1693/ Sc 4040 — 73*

Status: widow and wife   Husbands:
                                               first: Edward Barber
Children: ID#: 1043   *Sm# 221*
fisrt husbands: Luke   Death: 1694
marriage.   Edward   Occupation: planter
                Mary   TEV: 51.00   Lab: 0   DEbts Rec: 2.29
                an unborn child   Balance: 31.91
                                               Land:1500+a.
from second marriage: unk.

Inheritance:
first husband: Dwelling plantation for life and all personal goods. She was also the
               execr. of his estate.
Second husband: unk.

                                               Second husband: Willaim Hollins (Holmes)
                                               ID#: unk.   *Sm# 2046*
                                               Death: last record, 1698
                                               Career and status: unk.   *offc. App.*
                                               Land: what the marriage to Cibill brought,
                                                     the dwelling plantation.

Dr. Lois Green Carr
Men's Career Files
MSA SC 5094

Image No: sc5094-0230-1 Enlarge and print image (8K)   << PREVIOUS NEXT >>

Barber, Luke   Born: 1682   Died: 1743   Native

1st rec: 1693   last rec: 1708(this file)   2nd Generation
                  (cross rec, allow:1708 C + his f.(2)
Father: Edward Barber #1043 who d. 1694

Did not find him in 18th century inventory file.

Edward
Son of Luke Barber
d 1668
242

Dr. Lois Green Carr
Men's Career Files
MSA SC 5094

Barber, Thomas   b. ca. 1661   d. 1718   Native 1st Gen.   St. Mary's Co. *Chaptico Hundred*
10360
Date first record: ~~1694~~ *1694*   date last alive: ~~1718~~ *(202 CVMS file)* Mitcham Hills at ~~Chaptico~~   date last record: ~~1718~~ *1722*
Father: Dr. Luke Barber #0242, d. ~~1694~~ *1668*   *& DEC 18th C file # 10360*
Mother: Elizabeth, who mar. 2nd John Bloomfield
Siblings: Luke; Edward #1043 d. 1694; Elizabeth, mar. Joshua Buibert;

        Mary Nichols; & Ann who mar. Thomas Clark.
Wife: Mary Barber alias Jameston admr. with Mr. William Jameston. acct
Children: , daughter who married Thomas Sanders
        also Thomas; Luke; John; Elias d. w. i. 1743; Elizabeth. . One child died
                                before accounting.   *(LSW in Genealogy dept)*
Occupation: probably planter. Merchant.
Offices: appraiser. Commissioned to seek out a fugitive Indian 1697
Literacy: yes   Titles: Mr.
Householder: yes   Testate: no
Tev: £786.12.7½   Labor: 12 slaves valued £270.5.0

MCa SC 5094-232

195

Dr. Lois Green Carr
Men's Career Files
MSA SC 5094

Image No: sc5094-0231   Enlarge and print image (5K)   << PREVIOUS   NEXT >>

Barber, Luke

date first record   alive: 1727/8   2nd gen

Father: Thomas Barber d.1718 #10360

picture law km. Thomas Sanders - etc.

MSA SC 5094 - 231

196

Image: sc4040-0078-1 Enlarge and print image (2M)   << PREVIOUS NEXT >>

sc4040 - 78

Name: Mary Barber   First record: ~~1671~~ last: ~~1689~~

Status: daughter   Not married at time of father's will.

Daughter of:
father: Edward Barber
mother: Sibill

Not married...

Inheritance:
from father: a). plantation whereon Andrew Hilton now lives with ½ the land of the
                  fork whereon it lyes.
              b). the other ½ to child my wife is with if the child lives, otherwise it
                  goes to Mary
              c). 400 a. equally with Luke and Edward
              d). 1 feather bed and 1 iron pot at decease of wife.
              e). 1 cow.
              f). equal share of estate with her brothers and sisters.
              g). 100 L sterling to be paid on her marriage day from money in Eng.

197

sc 4040 - 77

Mary Barbier   WillsI, 534
Jul. 31, 1664
Jan. 4, 1674 /

Testator: Luke Barbier
to Mary Barbier

&100 sterling to be paid on day of marriage out of money in England

COPY - LAST WILL AND TESTAMENT, EDWARD BARBER (1693)

Copied (1927) by Rev. R.B. Owens from a certified copy belonging to R.P. Yates Barber of Sharps, Virginia. Original is recorded in the Maryland Land Office at Annapolis in Book (Will Book) No. 2, folio 287.

IN THE NAME OF GOD, AMEN

I, Edward Barber, being sick and weak in body, but in perfect mind and memory thanks be to god, do hereby make my last will and testament, that is to say first I bequeath my soul unto Almighty God, trusting through the merits of our Lord and Saviour Jesus Christ to find mercy and remission of sins, and next my body to the earth from whence it came, and a decent Christian burial.

First I give and bequeath unto my beloved wife Cibbill the plantation whereon I now live, with two hundred acres of land joining to it during her life, and after her decease to return to my son Edward.

Item. I give unto my son Luke all that plantation and land belonging to me lying in New Town Hundred upon Nevits Creek in Breton's Bay called Micham Hall, and all the rest of the dividit of land whereon I now live, except the plantation where Andrew Hillton now lives with three hundred acres of land belonging to it.

198

Item. I give unto my daughter Mary the plantation whereon Andrew Hillton now lives with half the land of that fork wherein it lies that belongs to me, the other half to my wife now being with child, I give unto that child if it lives; if not, the whole to my daughter Mary and her heirs forever.

Item. I give unto my brother Thomas Barber all my right and title of three hundred acres of land called Micham Hills and also of two hundred acres joining next to the plantation that was Mr. Jo Bearcraft's near Birds Creek.

Item. I give my right and title of the next two hundred acres of that tract to be equally divided between my cousins Thomas Nichols and Adam Clark and their heirs forever.

Item. I give unto the child my wife is now with the plantation near Birds Creek whereon Mr. Bearcraft did live with the two hundred acres of land it is on.

Item. I give the other four hundred acres to be equally divided among my other three children, to say my son Luke, daughter Mary, and son Edward.

Item. I give unto my children every one a cow properly to be their own not of my stock of cattle.

Item. I give unto my godson James Morris one cow yearling, and to my godson John Bratson one cow yearling.

Item. I give one cow yearling with her increase to between Mary and Martha Williamson, daughters of Samuel Williamson.

Item. I give unto my beloved wife Cibbill my household goods during her life, and after her decease I give unto my son Luke one feather bed and covering, and to my daughter Mary one feather bed and covering also, and to my son Edward one flock bed and covering, and to my child my wife is now great with my two chests and one brass warming pan, and to Luke, Mary and Edward to each one iron pot.

I appoint my beloved wife Cibbill to be my whole Executrix and to see that all my debts are justly paid, and my will and desire is that if in case the Lord Baltimore shall be desirous and appoint his agents to make restitution for the land belonging to me in Chaptico Manor, that it shall be in Beaver Dam Manor and to there received and divided as aforesaid peaceably, this my will and desire. And with all I also appoint that if my children shall die without issue, that the heirs of my sister Elizabeth Tuybert shall take proportionably to be coheirs with my brother Thomas, and in case Thomas dies without issue that the heirs of his sister Mary Nichols and Ann Clark shall take part in like manner. Lastly, I appoint Thomas Clark and Thomas Barber to be overseers of this my will and to see that my children be carefully brought up, this my will and desire is. As witness my hand and seal this second day of March 1693.

EDWARD BARBER (seal)

Signed and Delivered

in presence of us: Samuel Williamson - William Dutch - Stephen Cawood

On the back of the foregoing will was endorsed this viz.

MEMORANDUM.

That on the 21st day of this instant May 1694, came before me Samuel Williamson, Stephen Cawood and William Dutch and took their corporal oaths upon the Holy Evangelists that they saw the within mentioned Edward Barber sign, seal and deliver the within mentioned Will as his Last Will and Testament and that they know no other, and also at the same time was of perfect understanding and good memory.

As witness my hand this day, hear above specified.
Philip Briscoe

LAST WILL AND TESTAMENT, EDWARD BARBER (1764)

Son of Edward Sr., and grandson of Dr. Luke Barber of Micham Hall. Recorded in will book T.A. page 458 in the Court House at Leonardstown, Maryland. Copied by Rev. R.B. Owens, April 26, 1927.

IN THE NAME OF GOD, AMEN

I, Edward Barber, being very sick and weak in body, but in perfect mind and memory thanks to God, do here make my Last Will and Testament, that is to say first I bequeath my soul unto Almighty God, trusting through the merits of our Lord and Saviour Jesus Christ to find mercy and remission of my sins; then next, my body to the earth from which it came, and to a decent Christian burial.

First - I give unto my three daughters, Elizabeth, Sarah and Mary Barber liberty to work on any part of my land during the time of their living single.

Then I give and bequeath to my beloved wife Sarah, the Plantation whereon I now live, being a part of Westham, and a part of a tract of land joining on Westham where my son Luke now lives, being a part of Swans Forest, and LukeLand during her natural life, and after her death Westham and Swans Forest to be equally divided between my three sons - Edward, Luke and John Mivart, and after their deaths to the male heirs of their bodies lawfully begotten, forever, and LukeLand to my son Thomas and his heirs of his body lawfully begotten forever.

Item. I give unto my beloved wife Sarah, four negroes, Lige, Jude, Joss and Doll, for her use during her natural life, and then to return to my four sons, Thomas, Edward, Luke and John Mivart to be equally divided.

Item. I give and bequeath to my daughter Elizabeth Barber, two negroes, Eaton and Ester. I give to my daughter Mary the use of two negroes, Monica and Jenny during her natural life and then to her children to be equally divided.

Item. I give unto my daughter Sarah two negroes, Hagar and James during her natural life and then heirs, and if she dies without an heir, to return back.

Item. I give unto my granddaughter Rebecca, one feather bed and covering.

Item. I give and bequeath unto my beloved wife Sarah, Sons - Edward and John Mivart, Daughters - Elizabeth and Sarah, all the stock of cattle and hogs, to be equally divided.

Item. I give unto my beloved wife Sarah, daughters Elizabeth and Sarah all my horses and mares to be equally divided. I appoint my son John Mivart and my daughter Elizabeth to be my whole Executors and to see that all my just debts be paid out of what money I have by me and what is left of the money after my debts are paid to be equally divided between my beloved wife Sarah, son John Mivart, daughters Elizabeth and Sarah. This my will and desire is, as witness my hand and seal this_____day of April 1764.

EDWARD BARBER (seal)
His / Mark

Signed, sealed and published
in the presence of:

Edward Barber
Thomas Nettle
Mooviol Lock, Jr. Probated June 26, 1764

History of Neely and Allied Families

Neelys from Tyrone Ireland 1730 according to Pennsylvania records
Settled in York Co, now Adams Co; Samuel came to PA -4 sons
Richard Neely, earliest known ancestor to come to Rowan Co, NC
? Son of Samuel Neely; b. 1731 (on gravestone); m. Mary Duncan (b. 1732, d. 1791), d. 1801 (on gravestone), will in Rowan Co in County Clerk's office in old yellow book on highest shelf Deed in Rowan Co dated 1778 to Richard Neely for 627 acres on the waters of Hunting Creek, now Davie Co. It was in Richard Neely's home that General Green's hungary, defeated, worn out men rushed after being pursued by Cornwallis men at Renchus Ford January 19, 1791. Richard Neely opened a barrel of sorgum and fed them, he filled a new wagon with bacon, meal, molasses, home spun and woven blankets, shirts, britches, spun and woven by his wife and daughter, Betsy. They were lost in the swollen Yadkin River for which his son Francis later received pay.

ch Alexander (oldest), m. Margaret Barber (sister to William
Barber, grandfather of Mrs B.C. Clement and Richard N. Barber),

killed by one of Cornwallis officer's who went to his home and
told his wife she would find her husband down the road sitting
under an apple tree (served in American Revolution, 2nd Batallion,
North Carolina, his war service is recorded in North Carolina War
Records; he leaves descendents in North Carolina)

Francis, b. 15 October 1761 in Rowan Co, m. 2 December 1793
Mary Holeman (b. 30 October 1771, d. 16 July 1829, bur. in Van
Eaton Cemetery in Davie Co, dau. of Isaac Holeman who rendered
Revolutionary service; Mary lived near Old Samem Church in Davie
Co before she moved to her new home that Francis built near the
banks of Hunting Creek), bur. in Van Eaton Cemetery in Davie Co,
will in Book H, page 472 in Rowan Co (served in Revolution; he and
Carson Guffey were returning from collecting horses and mules for
General Green's Army when they rushed to cross the river unaware
that Cornwallis Army had camped there beside the swollen river.
Neely and Guffey were recognized and Guffey was shot from his
house and killed. Francis loosed his horses jumped into the cane
break and on down the river, where he remained until after dark
when he discarded his clothes and swam the swollen river and onto his home of his anxious
parents)

Arthur Neely ? son of Francis, b. 20 February 1795, m. 1826 Isabella
Welch (b. 20 November 1795, d. 1 January 1839, dau. of John Francis
Welch {b. in Rowan Co, m. 24 December 1802 Josephine "Fanah" Adams,
will dated 30 March 1842 recorded in Mocksville names his daughter
Isabella, son of Thomas Welch ((m. 28 October 1772 in Rowan Co Jane
Thompson {{dau. of Henry Thompson}}, killed 1781 by one of Cornwallis
men, friend and neighbor of Daniel Boone)), no siblings}, d. 12 May 1872
ch Rebecca, b. 16 January 1835 in Davie Co, m. 5 November 1853
Jacob Franklin Barber (b. 25 February 1826 in Rowan Co, d. 4
August 1878, son of **William Barber** {b. 12 March 1783 in St Mary's
Co, MD, m. Margarey Hughey ((b. 12 August 1793, d. 15 February
1855 in Rowan Co, dau. of Jacob Hughey and Margaret Cook)), d. 1
December 1854 in Rowan Co, son of **Elias Barber** and Elizabeth
Wainwright}), d. 22 May 1880 (ch. Lina Barber Clement, Lillie
Barber Summerell, William A. Barber, Richard Neely Barber, Edward
W. Barber)

The stairwell in the Jacob Franklin Barber house on the Richard W. Barber Farm is made of hand hewed heart pine. Becky Lloyd stands on the pine steps. The farm has been in the family since 1794. photo by Wayne Hinshaw, Salisbury Post

The Jacob Franklin Barber house on the Richard W. Barber Farm was built in 1854. The farm has been in the family since 1794 with many historic outbuildings still in good condition. photo by Wayne Hinshaw, Salisbury Post
By Lee Barnes

lbarnes@salisburypost.com

A statewide preservation organization has honored two Rowan County sisters for their decision to preserve their 200-year-old family farm.

Joyce Ann Barber and Rebecca Barber Floyd are among this year's Preservation North Carolina's winners of the Gertrude S. Carraway Award of Merit. The award is named for a New Bern activist who led the push to rebuild Tryon Palace in the 1950s.

The organization calls the sisters "heroes" for preserving their father's 241-acre farm instead of selling it for development.

The sisters worked with Preservation North Carolina and the Land Trust for Central North Carolina to get protective covenants for the property, which includes houses built in 1854 and 1870. The property is along U.S. 70 and has railroad access, which would have made it a prime site for redevelopment.

The covenants mean the sisters have essentially donated and sold development rights on the property to Land Trust, a Salisbury-based conservation agency that works to preserve farmland in 10 counties. Work on restoring the property began in earnest in 1989, after Hurricane Hugo made a mess of part of the farm. The Floyds, living in Athens, Ga., at the time, began splitting their between Georgia and the farm. For the past five years, they've lived in the restored 1854 house.

Elias Barber from Maryland started the farm in 1794. In 1939, Richard Wainwright Barber bought the land from other members of the family and introduced modern farming techniques. In 1947, his farm won awards for both its corn and cotton crops.

He died in 1977.

Floyd and her husband Charles now live in the restored 1854 Franklin Barber House. Joyce Ann Barber is in a nursing home. Handicapped since birth, she worked for 20 years in the N.C. Orthopedic Hospital in Gastonia.

A step back in time at first Rowan County Historic Landmark farm

No Original Caption
By Jessie Burchette

jburchette@Salisburypost

BARBER JUNCTION — Each day, thousands of motorists whiz by on U.S. 70, caught up in the rush to get to work, to shop or get from one interstate to the other.

A few hundred yards off one of the county's busiest roads, the Richard Wainwright Barber Farm has all the trappings of a trip back in time.

Its structures of heart pine and logs were built in the time of horse and mule power, a time when hand tools and muscles ruled.

The farm and its rich black soil sloping off the gentle hill are hemmed in by four-lane U.S. 70, Redmon Road and U.S. 801. A railroad track to Mount Ulla cuts through the 241-acre farm.

On the National Register of Historic Places, and designated a Century Farm by the N.C. Department of Agriculture, earlier this year the Rowan County Board of Commissioners designated it the first Rowan County Historic Landmark farm.

During discussions in July, commissioners admitted they were skeptical of designating an entire farm as a historic landmark, but they were won over by the evidence of the farm's agricultural significance.

And commissioners also hailed the family's do-it-yourself effort to preserve the land and the structures through permanent conservation and preservation easements.

The family waived a provision that would have given them a 50 percent reduction in taxes.

An official with the N.C. Department of Cultural Resources wrote a letter supporting the farm's designation as a landmark.

The coordinator noted the designation as a landmark means the community recognizes the property as an important historic resource worthy of preservation.

"The Richard Wainwright Barber farm is a remarkable surviving agricultural complex in Rowan County. In the ownership of the same family since the 18th century, it includes 17 identified resources including dwellings, farm buildings, and landscape features. The Barber Farm property is significant both historically and architecturally from the mid-19th century through the 1950s," wrote the coordinator.

The farm is also called Luke Land after the family's ancestral home in St. Mary's County Maryland.

Elias Barber (1754-1842) acquired the land after arriving in Rowan County from Maryland in 1794 with his brother. Barber Junction is named for the family.

The farm passed from Elias to his son, William (1783-1854). It then passed to William's son, Jacob Franklin (1826-1876) and then to Jacob's son, William A. (1856-1934).

William A. Barber's son Richard Wainright Barber bought the interests of other family members in 1939 and moved from Mount Ulla to the Barber farm.

The earliest buildings on the farm date to circa 1854 and were built by William's son Jacob Franklin Barber (1826 - 1876).

Here's a summary of the structures and other key information provided by the county's Landmark Commission:

- The Richard Wainwright Barber Farm has been in the continuous ownership of the Barber family since 1794.

- The farm is one of the most intact 19th and 20th century agricultural complexes in Rowan County.

- Jacob Franklin Barber house (1854) built by James Graham, who also built the main dwelling on the Knox Farm and the Hall Farm dwelling, both also on the National Register. All of the walls, except in the kitchen area, are hand-planed heart pine. All of the ceilings, the upstairs floors and downstairs bedrooms are also heart pine.

All of the windows except in the kitchen are the original 1854 windows.

The house contains five fireplaces. The chimneys which had deteriorated were totally rebuilt in 2002. They are faced with hand-made brick.

- Wheat house/granary (1855) — Two story granary covered by lapped pine weatherboard. First floor is divided into wooden bins for grain.

- Double crib long barn (1855) — Log portion of the barn was originally used for farm animals. A hay loft is over the stalls. The barn is currently under going restoration and rehab. Charles Barber, a relative, who operates a restoration business is doing the work. He's restored and rehabilitated several of the buildings.

- Log crib/barn (1855) — A half-dovetail log crib and barn with a gable roof and attached shed. Vertical pine siding sheaths the walls.

- Edward W. Barber house (1870s) — Stands on a knoll several hundred feet east of the Jacob Barber House, now serves as Charles Floyd's office. The modest two story house was built for Jacob Barber's son. For most of the 20th century it housed farm tenants.

Unoccupied for 30 years, it was heavily damaged by Hurricane Hugo.

During restoration, workers found siding on the interior kitchen wall that indicates the one-story kitchen may have been a free-standing kitchen that originally served the Richard W. Barber house and was later moved and attached to the son's house.

The massive restoration of the Edward Barber House included using freshly sawed heart pine, which as at least 100 years old. New windows were made from heart pine.

The house did get an update with electricity, plumbing, heating and air conditioning. The kitchen area serves as Charles Floyd's office.

The Edward W. Barber house is also on the National Register.

- Edward Barber well house (1870s) — A wooden well house featuring vertical oak board and batten. The rock-line well remains functional. (The well house is one of three on the property. Two other are stone.)

- Carriage house (1890) — Frame carriage house was heavily damaged by Hurricane Hugo but has been restored.

- Railroad (1898) — The N.C. Midland Railroad built a railroad through the Barber Farm. Two trains pass through daily.

- School (1900) — One-story, board and batten school with a gable roof stands a short distance from the Richard Barber house. William Barber built the structure to home school his children.

Farming practices

- Terraces (late 1930s) —Richard W. Barber had contour terraces constructed to prevent erosion, restore and improve the farm. The terraces remain and are protected by a conservation easement. Much of the terraced ares is in grass while the other is planted in crops.

- Check dam and gully system (late 1930s) — The Civilian Conservation Corps put in grassed greenways to carry water from the terraces to a large branch that flows into Withrow Creek. The CCC built concrete spillways at the ends of some of the terraces.

Looking for information on the family of Elias and Barbara Barber, who were the parents of Jesse Barber (1787-c1865). The records below show that Elias and Barbara were the parents of

Jesse, but it appears that there were several Elias Barber's in the area, so determining which is which is a bit difficult. If anyone has any information to share it would be greatly appreciated.

Chad
tw5@bellsouth.net

1800 Rowan County, North Carolina, p324, Elias Barber house hold: 1 male 0-10, 3 males 10-15, 2 males 16-18, 1 male 26-44, 3 females 0-10, 1 female 10-15, 1 female 16-26, 1 female 26-44, 1 female 45-up. No slaves.
Census was preindexed, so neighbors are unknown.

Aug 4, 1808: Christian Michael sold to Barbara Barber during her lifetime and to Jesse Barber, who was the son of Elias and Barbara Barber for 10 shillings, 92.25 acres on Dykers Creek and the Yadkin River adjoining John Biles, Hugh Cunningham, and Phillip Walser. After the death of Barbara, this land is to go to son Jesse. Witness: George Snider and Fredrick Walser. (Rowan Co, NC Deed Bk)

1810 Rowan County, NC, Carolina Township, p327, Barbary Barber house hold: 0 males, 2 females 0-10, 1 female 16-26, 1 female 26-44.
1. Henry Michael (sic?)
2. Jesse Langley

March 12, 1821: Jesse Barbee of Oglethorpe County, Georgia and Barbara Barbee of Rowan County sold to Phillip Walser for $220, 92.25 acres on the Yadkin River and Dyker Creek, adjoining John Biles, Hugh Cunningham, and this grantee. This transaction was not to be effective until after the death of Barbara Barbee. Witness: Thomas Barbee, William Walser. Proven by William Walser in May court 1821.

Moses Barber was my grgrgrgrandfather.
His fathers name Was William **Barber** from S.C.
Moses moved from Ga. to Backer Co. Fl. in the 1830's. He later moved to Orange Co. There is abook Called Florida'sFrontier The way it was. written byb Mary Ida Shearhart. She lives in Franklin N.C.Ph #704-524-3570 or 407-348-0103
she will send a copy for 25$

From Don Barber's Book on the Conn. Barbers

Don Barber
==
170. ISRAEL6 BARBER (Daniel5), b Simsbury CT 12 May 1765; d 1834; m 1801 ; r Simsbury until 1786, then at sea in 1786-1787, in Augusta GA 1787-1788, in Screven Co GA 1789-1800, in Tatnall Co GA 1801-1805, and in Camden (now Charlton) Co GA, on a plantation near the St Mary's River, after 1805. He received 600 acres of land in Screven Co in 1799, and in 1816-1818 he received 650 acres in Camden Co.

Israel must have been a restless soul. A letter from him to his brother Daniel, dated 1 Jan 1810, details his life story. Apparently his Uncle Thomas Barber in Simsbury caused Israel to leave there because of Uncle's "rascality". Israel went to sea at the age of 21, in the Sloop Commerce, which had a route between New Haven CT, Jamaica, and Savannah GA. This proved to be more of an adventure than expected, for they suffered a gale for nine days, which blew them off course to "Bermooda", where they nearly perished on the rocks.

Shortly thereafter the sloop was captured by a British Sloop of War. Israel was held prisoner for a while and then freed in Savannah. There he shipped aboard a Scotch brig. The Captain was "unsufferable" in conduct, feeding the crew very little and beating them without cause. A few months later when the brig reached Savannah the Scotch Captain "departed this life suddenly, to our great joy". The crew helped to bury him and then went to the grog shop and spent the remainder of the day drinking his health.•

Israel spent a year in Augusta, and then 10 years, probably in Screven Co Georgia. In about 1800 he traveled to the Altamaha River, probably Tatnall Co, where he bought a stock of cattle and some Negroes, and set up a small store of groceries. In 1801 he met and married the daughter of a planter who lived along the St Mary's River in Camden Co, (in what is now Charlton Co) Georgia. At that time the whole area below the Altamaha was called Guale, and served as a neutral zone between the English above the Altamaha, and the Spanish in Florida. Israel settled in 1806 as (he claimed) "the first white settler on the north edge of the Okefenokee Swamp". He stated he was 5 miles from the Spanish line, East Florida. Also he was 43 miles from St Marys, and 8 miles from the "Indian line".

Israel raised a family, and became a man of wealth, owning in 1810 1000 head of cattle, 300 hogs, 3 good horses, 9 slaves, and a good plantation. There he raised corn, cattle and rice. In 1809, after being cut off from his family for many years, one of his letters was answered by his brother Daniel. He was so overjoyed to hear about all his family, that he "killed the fattings of my flocks and made a great feast", which lasted 2 days. After a 30 years absence, he visited his New England boyhood scenes, but then returned to Georgia.

In 1817 Indians drove off 200 head of his cattle. This was part of troubles which eventually led to the first Seminole War.

In the years about 1825-30 there was an ongoing dispute between Florida and Georgia as to the boundary, in the region of the St Mary's River and the Okefenokee Swamp, where Georgia dips down into Florida. In 1831 a committee was named to establish the official boundary. Israel and his son Obediah were hired as guides in this project. Israel was later a "short-time resident" of Baker and of Nassau Counties in Florida. [~ Letter of Israel Barber, at Simsbury Hist Soc); CT State Lib:Buell Gen #2; Corresp:Carolyn Jarrard; "Baker County, the Way It Was", weekly articles by Gene Barber, Baker County Historian, in 1975-1978 ~]

Children of Israel, born in Tatnall and Camden Counties, 1802-181?:

    i GRANDISON7, ; m 1828 Sarah HAWTHORNE. In the days of the border dispute between Florida and Georgia, Grandison "wore out his cart and his wife" moving back and forth between Ware Co GA and Columbia Co (now Baker Co) FL. Every time the   political climate changed and Georgia claimed this part of Florida, Grandison   would move down into it, but later when the political tide turned against Georgia, Grandison would move back up, because he would be "damned to hell rather than live in Florida". When the State Line was finally established, Grandison built a house on this Line, one half of the house in each state.

    At this time he was doing some business on the sly, namely cattle-rustling,   and when things got too hot for him and the Sheriff came out, he would move to the   other side of his house, into the next state, to avoid arrest. This worked for a while, until the fateful day when both Sheriffs showed up at the same time!
    ii ELIZABETH7, ; m 1842 Cornelius VOORHEES.
    iii JEMIMAH7, ; m 1836 John PEOPLES.
    iv OBEDIAH7, b probably before 1814; d Ware Co. A different, unrelated Obediah, b 1825, was known as the "King of the Okefenokee". His log cabin has been preserved, and can be seen at the Okefenokee Homestead, about 8 miles southwest of Waycross, Ware Co GA. This other Obediah was supposedly married 3 times, and had 20 children. [~ 1850 census:Bryan Co; 1860 census:Pierce Co; IGI:GA; Early American Marriages:GA; "Baker County, *The Way It Was*, weekly articles in 1975-1978 by Gene Barber, Baker County Historian ~]

v ??SARAH JANE7, ; m Mark ROBINSON, b Wayne Co GA 17 Jan 1835, son of James and Easter (O'STEEN) ROBINSON. From the birth date, perhaps Sarah Jane is a grandchild of Israel. [~ Kindred Konnections:Celia Davis-Taylor ~]

Article by Norman Alford of Round Rock Texas

Article from Norman Alford in Round Rock, Texas History of Jared Phelps Barber and his wife, Mary Eliza (Morris) Barber, who lived at Barber's Crossroads in Crenshaw County, in the period of before 1860 to when J.P. Barber died in 1893.

Jared Phelps Barber and Mary Eliza (Morris) Barber had a store and plantation at Barber's Crossroads in 1860, in then Butler County, Alabama, where in the 1860 Census he was listed as a "planter" with considerable real estate and personal property value shown. Living next to him in 1860 was his widowed sister-in-law Sarah Barber, with three children, widow of his brother Grandison Barber.Also, living in J.P. Barber's household in 1860 were two children of his sister Charlotte (Barber) Bellamy. In 1850 in Jefferson County, Florida, the families of Grandison and Sarah Barber and of John and Charlotte (Barber) Bellamy lived near each other, and they were natives of Camden County Georgia in 1860, Georgia, so Grandison Barber must have died and something had happened to John and Charlotte Bellamy, since their youngest children were living with their uncle J.P. Barber at Barber's Crossroads.

Barber's Crossroads became Rutledge in 1867, in Crenshaw County.
Jared Phelps Barber was born in 1812 in Camden County, Georgia, near the St. Mary's River, and he was the son of Israel Barber, born in 1765 in Simsbury, Connecticut. The 1880 Census in Crenshaw County says that J.P. Barber's father was "born in Connecticut."

His father, Israel Barber, was the son of Daniel Barber and Martha (Phelps) Barber of Simsbury, CT, and Daniel Barber was in the American Revolution. Israel Barber, at age 21, left Simsbury in 1786 as a sailor on a ship. After about a year, he left the ship at Savannah, Georgia, then went to Augusta, then eventually by about 1804, was in Camden County, where he married the daughter of a Georgia planter and gained land and a large herd of livestock. Israel Barber of Camden County, GA, wrote his brother around 1810, and some of the correspondence, or references to this correspondence, is in the Simsbury Historical Society archives today. After serving as a guide when the Georgia-Florida line was surveyed, Israel Barber died in Camden County in 1833. Both the Barber ancestry and Phelps ancestry is well known today at Simsbury, Connecticut, since both families helped establish Simsbury.

Jared Phelps Barber married Mary Eliza Morris on 16 Feb 1837 in Thomas County, Georgia, and by 1840 and in 1850, they farmed and had slaves in Barbour County, Alabama. In 1850, Virgil Barber, probably a brother to Jared Phelps Barber, lived with Jared and Mary Eliza Barber in Barbour County. Before 1860, Jared and Mary Eliza Barber moved, with their two sons, and had the store, plantation, and slaves at Barber's Crossroads in Butler County. Their son Peyton Phelps Barber was born in Barbour County, Alabama on 13 April 1849 and their son, James Israel Barber, was born in Barbour County on 9 July 1851. James Israel Barber later went by the name of James J. Barber, and he married a woman named Hattie R. Johnson about 1874, and before 1879 they moved to around Winnsboro in Wood County, Texas, where they had more children, where James J. Barber was a "census enumerator" in 1880 and a "stock tender" in 1900. James J. Barber died in 1906 and his widow Hattie and some of the family moved across into Oklahoma.

Their son Peyton Phelps Barber married Tallulah Agnes Davis at Rutledge, Crenshaw County, Alabama on 14 Nov 1867, and in 1870, Peyton Phelps Barber was age 21 and a "dry goods merchant", probably in his father's store at Rutledge. Tallulah Agnes Davis was born 9 Jan 1851 at Pleasant Valley in Murray County, Georgia. She met Peyton Phelps Barber at Barber's Crossroads in 1864, after her A.J. Davis family fled from Pleasant Valley during the Civil War, from near where around Dalton the Union Army of General William T. Sherman massed in May 1864, prior to marching on Atlanta. Tallulah was the daughter of Alfred Jasper Davis and Sarah Olive (Packard) Davis, who with their five daughters fled in 1864 from Murray County, GA to Butler County, AL, where they lived on the Jared Phelps Barber plantation for awhile, and the family story says that "some of their things were burned on a train." The special census taken in Butler County in 1866 records the A.J. Davis family living next door to J.P. Barber. The A.J. Davis family did not return to Murray County, GA after the war, and A.J. Davis died at Rutledge in 1859. Peyton Phelps Barber, after he moved to near Staff in Eastland County, Texas, helped build the Staff Methodist Church around 1895. In 1940, after the population of Staff had declined, Robert Peyton Barber, bought the old Staff Methodist Church, tore it down, and used the lumber to build a new farm home of their place west of Staff.

After the Civil War ended in April 1865, the only son of A.J. and Sarah Davis joined his parents and five sisters at Barber's Crossroads. His name was Charles Chilion Davis and he had served as a corporal in the 39th Georgia Infantry, Company A, was taken prisoner at Vicksburg on July 4, 1863, but fighting again in battles in Tennessee in late 1863 with the 39th Georgia Infantry. Young C.C. Davis, according to the record, deserted the 39th Georgia Infantry, Company A, in 1864 and was found and arrested by Union soldiers in Murray County, and taken to the federal prison at Louisville, KY, where he was released and ordered in July 1864, to "stay north of the Ohio River." C.C. Davis, born 16 June 1844 at Pleasant Valley, GA, married Lula Adelle Cross on 11 June 1871 in Crenshaw County. In 1880, C.C. Davis was a school teacher at Fuller's Crossroads in Crenshaw County. The C.C. Davis family stayed in Alabama, where he later farmed at Davenport on the Lowndes- Montgomery county line, and he died in 1923. In February 1893, C.C. Davis made a train trip from Davenport, AL, after nearly thirty years of absence, back to Pleasant Valley in Murray County, GA, where he met old friends whom he served with in the Civil War. He wrote a long letter about this trip, which we have, to his sister Corinne in Eastland County, Texas. The grandson of C.C. Davis was Charles Davis Powell (1907-1989) and Charles Davis Powell lived in New Orleans for over sixty years. He did much of the research that led to him contacting descendants of Peyton Phelps Barber in Abilene, Texas around 1970, and telling them of the ancestry of Sarah Olive (Packard) Davis, being a Mayflower descendant. The family already knew that Sarah Olive Packard's father was Charles Chilion Packard (1791-1851) and that he had married Sarah Gordon (Roulain), a widow, in Charleston, SC in 1818. After Chilion Packard's wife Sarah died at Aiken, SC in 1839, Chilion Packard and his only remaing child, Sarah Olive Packard, moved on the Pleasant Valley in Murray County, Georgia, where Chilion Packard had a store and was postmaster, and his daughter married A.J. Davis on 16 August 1842. Chilion Packard died at Pleasant Valley in 1851. A.J. Davis was the son of Henry Davis and Elizabeth (Miller) Davis, who moved to Murray County from Roane County, TN before 1834. A.J. Davis, at about age 20, served in the "Cherokee Indian Disturbance of 1837-1838", in the Georgia militia, and his widow, Sarah Olive Davis, in 1894 in Eastland County, TX, applied for a government pension based on this service. Peyton Phelps Barber and Tallulah Agnes (Davis) Barber had a large family at Rutledge that grew to eleven children between 1868 and 1891. In 1880, Peyton Barber was farming at Rutledge, and we have a letter written by Corinne Davis in 1884 that relates some of the family daily events then. In 1889, Peyton and Tallulah Barber decided to move their large family of ten then, to near Staff in Eastland County, Texas, where some neighbors and family had gone. Peyton went to Texas ahead of the family to find a farm and in October 1889, the rest of the Barber family joined him, along with their grandmother Sarah Olive (Packard) Davis and Tallulah's sister, school teacher, Margarette Corinne Davis.

Their oldest son, William Selwyn Barber, stayed in Crenshaw County for about a year to attend college at Highland Home College in 1889-1890. He came to Eastland County where he became a good farmer and school teacher near Gorman, Texas, and married Jennie Dulin. The eleventh child, a son, Jared Phelps Barber, was born in Eastland County in 1891. Jared Phelps Barber (1891-1944) served in WWI, as an ambulance driver and was greatly effected by his war experiences. He became the highest educated of the 11 Barber childen, gaining a master's degree at SMU in Dallas, and he became a school teacher in Houston, where he taught debate at San Jacinto High School. His debate class debated the class taught by Lyndon Baines Johnson, when Johnson the future U.S. President, taught at Sam Houston High School about 1931, before he went to Washington, D.C.

Mary Eliza (Morris) Barber, wife of Jared Phelps Barber died at Rutledge on 23 Jan 1871, and she was buried in Vernledge Cemetery in Crenshaw County. Jared Phelps Barber, born 1812 in Camden County, GA, died on 18 Nov 1893 in Crenshaw County, and he was buried at Vernledge Cemetery, and their names appear on the Vernledge Cemetery listing . By 1880, J.P. Barber had remarried to a much younger woman, named "Anna", who was age 36 in 1880 and born in Alabama. The Barber family in Texas did not have any record of who "Anna" was, and I found this out only through the 1880 Census.

We have a family letter that states that the obituary of Jared Phelps Barber in 1893 stated that he was born in Camden County, **Georgia**, although the obituary is lost. We have family Bible pages and family history that records the names, births, and deaths of all of the eleven children of Peyton and Tallulah Barber, and of the family of A.J. and Sarah Olive (Packard) Davis.

The fifth child of Peyton Phelps and Tallulah Agnes Barber was Robert Peyton Barber, born in 1879 in Crenshaw County, my grandfather. Robert Peyton Barber married Mary Effie Greenwaldt in 1905 near De Leon in Comanche County, Texas. Their only child and daughter, Sarah May Barber, was my mother and she was born 17 May 1917 near Mobeetie in Wheeler County, Texas, and she was living at Eastland, Texas on 5 January 2002, when she died.

Sarah May (Barber) Alford, my mother, studied family history extensively and she kept many family papers,some of them very old. The ancestry of her great-grandmother Sarah Olive Packard goes back through Charles Chilion Packard, born 1791 in Plainfield, Massachusetts, to Noah and Molly Packard of the American Revolution, and on back to John and Prisilla (Mullins) Alden, who came to America on the Mayflower in 1620. In my lineage, their are only five names back to the Mayflower: Alden, Packard, Davis, Barber, and my name, Alford.

The Barber ancestry of Peyton Phelps Barber (1849-1929), his father Jared Phelps Barber (1812-1893), and his father **Israel Barber** (1765-1833), and his father Daniel Barber (1732-1779), goes back to Thomas Barber, who came at age 21 in 1635 to Windsor, Connecticut, as a carpenter's apprentice to build houses for the English people who were coming to Windsor. Genealogist, Dr. Donald S. Barber, has published a book, The Connecticut Barber's: A Genealogy of the Descendants of Thomas Barber of Windsor, Connecticut, published 2001, and he has a Web page.

Tallulah Agnes (Davis) Barber died in 1906 near Staff in Eastland County, Texas. Her mother, Sarah Olive (Packard) Davis died in 1908 near Staff, and Peyton Phelps Barber died at Cisco, Texas on 26 Nov 1929. After Tallulah died in 1906, Peyton married Tallulah's sister, Margarette Corinne Davis, and she died in 1932 at Plainview, Texas, where she was being cared for by Fred and Neil Barber. They are all buried in the Barber-Davis plot at the

Eastland Cemetey in Eastland County, Texas, where there are 18 Barber-Davis family graves, including the graves of my grandparents, Robert Peyton and Mary Effie Barber. When my grandparents, Robert and Mary Effie Barber, returned from the plains of Texas to Eastland County in 1935, they bought a 178-acre farm on the Leon River, land formerly owned by the descendants of Rev. Caldwell Brashears, the farm where Ary Ann (Davis) Williamson died in 1880. Caldwell Brashears was a very early pioneer on the Leon River at Providence Crossing, where natives of Crenshaw County had come as early as 1870, including the names of Williamson, Hazard, and Duncan.

George W. Williamson, a Civil War veteran from Crenshaw County, came to Eastland County in 1870, and he is buried in Providence Cemetery on the Leon River, now Lake Leon. His brother, also an Alabama Confederate veteran who served with his brother George, was Esquire T. Williamson, who came to Eastland County near Providence Crossing in 1874, with his wife, Ary Ann (Davis) Williamson (1846-1880), one of the daughters of Alfred Jasper Davis and Sarah Olive (Packard) Davis. E.T. Williamson and Ary Ann Davis married in Crenshaw County on 16 May 1867, and they left Crenshaw County in 1874, first farming for one season in Hill County, Texas, then moving to near Providence in Eastland County. Ary Ann Williamson had two more children on the farm near Providence, and she died in 1880, one of the early burials in the Eastland Cemetery, the first burial in what became the Barber-Davis plot in the Eastland Cemetery. Another of the A.J. Davis daughters was Olive Lenora Davis (1848-1934) and she married Julius George Cross in Crenshaw County on 11 June 1871, and they are buried at Stanton in Martin County, Texas.

I hope you enjoy all this information. Barber's Crossroads, now Rutledge, was probably named for Jared Phelps Barber, who had the store and plantation there before 1860. I noticed that in 1890, in the list of Rutledge residents published on the Web from the Rutledge Wave, that in 1890, he was not listed as a resident of Rutledge, but he must have been living nearby, since he was buried in Vernledge Cemetery.

(2) FAMILY OF GEORGE BARBER of Maryland

Ref: Richard Warner: peterpan@neverlandsite.com

First Generation

1. GEORGE BARBER[1], 1802; m/1 Mary **Cullison**; m/2 Ann ---; r Baltimore MD.
   2   JOHN WESLEY[2], 1826; m Elizabeth **Bowers**.
        ELIZA ANN[2], 1833
        ELIZABETH[2], 1837

Second Generation

2. JOHN WESLEY BARBER[2], 1826; m Elizabeth **Bowers**; r Smallwood MD.
        WILLIAM H[3], c 1849
        MARY C[3], 1850
   3   GEORGE W[3], 1852; m Mary Catherine **Davis**.
        ANN[3], c 1855
        HELENA[3], c 1859
        JOHN Q[3], 1862; m Elizabeth Ellen **Wagoner**; m/2 Fannie P **Williams**.

First wife:
LILLIE M^4, 1887
MINNIE V^4, 1888
Second wife:
JOHN C^4, 1895
CHARLES M^4, 1896
EVA B^4, 1897
GEORGE EDWARD^4, 1908; d Westminster, Carroll Co MD; m Edna L **Brilhart**.
JAMES M^3, 1864; m Julia A **Williams**.
J HERBERT^4, 1885
ALVERTA M^4, 1888
ELIZABETH A^4, 1893
ELIZA^3, c 1867
FANNIE B^3, c 1871

Third Generation

3. GEORGE W BARBER^3, 1852; m Mary Catherine **Davis**; r Bird Hill, in Gamber, Carroll Co MD.
WILLIAM NICHOLAS^4, 1875; m Caroline C **Bitzel**.
BERTHA VIOLA^5, 1896; m George E **Miller**.
MARGARET ANN^5, 1910; d Westminster, Carroll Co MD; m Earl D **Fleming**.
GLADYS MAE^5, 1913; m Frederick W **Richter**.
EDITH^5, ; m --- **Master**.
MARY E^5, ; m --- **Lambert**.
RUTH A^5, 1919; m --- **Hoff**.
WILLIAM W^5, c 1921; m Anna M ---.
EDNA^5, ; m --- **Myers**.
ELVA^5, ; m --- **Flohr**.
NELLIE^5, ; m --- **Gorsuch**.
DAUGHTER^5, ; m --- **Hoff**.
DAUGHTER^5, ; m Charles Emory **Green**, Sr.
DAUGHTER^5, ; m --- **Brauning**.
DAUGHTER^5, ; m --- **Wilburn**.
JOHN HARVEY^4, 1877; m Rosa Bell **Harris**.
JESSIE PAULINE^5, 1901; m Edgar Dewey **Bair**.
ADALINE^5, 1902
EDGAR GEORGE LEVI^5, 1903; m Ruth Marie **Wimert**.
DAUGHTER^6, ; m --- **Talmadge**.
DAUGHTER^6, ; m --- **Zepp**.
HILDA GRACE^5, 1905; m Harold Edward **Stoner**.
BESSIE FRANCIS^5, 1907; m C William **Lowe**.
CATHERINE LOUISE^5, 1910; m/1 Charles Elmer **Jenkins**; m/2 Nimrod
Howard.
DAUGHTER^5, ; m Guy Irvin **Miller**.
ETHEL MAE^5, 1915; m --- **Stonesifer**.

JOHN HARVEY[5], 1918
OSCAR MONROE[5], 1924; m --- **Redding**.
DAUGHTER[6], ; m --- **Frizzell**.
HARRY A[4], 1882; m Bessie M **Foffett**.
EFFIE MAE[5], ; d Westminster.
DAUGHTER[5], ; m --- **Brown**.
DAUGHTER[5], ; m --- **Boone**.
EVELYN VIRGINIA[5], 1924; m/1 Howell **Davis**; m/2 --- **Cody**.
CHILD[5]
CHILD[5]
RAYMOND A[5]
FRANCIS[5]
CHILD[5]
DAUGHTER[5], ; m --- **Close**.
WILLARD GEORGE[5], c 1923; d Westminster; m ---.
GEORGE CALVIN[4], 1883; m Della Mae **Lippy**.
DAUGHTER[5], ; m --- **Muller**.
HARRY CALVIN[5], 1907; d Baltimore 1983.
ELMER SYLVESTER[5], 1908; m Mary C **Sherfey**.
DOROTHY LOUISE[5], 1915
LOUIS M[4], 1885; m Effie M C **Frizzell**.
DOROTHY LaRUE[5], 1916; m James Ray **Swartzbaugh**.
GEORGE LEONARD[5], c 1919; m ---.
CHARLES WESLEY[5], 1930 - 1955
ELLA MAY[4], 1888
HENRY HERCHEL[4], 1894

MOSES & ELIZABETH BARBER

Below is the grave marker erected by relatives for Moses Barber and Elizabeth Barber and son Zadock Barber & wife Tempie Stinson at Barber Family Cemetery near Goldston, Chatham County, NC. Moses was born in 1745 and died 1795. Elizabeth was born 1750 and died 1825.

Zadock Barber, b. 17 Oct 1785, d. 1 Aug 1848, Chatham County, NC; m. Tempie Stinson, b. 1787, d. 1850, Chatham Co., NC.

1.   Moses Barber, b. 1813, Chatham County, North Carolina, d. 1880, Chatham County, North Carolina; m. Hanah Barber, b. 1812.
         a.   Rebecca Barber b. 1836
         b.   Margret Barber b. 1839
         c.   Sallie Barber, b. 1842
         d.   Bethany Barber b. 1844

2.   Tyson Barber b. 1816, Chatham County, North Carolina, d. Fayetteville, Cumberland Co., NC; m. Sarah J. Barber, b. 1828.
         a.   Wesley Barber b. 1860
         b.   Zedriah Barber b. 1865
         c.   Thomas Barber b. 1871
         d.   Lony Barber b. 1873

3.   Jane Barber b. 1819

4.   William F. Barber b. 1821, d. 1893

5.   Lydia Barber b. 1824

6.   Wesley B. Barber b. 1831, d. 1882
7.   Archibald Barber b. 1831, twin?
8.   Moses Barber b. 1835

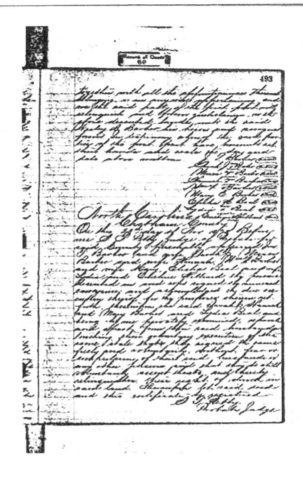

WESLEY BARBER
BORN 1831   DIED FEB 16, 1882
HIS WIFE
RODIE EMALINE HATCH
NOV. 3, 1832 – DIED NOV. 21, 1907
MARRIED AUG. 3, 1852

07/11/2008

Heritage Books by Betty Jewell Durbin Carson:

Barber/Barbour Genealogy:
Thomas Barber, The Emigrant, 1614–1662, Book 2

Barber/Barbour Genealogy:
Samuel Barber, 1655–1704, Book 3

The Brice Family Who Settled in Fairfield County, South Carolina,
about 1785 and Related Families

From D'Aubigny of Normandy, France to Robert Durbin of England
and Thomas Christoper Durbin of Baltimore, Maryland

Descendants of Thomas Mattingly (Born 1623, Omny, Sussex, England;
Death 24 July 1664, Newton, Charles, Maryland)

Durbin and Logsdon Genealogy with Related Families, 1626–1991

The Durbin and Logsdon Genealogy with Related Families, 1626–1991,
Volume 2

Durbin and Logsdon Genealogy with Related Families, 1626–1994

Durbin and Logsdon Genealogy with Related Families, 1626–1998

Durbin-Logsdon Genealogy and Related Families from Maryland to Kentucky,
Volumes 1–2

CD: The Durbin and Logsdon Genealogy with Related Families, 1626–2000,
3rd Revised Edition

History of the Barclay/Barkley Clan; Roger de Berchelai, Scotland
Barber/Barbour Genealogy: Book 1

History of Curtis Land, 1635–1683; with Excerpt on Francis Land

Jean (John) Gaston of France

Our Ewing Heritage, with Related Families, Part One and Two, Revised Edition
Betty Jewell Durbin Carson and Doris M. Durbin Wooley

CD: Our Ewing Heritage, with Related Families, Revised Edition
Betty Jewell Durbin Carson and Doris M. Durbin Wooley

Patterson Family History